Social Education:
Principles and Practice

EDUCATIONAL ANALYSIS
General Editors: Philip Taylor and Colin Richards

CONTEMPORARY ANALYSIS IN EDUCATION SERIES
General Editor: Philip Taylor

Contemporary Analysis in Education Series

Social Education: Principles and Practice

Edited by
Chris Brown, Clive Harber and Janet Strivens

 The Falmer Press

(A member of the Taylor & Francis Group)
London, New York and Philadelphia

120795

UK   The Falmer Press, Falmer House, Barcombe, Lewes, East Sussex, BN8 5DL

USA   The Falmer Press, Taylor & Francis Inc., 242 Cherry Street, Philadelphia, PA 19106-1906

First published 1986

Library of Congress Cataloging in Publication Data

Social education.

    (Contemporary analysis in education series; 12)
    1. Education, Humanistic—United States. 2. Education
—Social aspects—United States. 3. Social skills—
Study and teaching—United States. 4. Life skills—
Study and teaching—United States. 5. Humanitarianism—
Study and teaching—United States. I. Brown, C. H.
(Chris H.). II. Harper, Clive. III. Strivens, Janet.
IV. Series.
LC1011.S63 1986 370.19 86-13392
ISBN 1-85000-112-X
ISBN 1-85000-113-8 (pbk.)

Jacket design by Leonard Williams

Typeset in 11/13 Garamond by
Imago Publishing Ltd, Thame, Oxon

Printed in Great Britain by Taylor & Francis (Printers) Ltd, Basingstoke

Contents

v

Contents

General Editor's Preface

There can be little doubt that education is being pressed to concentrate more and more on instrumental skills and marketable capabilities. The idea of a balanced, liberal education in which all sides of the human character finding scope for development is being de-emphasized. Vocational education with its emphasis on the workplace, on job experience and the labour market, is increasingly the order of the day.

Despite this trend there is a real and genuine concern within schools that they should provide a social education for all their pupils. The concern to teach morality, and support for a caring and civil community remains strong. It is to this issue that this book is addressed. It addresses both the theory and practice of social education and does so out of a realization of the practical problems which face teachers.

In its two sections — Principles and Curriculum Development — this book examines the grounds for social education and its practices in a direct and readable fashion, and uniquely. No other book does so across the curricula range achieved in this book. On this and the practical usefulness of the book, the editors and contributors are to be congratulated.

P.H. Taylor
University of Birmingham, 1986

Preface

As the references and bibliographies is this book indicate, much has now been written on social education. This volume is an attempt to bring together the many diverse curriculum approaches to social education that now exist in order to provide a practical handbook of methods and resources.

The book is divided into two sections: Principles and Curriculum Developments. Common to both sections, however, is a concern for method in social education based on participation and discussion. Such an approach assumes equality between participants and respect for all individuals. Prejudice and discrimination based on such factors as gender, race, class, age etc. have no place in a critical social education though it is the task of social education to enable learners to examine such attitudes in the classroom.

Chris Brown, Clive Harber and Janet Strivens 1986

Part I
Social Education: Principles

Social Education in Secondary Schools: Principles and Practice

Chris Brown

The vulnerability of schooling to short-lived bandwagons is matched only by teachers' imperviousness to them! It is easy enough to understand how the education of the young can attract the attention of political or moral campaigners. The young are the citizens of tomorrow; what they are taught in school might determine how they think and behave as adults. But the ability of teachers as a group to resist these pressures is usually quite effective. On balance we should probably be thankful for the strong professional cynicism towards bandwagons. It can be very frustrating for reformers to encounter such cynicism but it does ensure some continuity in educational life and protects the young from the wilder excesses of both reformers and reactionaries.

On the other hand, there is no obvious reason why long established customs of mass schooling should be immune from criticism or even change. There may be no virtue in change for itself but nor is there much rationality in refusing to consider whether change is needed. The practices acted out daily within classrooms have endured over time but they did not spring up fully fledged in the guise we now recognize. The problem is to identify changes which are part of a long-term evolution and those which are merely ephemeral.

How, for instance, can we best understand social education, the subject of this book? The term itself is certainly not new; it was used as the title of a book published by Scott in America in 1908. The book lucidly sets out principles of education which are easily recognized in the more prosaic language of today's official reports:

The school as a special organ for education must fit into the rest of society, must supplement it where necessary, and learn from it on every side. It must prepare the children to live the best possible lives both for themselves and others in the world which they are to enter. In order to do this the school must be adapted not only to the present state of society, but it must select the influences received and perpetuate those which are best. It must carefully avoid fitting children for a past or lower order of things. It must indeed do more than this, because society itself is constantly changing. Not only the industrial and business world, but the whole life of today is quite different from what it was thirty or even ten years ago. To be really effective the school is forced to idealize the present activities of society, and prepare the young for a future world which exists only in the minds and hearts of the community. The school at its best is a prophecy, as every embryo is a prophecy of a better and nobler life.

Scott's account is not essentially different from many attempts to characterize social education today. The only difference is that whereas Scott was an individual in the tradition of education reformers, advocates of social education in Britain today often have the backing of the most powerful and the most monied influences in education. For instance, much of Scott's argument can now be found in HMI documents, MSC guidelines and employers' recommendations. Perhaps, then, social education is neither new nor ephemeral; it has simply been rediscovered.

The Students' Perception

Before considering definitions of social education, it is worth viewing the issue from the perspective of students. David Hargreaves (1982) has argued that much of students' resistance to schooling which is experienced daily by teachers, is caused by the way in which so much of the ordinary routine of school constantly detracts from pupils' dignity: '. . . pupil opposition is a rejection of school because schooling destroys their dignity. In response, the pupils set up an alternative means of achieving dignity and status by turning the school's dignity system upside down'.

Time and again when asked what they think about secondary school, young people say the same thing: in response to Paul Corrigan (Corrigan, 1978), Albert said (p. 27)

Question: What do you think about boys that play truant?
Albert: I've played truant, it's just because you get so sick of

school. In engineering drawing I stopped off because
there's this teacher and he is always picking on you and it's
hard and I don't know what to do, so I just stay off.
Question: Why do you think boys play truant?
Albert: It's just like with teachers who are saying things are
too hard to do. They get sick of teachers who are just
picking on them and sending them out of the class and that;
so they just don't go.

But it is not only the hard cases who experience school as an attack on
their dignity. Mandy told Roger White (White, 1983)

You can't put up your hand and say, 'Sir, this lesson's very
boring'. You just aren't allowed to do that in school. If you
feel it's boring, you think there's something wrong with *you*;
you get worried because everybody else is writing things
down. Everybody else is telling you what's best for you and
what ain't, but you're never taught to question anything.
You're never taught to think like that. If you do question
anything, there's something wrong with you: you're insolent,
you're naughty, you're a thug. I remember once being so
bored with geology that I started reading my book, *Fantastic
Mr Fox*, and the teacher called me out. 'Mandy, what are you
doing?' 'I'm reading *Fantastic Mr Fox*'. He told me to get out.
When I said, 'Actually I find your lesson very boring', he
thumped me and sent me to the Deputy Head. He could at
least have took it that I found the lesson very boring.

Geoff implies that the problem is not just one of a few disaffected
troublemakers:

Obviously you need a certain amount of discipline, otherwise
everything's going to pieces, and it must be hard to draw the
borderline between discipline and relaxation. More consultation with the kids would be better, because a lot of decisions
are made just by teachers and they do affect the pupils.
Teachers think pupils aren't old enough, but most of them are
really, and some are older than the teachers in some ways.
Perhaps having a body of pupils who could speak at staff
meetings would help.

The hidden curriculum of school initiates children into a future
institutionalized world where as adults, their opinions will count for
little but so long as they abide by the rules they will be rewarded. The

trouble is that this sort of social education is no longer appropriate. It was probably never ethically sound in an erstwhile democracy but now, when work is more problematic than it has been for a long time and thus the system cannot deliver the rewards for conformity, it is not expedient either.

However, it is not easy to change the habits of decades merely because the MSC is prepared to hand out cash. The problem is also wider than education. The position of young people in modern societies is characterized by low status and relative powerlessness. Some people feel that the young are always 'getting away with it'. Their music drowns the sensibilities of many adults; their sexual activity offends; their fashion can reduce even the most sympathetic adult to apoplexy. But, insofar as this picture of the young reflects the reality of life for the average young person it is the same response as truancy or disruption in school — an attempt to assert status, self-respect and dignity in the face of persistent repression. Social education is a response to this situation.

What is Social Education?

One way of attempting to understand social education is to contrast it with the sort of academic programmes which currently characterize vast tracts of the secondary curriculum. In these programmes learners are required to attend to a mass of detailed data with which they are totally unfamiliar partially derived from some of the disciplines of knowledge of higher education. The object of their activity is to remember as much as possible of what they are told or read and faithfully reproduce it at some future date. The bulk of their experience in school is taken up with this activity which is undertaken in little time pockets divided by the ringing of a bell. Work is nearly always individual rather than cooperative and failure to remember adequately is attributed to low intelligence ('thickies') or to opposition, whether apathy ('laziness') or resistance ('disruption'). Valued knowledge is always cognitive, never affective or practical and it always therefore involves writing and/or reading, never any emotional commitment or practical expression.

Carl Rogers (1983) has suggested that teaching like this is based on several basic assumptions:

(i) pupils cannot be trusted to learn;
(ii) passing exams is the best criteria for judging potential;

(iii)   what teachers teach is what pupils learn;

(iv)   learning is the accumulation of information;

(v)   pupils are best regarded as manipulative objects, not as persons.

So how can we define social education? Between them, the following say as much as can be said in a short definition:

> The term 'social education' will . . . be used to cover all those teaching or informal activities which are planned by curriculum developers, teachers, or other professionals to enhance the development of one or more of the following: knowledge, understanding, attitudes, sensitivity, competence, in relation to:
> — the self and others, and/or
> — social institutions, structures and organisation, and/or
> — social issues. (Lee, 1980)

> Social education is the conscious attempt to help people to gain for themselves the knowledge, feelings and skills necessary to meet their own and others' developmental needs. (Smith, 1981)

In their different ways, these definitions arrive at much the same point. Both stress feelings and skills as well as knowledge and both regard the personal development of the learner as the purpose of social education. However, Lee puts emphasis on certain issues external to the learner while Smith regards the learner's needs as the determining factor in planning social education. In this Lee reflects the more formal structures of schooling while Smith draws on the more open traditions of youth work. However, for our purposes, these two definitions are complementary because in practice social education takes two forms. It can be a *curriculum* or it can be a *pedagogy*. Lee's definition relates more to the social education curriculum while Smith's refers more to teaching/learning methods and to questions of general relationships. We will pursue these two directions separately.

The Social Education Curriculum

The curriculum is the main focus of this book. Indeed, the book is designed to explore the major areas of the social education curriculum and suggest ways of tackling them which encourage 'good practice' by helping teachers to think through the nature of what they are attempting to do and to construct effective and enjoyable learning experiences.

Since the seventies the secondary curriculum has been invaded by courses which focus on aspects of living in contemporary society and there are probably few schools today which do not offer some such course. While we can use the label 'social education' for these courses, there are wide variations. At the most rudimentary level social education may be little more than short courses in careers education or health education. Other courses are more elaborate and may incorporate careers and health along with other topics such as moral education and political education in programmes with titles like 'preparation for life' or 'design for living'. Alongside these courses, but not integrated with them, are likely to be courses in child care and parentcraft which have sprung up as an extension of home economics for the 'less able'. Even more elaboration is usually indicated when titles like 'social education', 'social studies' or 'community studies' are used. In these courses there is likely to be a planned syllabus and a higher level of commitment on the part of staff.

Social education, whatever its degree of elaboration, tends to appear at fourth and fifth-year level and is offered frequently only to 'less able' pupils. In some schools, however, there is a firmly held view that social education should be compulsory for all pupils. Another strongly held view by some teachers is that social education should not be examined in any formal sense but the more elaborate the course and the larger the range of pupils who take it, the greater is the pressure to introduce a mode III exam or even a mode I for the 'more able'.

A powerful driving force behind social education is a concern within the school that modern society has become too complex for 'children' to be let loose in safety without some sort of preparation. While this underestimates the resilience of most young people, it must nevertheless be said that social education in many schools is firmly based on a genuine caring motive. It is no accident that much social education is seen to lie within the province of the RE staff and where RE has been left to wither in the formal curriculum, the staff thus displaced may well be relocated into moral or social education.

For 'less able' pupils the traditional curriculum has come to appear moribund in recent years, a perception hastened by ROSLA and the spread of comprehensive education. Some consideration of contemporary life and experience seems to many teachers to be more relevant for pupils who will not be going on to further or higher education. Moreover, if the curriculum of the 'less able' pupils can be made more interesting for the pupils themselves it relieves the pressure of classroom control on the teacher.

A lot of social education is also a direct response to outside pressures. Health education is vigorously backed by the Health Education Council. Development education is financed by the EEC. The biggest impact on the social education curriculum recently has been the government itself, particularly through the MSC and its attempt to shift schools away from subject-based curricula and didactic teaching methods. The motives behind this are closely tied up with youth unemployment and a concern to shore up the work ethic.

In the schools, the social education curriculum has low status and few resources. The consequences are that, because it does not fit into a 'subject' definition it is implemented without much thought to aims or to a coherent plan of learning. Such principles as are applied are often not examined closely and the whole enterprise takes place in an ethos of utilitarianism and 'common-sense'.

There are several grounds upon which a critique of the social education curriculum can be based:

(i) There is a tendency for material to be underscored by implicit values of one sort or another. For instance, whatever attitudes a geography teacher might hold personally, in teaching geography he/she is confined to a technical and validated body of knowledge. But in social education it is much harder to be so detached and students are frequently suspicious that teachers are just grinding their own axes.

(ii) It is quite common for much social and personal education to focus on individual behaviour like 'choosing', 'making decisions', 'forming relationships' and so on, as if these were activities which could be isolated from environmental and situational factors. In reality, the peer group and the neighbourhood are more powerful influences than most teachers recognize.

(iii) Often social education courses are called 'preparation for life', which is perhaps one of the more insulting aspects of social education for young people. Are they not living? Is their present life less valid than their teachers? Or does the phrase carelessly admit the poverty of much of 'life' in school?

(iv) Social education is often overtly an attempt to be 're-levant'. Unfortunately, relevance is often only what is perceived as relevant to pupils by adults. What is perceived as relevant by pupils (sex, the police, parents etc.) is usually ignored or infused with moral prescription.

(v) One of the strengths of conventional social education is that however value laden or irrelevant it may be, teachers often recognize that they cannot always 'teach' it in the usual way. Some space must be found for pupils' opinions and for debate and discussion. Unfortunately, unless there is also some substance, debate may just deteriorate into superficiality and the exchange of slogans from newspapers.

(vi) Another feature of social education is that it usually involves issues which, in public life, are controversial. This leads teachers to reduce issues to the lowest common denominator (for example, political parties rather than political arguments) or to avoid the dangerous areas (for example, racism) altogether. Thus they become unreal or boring or both.

(vii) The social education curriculum is frequently a mess in the way it is organized. 'Leisure' courses give way to tobacco and drugs. This may be followed by the long-awaited but disappointing sex education. Then it is all downhill — civics is followed by personal budgetting which heralds the most ironic of all the social educations — careers. To achieve any credibility a better organizing principle is needed.

(viii) Social education is extraordinarily susceptible to the prevailing moral panics. Is the illegitimacy rate increasing? Then we need better sex education. Is divorce rising? Then we need family life education. Is there a growth of political extremism? Then more political education is the answer. Is there no work for school leavers? Then urgently develop vocational education. Social education will be defenceless against such tendencies unless it has a positive rationale in an educational context.

There is no easy solution to finding a coherent way of organizing a social education curriculum. This book sets out to examine some of the more common components of the social education curriculum, to explore the problems faced by those who want to teach them well and

to suggest 'good practice'. Richard Pring (1984) outlines the principles by which 'good practice' might be judged:

> We might therefore ask of the curriculum and of the other
> experiences pupils are receiving in schools: does the curricu-
> lum, for example,
>
> (i)   respect pupils as people who can think, that is, have
>   their own ideas and points of view, capable of contri-
>   buting to the various explorations, enquiries, or activi-
>   ties that children and adults engage in?
> (ii) assist pupils to see others as persons whatever their
>   colour, creed or appearance?
> (iii) enable pupils to see themselves as persons, able not only
>   to think and to reflect and to develop a point of view,
>   but also to accept responsibility for their own be-
>   haviour and future?
> (iv) foster that attitude of respect for oneself and others as
>   persons, that is, as people that have legitimate points of
>   view and that can and should be held responsible for
>   what is done?

Social Education Pedagogy

The trouble with the social education curriculum is that however
good the components, it has to seen in a wider context. There is little
point in fostering 'open' classrooms in health education if maths
lessons remain coercive and threatening. Political education skills are
meaningless if they are ignored in the school generally. Smith's
definition of social education emphasizes the personal development
of the learner. From this perspective social education is method rather
than curriculum. Indeed, it may be that the best practice in social
education is not expressed through a curriculum at all but through the
quality of the learning situations created throughout the curriculum
as a whole and the quality of the relationships which pervade the
entire school. Implementing social education along these lines is
vastly more difficult than introducing a new 'subject' (though that is
difficult enough!). A majority of staff have to believe in the need for
new methods and experience adequate in-service training whereas a
new subject can be pioneered by a small group of enthusiasts who can
be left to get on with it while everyone else does what they have
always done. Moreover, any serious school policy on social education

requires organizational and managerial skills from senior staff who, even if they can persuade the teachers, must still convince governors, LEA and parents if they are to be successful.

The methodologies of social education can be characterized in a variety of ways.

Person-centred Teaching

This is 'an approach to teaching which attempts to relate formal learning in school to the wider process of personal growth and development. It emphasizes learning rather than teaching and places the relationship of the teacher to the pupils as the key factor in the process' (Whitaker, 1984).

Person-centred teaching involves respect for learners independent of their skill or success. It assumes that learners have skills, knowledge and experience not possessed by the teacher and thereby places the relationship of teacher/learner in a more equal context of mutuality. Thus learners are not perceived as ignorant and cannot be labelled 'thick'.

The test for good social education teachers may be the extent to which they subscribe to either one of the following assumptions:

A   Pupils dislike learning and try to avoid it. They have to be coerced and controlled and even threatened with punishment to do it properly. Most pupils wish to avoid having to take responsibility for their own learning and prefer to be directed.

B   Pupils enjoy learning and find it as natural as any other part of life. If allowed to pursue learning which is relevant to their needs and interests they will work with energy and enthusiasm. They will willingly and ably take responsibility for their own learning and prefer to work this way.

Teachers whose gut feelings lead them to support A may find social education idealistic in conception and impossible to implement in practice. Teachers who can see that B is at least possible will find it easier to struggle to understand what social education means in practice.

One logic of person-centred teaching is that age-related grouping as well as ability-related grouping becomes irrelevant. What matters is motivation on the part of the learner, commitment by the facilitator and a shared interest between all concerned. Within some limits determined by maturity and prior learning, age ceases to be the all-important factor it usually is in formal compulsory education.

Groupwork

A characteristic of good social education is that a great deal of it will be done in groups. This is not to say that individual learning should never take place. There will be many times when learners will wish to reflect on their learning privately; there will be times when they may wish simply to be away from the interactions with their friends. There will even be times when some individual study will be the best way of moving forward.

Nevertheless, groupwork offers a framework for all sorts of learning. For a start it encourages learners to see that there is not a single source of authority for learning because groupwork involves some, if not all, the participants in contributions which help others to learn. In this way learners see that they can also be teachers.

Another feature of groups is that they encourage a deeper level of learning than is usual in didactic learning methods. Group discussion, if participants are skilled, enables ideas to be bounced around and the range of understandings to be uncovered so that knowledge is recognized as many-sided and subtly-shaded.

Group learning has a crucial role to play in the emotional aspects of learning. Participants can share their feelings about not under-standing and of feeling inadequate. No one need be isolated with a sense of personal inferiority. Moreover, personal effectiveness can be greatly enhanced in groups rather than in more common isolated learning methods. Finally, group activity can be structured to engage participants in a range of active learning situations, from ranking a series of propositions to implementing a political pressure campaign. Effective and enjoyable learning occurs when learning experiences are varied and shared and the group structure facilitates this.

However, it should not be assumed that individuals possess the skills to make the most use of groupwork automatically. On the contrary, although most young people have experience in family groups and peer groups, their experience of more formal groups is limited. The skills of groupwork therefore need to be developed and practised deliberately and self-consciously. The traditions of formal education are so strongly rooted in a one-way, individualistic transmission pedagogy that the acquisition of groupwork skills can only be achieved by a long-term programme of development for both teachers and learners.

Experiential Learning

This is a rather more complex concept than is often thought. In the first place it is helpful to distinguish between experiential learning, which refers to situations specially constructed in the classroom by teachers; and experience-based learning which refers to occasions when learners are deliberately put into situations which already exist, probably outside the learning environment. Thus a group exercise, a role play or a simulation are experiential, but work experience, community service or observation are experience-based. However, while these two situations are in many ways very different (for example, in the amount of control learner and teacher have) in terms of their potential for learning, similar criteria apply.

The claims for experiential learning rest on the argument that learning has three components — knowing; doing; and feeling. Formal education is overwhelmingly focussed on knowing, with the result that when people feel badly about their experience of learning there is no chance to air these feelings. This then may interfere with any further successful 'knowing'. By tradition, 'doing' learning, for example PE, drama, craft, is consigned to the peripheries of 'proper' learning. To all intents and purposes, 'feeling' learning is banished altogether. Experiential learning combines all three. 'Content' is not lost; experiential learning is not some mindless, mad frenzy of action but nor is it a solemn ritual of isolated intellectualism. At the same time the emotional impact of the experience and the learning can be explored and shared.

In experiential learning, action, whether it is discussion, brainstorm, problem-solving, etc, goes on at the same time as reflection. The two occur simultaneously. Thus in a discussion of say, abortion, participants are not only hearing the words of others on the issue but they are monitoring the interactions, attitudes and emotions of members by observing all the non-verbal cues and asking what part they are playing in the discussion and what they are learning. In a discussion experience such as this there may be times when it is necessary to stop the talk (ie the discussion of abortion) to check out how group members are feeling about the experience of the discussion itself.

Experiential learning then, is more than 'active' learning. Students who are familiar with transmission learning often complain that active learning is not 'real' learning. Once the element of reflection is added, however, they are able to share their feelings about the experience while it is happening and then perhaps influence its future course or recognize that it is different to the sort of learning they are used to but nevertheless real in its own terms.

Experiential learning demands skills of teachers that few possess. For instance, there can be no question of the teacher determining a precise learning schedule. The outcomes of experiential learning can never be predictable. The teacher must be ready to follow a lead set by learners, though at the same time be ready to suggest or guide if it seems necessary. Teachers must take part in a cooperative learning exercise rather than a continuous formal teaching strategy. Of course, there will always be times when a formal input is needed. As part of a whole repertoire of learning strategies didactic teaching has a place. But teachers who are seriously concerned to engage in social education must become skilled practitioners in a whole range of learning processes. Experiential learning is not a free-for-all and structuring it properly is not an easy task.

Problem-solving

Social education treats knowledge as problematic, tentative and many-faceted. This is not how we normally treat knowledge. The most common perception of knowledge is that it is certain, fixed and straightforward. The dominant teaching mode simply involves transmitting a body of knowledge from a teacher to a learner. Now, there may be occasions within a social education programme when knowledge is appropriately thought of in this way. When it comes to technical instructions, such as using equipment or learning French verbs, the room for doubt may be limited or pointless. At other times it may be convenient to transfer information as if it were unproblematic and straightforward. However, for the most part, social education knowledge is validated within the learning process and is always under the control of the learner rather than imposed from an external 'authoritative' source.

A good example of the difference between social education and traditional learning is the role of 'mistakes'. Conventionally school pupils seek to avoid mistakes. When they are made they invite punishment or censure of some sort. They are seen as a mark of failure and an indication of lack of ability. In problem-solving education, there will be many mistakes before a solution is reached. In a problem-*posing* approach, there may never be a solution in any conventional sense. Mistakes are a necessary feature of problem-solving — they are to be sought after and welcomed. They are a mark of 'success' insofar as they represent an attempt to pierce the unknown and provide data and experience with which to tackle the problem afresh. Unless people have the courage to make mistakes their learning will be shallow and fragile and they will always remain dependent on others.

Human Relations

One feature of all these methodologies is what might be called their human relations element. Teachers are used to separating out the 'academic' from the 'pastoral' or 'tutorial'. Cognition reigns supreme. Writing, reading, listening, memorizing, copying out are the dominant features of most classrooms. These would not necessarily disappear if new methodologies were used widely but they would become just part of the repertoire of facilitating learning.

Behind the methodologies of social education lies the belief that learning 'subjects' should go hand-in-hand with learning about oneself and others at the interpersonal level. Of course, such learning goes on continuously even in our present schools but it is usually negative as we saw earlier. Pupils learn that they are 'thick' or 'lazy' or 'selfish' or 'cheeky' and so on. Today's school offers no systematic framework for developing consciously the skills that go with good human relations. Social education should not ignore this dimension.

At the same time it should not ignore the more traditional subject matter. Social education is not *just* 'lifeskills'; it can also be about simultaneous equations. What is interesting and relevant to learners does not float down from heaven but arises from concrete experiences. Social education is still about leading students into new areas, expanding horizons, challenging existing beliefs and perceptions. It will embrace learning outside the existing conventions of the curriculum — painting and decorating, astronomy, the history of football and so on— but more recognizable school subjects are equally valid. Indeed is there any reason why the methodologies of social education should not be applied to the whole range of examination subjects on offer in school? If learners want to attain exam success, if the learning environment is person-centred, if learning methods are cooperative, collaborative and experiential, why should teachers not use social education methods to achieve exam success?

Learning and Study Skills

An approach to learning that is part of social education, is to teach learners how to learn. There is no point in dumping a class of fourth or fifth years into a brainstorm or a rank-ordering group exercise, if the methods have not been fully explained. Learners who have never known anything but 'chalk and talk' will not be suddenly transformed into competent role-players or cooperative team members. It needs explanation and practice to shift from the passive pupil role to the active learner one.

But if social education is to seriously embrace a goal involving mastery of a body of knowledge as well as the human relations skills, then attention will need to be paid to the more limited range of academic study skills as well. Study skills have been described as:

    (i)   formulating and analyzing the range and nature of information to be gathered;

    (ii) identifying and appraising the most likely sources;

    (iii) tracing and finding them;

    (iv) examining, selecting and rejecting what is found;

    (v) using or interrogating resources;

    (vi) making notes or otherwise recording any information found;

    (vii) interpreting, analyzing, synthesizing and evaluating it;

  (viii) presenting and communicating it in an organized way;

    (ix) evaluating personal performance to improve future efficiency.

All the social educations are likely to be involved here — it is person-centred because learners themselves discover and evaluate knowledge; it is experiential because knowledge is not just transmitted but has to be found and interpreted; it is likely that most, if not all, of these study skills will be best achieved in cooperative group activity; and it is problem-solving because the knowledge is not given but has to be found, analyzed and communicated.

Indeed, if a school got no further than a whole-school policy on study skills it would have gone a long way towards social education, even if the human relations aspects is not explicitly tackled. The failure to foster skills of learning is perhaps one of the greatest indictments of traditional schooling. The effect has been that students whose cultural background already contains the social skills and mental dispositions required for learning are automatically, if unwittingly, advantaged despite the fact that those without the skills could be taught them relatively easily. Our complete failure in this respect demonstrates how lightly we regard learning. For all the claim about the serious nature of learning, the school system has largely ignored the means by which learning is achieved.

Conclusion

Up to this point, this chapter has been largely positive about the potential of social education; in places, it may even have been eulogistic; there is little point in approaching social education without enthusiasm. Nevertheless, some realism is necessary.

Firstly, the principles and practices of social education as discussed in this chapter are not widespread outside schools. Most societies which can afford and which need systems of mass schooling have them in order to produce citizens who accept prevailing norms as natural and who are oriented to the large scale bureaucratic structures which dominate adult life. Social education might not be very helpful here.

On the other hand, much of the pressure for versions of social education is coming from outside the school. Societies are changing; there is more emphasis on the diversity of culture rather than the uniformity of morality. Social and cultural life is more varied and less defined by role and custom than it used to be. A working lifetime will almost certainly contain more change and innovation than in the past. Longer periods of non-work may be in prospect, again demanding more personal resources in individuals and more cohesive structures in communities. This is one rationale for social education but whatever the future prospects, the present is still in the shadow of the past and in this light social education looks either idealistic or subversive.

Moreover, if social education is the child of economic forces, teachers are obliged to ask very searching questions. Is it a device for just another species of factory fodder? Is it just a more subtle version of social control in a workless society? But how social education is delivered in classrooms is not entirely under the control of outside forces. Whatever the motives of employers and politicians, the practices of teachers could give young people a worthwhile experience in schools which most do not get now. Even as radical a critique of official educational responses to youth unemployment as the collection of essays entitled *Schooling for the Dole?* (Bates *et al*, 1984) concludes by recognizing that much of the 'new realism' symbolized by the concept of 'social education' is at least a recognition that the traditional subjects and techniques have been rejected by many young people. They point out that much of the MSC rhetoric concerning race and gender equality can be taken at face value and pushed to its limits by teachers. They suggest that social education might offer greater possibilities for educational and personal development than the narrower, vocational forms of social and life skills training, assuming teachers with the sophistication and sensitivity which the following chapters encourage.

Mark Smith (1981) concludes his lucid discussion of social education as follows:

> ... much social education has been uncritical of the society and time it has been borne of. It has accepted the powerless position of those it is supposed to help and done little to change that situation, even though this would appear to be a direct contradiction of its core values. In an unjust society social education has to be critical ...
>
> In a sense it should be unnecessary to put the word *critical* in front of the phrase 'social education', for what is education if it is not a critical process? Unfortunately much of what passes for social education neither questions nor develops.
>
> ... Helping people to meet developmental needs must involve educators in politics and in making plain the values and assumptions that inform their work. Personal problems and experiences can only be fully understood and acted upon when they are seen as *both* private 'troubles' and public issues. This is the task for a critical social education and whilst the problems are formidable, the opportunity for action is always with us.

Social education is not a panacea for society's ills. It is almost barren as a form of social engineering. So social education will not undermine the class system, it will not end racism and it is not a cure for football hooliganism.

Social education is aimed at offering young people a better deal in their immediate life at school and perhaps in the other areas of their lives. It is not ultimately a preparation for an unknown future but a more rational and a more civilized policy for the present. It is not only students who would find school a different place; teachers also might find that a whole-school approach to social education could transform their own professional satisfaction. But they will need braver and more imaginative leadership than they are presently getting from senior management in schools, in the LEAs or in central government agencies.

Teachers will also need in-service training and staff development. Most good practice in social education is a radical departure from traditional skills. Those who are good at these will need a lot of persuading before they even consider supplementing them. Those who are less good may find the new methods and attitudes even more threatening. Nevertheless, the various chapters in this book suggest how some of the subjects commonly defined as social education can be approached and in illustrating the techniques that go with the principles and practices outlined in this chapter, will show how all subjects could become social education.

References

BATES, I. *et al* (1984) *Schooling for the Dole?*, London, Macmillan.

CORRIGAN, P. (1979) *Schooling the Smash Street Kids*, London, Macmillan.

HARGREAVES, D. (1982) *The Challenge for the Comprehensive School*, London, Routledge and Kegan Paul.

LEE, R. (1980) *Beyond Coping*, London, Further Education Unit.

PRING, R. (1984) *Personal and Social Education in the Curriculum*, London, Hodder and Stoughton.

ROGERS, C. (1983) *Freedom to Learn for the 80's*, Columbus, Charles E. Merrill Pub. Co.

SCOTT, C. (1908) *Social Education*, Boston, Ginn and Co.

SMITH, M. (1981) *Creators not Consumers*, Leicester, National Association of Youth Clubs.

WHITAKER, P. (1984) 'The learning process', *World Studies Journal*, 5, 2.

WHITE, R. (1983) *Tales Out of School*, London, Routledge and Kegan Paul.

Social Education: Some Questions on Assessment and Evaluation

Robert Stradling

Introduction

Those of us within the teaching profession who are concerned with the provision of social education programmes, whether this be in secondary, further or tertiary education or teacher training, seem to have very mixed feelings about the desirability, educational value and practical feasibility of systematic course evaluation and student assessment.

Some schools and colleges have introduced course monitoring procedures: colleagues observe and discuss each others' lessons and course teams meet regularly to consider changes and improvements. In some other schools course teams start off with good intentions regarding evaluation but soon find that the usual organizational constraints and problems take up an increasing amount of their non-teaching time leaving little time for mutual reflection on the way the course is going. There remains a sizeable minority of teachers who eschew any kind of systematic evaluation preferring, pedagogically speaking, to 'fly by the seats of their pants' and rely on 'gut reactions', just as they always have done.

Provision for student assessment in social education ranges from the complete absence of any form of assessment at one end of the spectrum to formal examinations and continuous assessment for CSE mode I and III syllabuses at the other end. Somewhere between the two poles one finds schools and colleges employing student self-assessment schedules or utilizing the student profiles developed for TVEI schemes or City and Guilds Foundation courses, or developing their own profiles loosely based on the models developed by the Further Education Unit or the Schools Council.[1]

In this chapter I shall be arguing that some form of course

evaluation and student assessment is necessary in all social education programmes and should be regarded as an integral element in curriculum design and lesson planning. However, the kind of course evaluation I have in mind is *formative*, i.e. aimed at developing and improving one's teaching rather than judging it against some notional standard; and the type of assessment argued for primarily is student self-assessment. Beyond this I shall also suggest ways in which both formative evaluation and self-assessment can be integrated into social education courses.

Some Definitions and Terms

I shall be using the term social education throughout the chapter as a kind of catch-all label not only for those courses which have proliferated in the 1980s with titles such as social education, personal and social education and design for living, but also for those areas of the curriculum for which 'social education' might be said to be an umbrella term. Here I have in mind political education, moral education, media studies, peace studies, health education and so on.

The term 'evaluation' is used here to refer to the processes of collecting information and making judgments about the feasibility, effectiveness and educational value of a course, unit or lesson in order to make further decisions about provision, course structure, learning activities, teaching methods or classroom organization. Judging 'feasibility' involves asking questions about whether the approach adopted was suitable for a given group of students; whether one could reasonably expect the students to fulfil what was demanded or expected of them; and so forth. Judging 'effectiveness' involves considering whether practice is matching up to intentions; whether the teaching method used is suitable for the ends desired; whether the constraints within which the teacher is operating are surmountable or can be circumvented, etc. Judging the educational value is self-explanatory although it does rather depend on the criterion one adopts, for example, relevance, intellectual or emotional development, etc. As noted earlier, evaluation in this sense can be formative, intended to provide useful feedback on how the course is developing, or it can be summative, intended to establish what the innovation has achieved. The emphasis can be on the teaching and learning process — what is happening in the classroom — or on the product — what was learned.

The term 'assessment' is used here to refer to the processes of appraising and judging the students' learning potential and what they have actually accomplished. Here too one can draw a distinction between 'formative assessment' — which may involve diagnosis of strengths and weaknesses, and identification of emerging needs and interests — and may be undertaken by teacher or student alike; and 'summative assessment' which is more usually judgmental and formal and often involves marking and grading students' work and making finely-drawn distinctions between them.

Of course the distinction between evaluation and assessment tends to be blurred at the edges and there is a good deal of overlap between the two. Assessment, whether it be formative or summative, could be said to provide useful information for evaluating the course. But one of the questions considered later in this chapter is whether the main function of such information should be to legitimize the social education programme or to help teachers and students learn from experience. At present most of us work in an educational system which tends to reward us for promoting and defending what we do but seldom hands out prizes to those who are self-critical or appear to be so 'naive' as to encourage students themselves to contribute to the evaluation of the lessons. One suspects that this climate, which threatens to be all-pervasive in education, is unlikely to be significantly changed by social educators alone.

Course Evaluation: Some Issues

In many secondary schools social education is a high-risk, low-status area of the curriculum. It tends to be perceived as low status by many pupils, parents and colleagues because it is often non-examined, seems to be non-academic, often has no departmental base, the staff involved are often 'drafted' on to the course because they happen to be free on the timetable, and sometimes students are 'creamed off' to do more academic and specialist subjects. In part it is at risk because some lessons or units of lessons may be potentially controversial and arouse the anger or suspicions of some parents, governors or local politicians. This has certainly proved a major constraint on the provision of political and peace education in some schools and has no doubt influenced the thinking of teachers involved in other areas of social education. But social education is also at risk in a different and even more critical sense. The very circumstances which exist in schools to enable social education to be introduced in the first place — the availability of staff and resources, the flexibility of the curriculum and the timetable, etc. — often mean that in subsequent years the school is also expected to respond to calls for other curricular innovations. The result is either that social education becomes a mere label for a changing ragbag of units — described to me by one Deputy Head as 'our dustbin course' — or it is liable to be replaced by the latest innovation.

Now clearly the tendency for social education programmes to be perceived as low-status, high-risk areas of the curriculum has implications for course evaluation and student assessment. Traditionally the solution to these twin problems has been to opt for some form of publicly-acknowledged and accredited assessment. This may take the form of an end-of-course examination, or externally-moderated continuous assessment, or, more recently, the standarized profile or record.

In such circumstances the value of the course and the effectiveness of the teaching tends to be measured by results. What this does not provide is information about why the course proved successful or unsuccessful, what the strengths and weaknesses of different units or teaching methods were, nor does it identify the potential problems and the scope for improvement and change. And yet where a curriculum innovation is making new demands on teachers and students alike the need for information and feedback of this type, particularly about teaching and learning processes, is much greater than the need for some kind of summary indicator of the overall success rate of the students.

I shall say more about the limitations of formal assessment in social education later but for now it is sufficient to point out that there are other tried and tested ways of raising the status and lowering the associated risks of a new course which do not necessitate the formal assessment of students. Good consultation with parents and governors; involving senior members of staff in course planning and teaching; ensuring that there is a secure departmental or organizational base and adequate resources; and introducing some procedures for negotiating course content with students can all, separately and jointly, help to give the new course status, legitimacy and a secure place in the curriculum.

There are a number of other typical features of social education in many schools and colleges which also have implications for course evaluation. Social education has developed — is developing — in widely different directions and most of these developments have been initiated by individual teachers or groups of teachers, often quite isolated from others engaged in similar work. At present there is no shortage of missionaries for their own approach whether it be values clarification, counselling, social skills training, residential learning and experiential learning, team teaching or whatever. What we lack in social education and its associated areas of the curriculum is an established body of good practice which is not simplistically prescriptive but actually offers alternative strategies for dealing with typical classroom problems and constraints. In the absence of such evidence, and given that there is considerable conflict amongst educators on whether we should be educating young people for conformity, work, autonomy, survival, involvement or social change, it seems to me that the only appropriate stance for social educators is to regard competing ideas about the suitability of different teaching methods and approaches as nothing more than plausible hypotheses to be tested in their own classroom rather than gospels to be preached regardless of experience. All too often the latter kind of teacher, when confronted by problems, tends to attribute them to the failings of students or colleagues rather than reflecting on the appropriateness of the overall strategy. At this stage in the development of social education programmes it is only common sense to assume that no-one has a monopoly of wisdom and experience on sound teaching practice.

Another feature of social education which has implications for evaluation is the growing emphasis on process-based rather than product-based teaching. That is, the teacher is concerned less with the transmission of information or the understanding of 'received' ideas and opinions, and more with helping students to develop certain desirable skills and ways of thinking, organizing knowledge, acting and feeling, and a capacity to transfer these from one context or social situation to another. Process-based approaches are much more difficult to evaluate than product-based courses. The gains for the learner are sometimes less tangible and certainly less immediate; and individuals tend to learn process skills at widely differing rates. Yet for that very reason some kind of evaluative feedback is essential. When teaching is mainly product-based the pace of a lesson or a specific learning activity is usually set by the average student. When teaching is process-based it may be necessary to think in terms of individually-paced learning. In such circumstances systematic feedback is useful for diagnosing individual learning problems or the specific needs of individual learners.

Student profiles can be very useful here and I think it is a matter for regret that much of the current concern with profiling focusses on the problems of comparability, reliability, grading, aggregation of grades, and public certification. From the point of view of social education (and why not all forms of process-based learning?) the real value of the profile lies in the need for teachers to discuss with each individual her or his progress and learning problems, negotiate new 'targets' and goals and decide on the value of what is being learned or the appropriateness of the learning activities employed. As such, this kind of profile offers feedback to the teacher on what is happening, and feedback to the students on how they are getting on.

When social education involves skills-based learning this kind of feedback ought to be an integral element of course design. As Len Masterman has pointed out: 'It ought to be axiomatic in any teaching based upon developmental processes rather then content transmission that pupils themselves should have some idea at each stage of the process they are passing through, and of the abilities they are acquiring'.[2] One could also add that it ought to be axiomatic in this kind of teaching that the teacher has a clear idea of the stages of the process each learner is passing through.

One other typical feature of social education that has implications for course evaluation is the new demands which it is making on many of the teachers involved for which they have not been trained. The curriculum innovators in social education put great emphasis on the need for teachers to have a wide repertoire of teaching methods (often much wider than they would employ in teaching traditional subjects). They are encouraged to use some of the techniques of counselling; to devise or supervise role plays and simulations; to think up ways of promoting experiential learning; or to become an 'enabler' and risk the consequences of a genuine shift in the distribution of power within the classroom. For many teachers this kind of teaching represents new territory salted with potential boobytraps and minefields.

This is particularly apparent in social education where so many of the teachers involved have been 'drafted in', may be specialist teachers in subjects which have not best prepared them for these new demands, and may not be particularly committed to the innovation. Of course this is not the case in all schools and I would not wish to give the impression that all 'drafted' teachers are uncommitted, or that all of the mathematicians, craft teachers or PE instructors contributing to social education programmes are inflexible and unable to learn new teaching methods. Nevertheless the situation described above is by no means atypical and highlights the need for teachers to monitor their own (and each other's) lessons and evaluate their own teaching.

Evaluation Techniques

The gist of the argument in the previous section was that social education programmes, particularly those which are innovative, emphasize the learning of processes rather than the transmission of content, and make new demands on many of the teachers involved, require:

(i) — an experimental frame of mind on the part of the course teams;

(ii) — the introduction of monitoring procedures (albeit fairly rough-and-ready and informal ones) to see if what is happening in classrooms is effective and matches up to intentions and if not, why not;

(iii) — and an emphasis on feedback from students to teachers and from teachers to students.

In essence then what is called for here is formative evaluation aimed at modifying and improving classroom practice and adjusting it to the needs, interests, experiences and potential of the students. By contrast, attempts at a summative evaluation of social education are likely to bear little fruit. Social education is essentially a long-term enterprise which at best only intervenes in a well-established learning process. In such circumstances there seems little point in seeking to isolate the specific impact of a particular course. As Professor Lunzer, the evaluator of the Schools Council Social Education Project puts it:

> One can hope that what was done in a limited number of sessions spread over the quite limited period of one to three years will have contributed something towards these ends (i.e. of social education). But clearly there is no means of establishing this. Clearly too, it would be too much to expect that the very tentative reorientations that were achieved in varying degrees ... should result in long-term changes which would be clearly discernible in the context of the many other influences which interact in the process of socialisation.[3]

The same could be said of peace education, multi-ethnic education, political education or attempts to combat racism and sexism. The gains cannot really be measured, nor are they attributable, but the enterprise may still be educationally valuable and valid if classroom practice is responsive to students' reactions and not allowed to become ossified.

The need for self-evaluation has already been stressed, but in spite of efforts to be objective most of us find it difficult to stand back and appraise our own work with some degree of cool detachment. It is a skill that has to be learned through practice and reflection on practice. However, this learning process can be enhanced by getting colleagues to sit in on some lessons and discuss them later or swap tutor groups and compare the experiences afterwards. Apart from providing a more objective appraisal and introducing fresh perspectives, this process is likely to have useful spin-offs. Colleagues may be more sympathetic to your ideas if they see them in action and feel they can discuss them, be critical and make a contribution. This can also help to build up a more supportive climate towards social education within the school.

Often the best source of criticism and judgment on the course is the students themselves. Students' opinions on what one is doing and why, and its relevance to them and to others, and their opinions on the materials and specific learning activities, and attempts to involve them in the design and development of the course all provide useful evaluative feedback. The spin-off here is that people tend to learn more effectively when they know what they are supposed to be doing and why, and when they feel they have some control over the learning situation.

What is sometimes referred to as 'peer evaluation' is another useful source of feedback. Eliot Eisner has recommended the 'group critique' method for teaching art. Each student displays one or more pieces of work, explains what he or she was attempting to do, and solicits reactions from the others. Eisner suggests that this is a useful way for the teacher to pick up what students see and react to and, above all, what they *miss* seeing.[4] There is scope here for developing this approach in social education. Instead of just organizing a role play, for example, and then either leading the subsequent discussion or merely explaining the point of the exercise, it should be possible to get the role players to describe what they were trying to do and how they felt, and get them to solicit reactions, comments, criticisms and alternative suggestions from the rest of the group.

There is also a growing trend in some areas of adult education to reserve the last few minutes of a seminar for a group evaluation which can range over the contributions of individual members of the group, the role of the tutor, the value of the topic, etc. This too has potential for social education. Just how systematically it is done depends on the particular group of students. One group may appreciate the opportunity to have their say, particularly if they can see that their comments are genuinely taken into account. For some others it may be so alien to normal practice in the school that they find it difficult to respond to. Others undoubtedly reject it out of hand. How one uses group evaluation therefore is a matter of professional judgment.

In the FEU document *Developing Social and Life Skills* my co-authors and I suggested that SLS tutors could evaluate their own courses or schemes and their own teaching through a form of profiling. We suggested that there are a number of different models of social and life skills development which underpinned these schemes. There is the deficiency model, which assumes that certain basic deficiencies need to be remedied (for example, poor social skills, poor self-image, etc.); the competency model, which emphasizes mastery of specific skills; the information-based model, focussing on knowledge for survival in the adult world and 'practical knowhow'; the socialization model emphasizing social adjustment; the experiential model, laying stress on practical activities and action; the reflective model, focussing on ways of thinking and problem solving; and the counselling model, which gives importance to the exploration and expression of emotions and feelings.[5] It is rare in SLS schemes, as in social education in general, to find a pure example of one of these models being put into practice to the total exclusion of the other six. The typical scheme tends to include elements of several models but giving greater weight or priority to some elements than to others. So, for example, the SLS tutor might feel that her group of learners have 'missed out' at school, need some help with basic skills and social skills, will find the absorption of information difficult or boring, and will respond well to opportunities to learn from direct, indirect and even vicarious experience. Another tutor with a different group may feel that his learners need opportunities to examine their behaviour towards others, need to be aware of other people's expectations of them, and need skills and knowledge for 'survival' in the adult world.

We suggested that each SLS tutor or course team could draw up a kind of profile of the scheme which demonstrates the respective priorities and weight given to the various elements within the scheme. An example of just such a profile is reproduced in figure 1. The height of the profile indicates the degree to which the scheme reflects the characteristics of each model.

In order to draw up a profile such as this one needs to know *what, how, why* it is being learned, and *how much* attention is being given to it. A profile could be constructed for a single session, a unit or an entire scheme.

The process by which the profile is arrived at involves discus-

Figure 1: Profiling Social and Life Skills Schemes

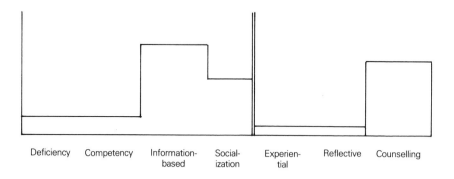

| Deficiency | Competency | Information-based | Social-ization | Experien-tial | Reflective | Counselling |

sion and reflection on:

(i) why a particular learning activity or set of activities is included;

(ii) whether these activities will be sufficient to develop the skills, knowledge, attitudes or learning processes desired;

(iii) whether the profile for a scheme should change during the course of the scheme, for example, should there be more emphasis on counselling and remedying skills deficiencies to begin with and then a shift towards social skills development and experiential learning later in the scheme?

In essence the idea behind this kind of course profile in relation to a single scheme or programme is that it enables the staff involved to construct a theoretical profile, based on the assumed characteristics of their learners and their needs; to compare this with the profile or sequence of profiles which emerges during the teaching of the course as a result of personal reflection and course team discussions; and decide whether any mismatch which is revealed should be resolved or simply reflects an acceptable shift in good practice. We felt that this kind of procedure might be not only a useful device to aid the development and evaluation of curricula, but could also serve to focus discussion on the course between members of the course team and perhaps even initiate some school or college-based in-service training.

Although this approach may have been developed specifically for social and life skills development in FE colleges, work places and, to a lesser degree, in youth clubs, the principle could also apply to social education in the broader sense in secondary schools. Some teachers may recognize in their own course some of the assumptions in the models which we developed to characterize SLS schemes. Others may feel that these particular models are not applicable to their approach to social education. However, whatever the approach there are likely to be a number of basic educational aims and assumptions which underpin it (for example, any permutation from the list in figure 4) and some of these will be given priority over others. A useful first step to course evaluation then would be to attempt to profile these assumptions, aims and priorities and start matching them against actual practice.

It is also possibile to profile pedagogy in a similar way with similar benefits. Figure 2, for example, is taken from an evaluation study of political education provision conducted by my colleagues at the Curriculum Review Unit.[6] It compares two teachers involved in teaching the same course and contrasts the way they use questions in the classroom. Both saw themselves as creating a classroom climate in which students would feel free to express their own views and opinions and where the process of 'asking the right questions' was more important than 'giving the right answers'. The profiles, particularly the one on the right, suggest some mismatch between intentions and practice.

Focal Points for Evaluation

Already in this chapter a number of suggestions have emerged concerning what could be looked for when evaluating social education programmes. It is not my intention here to attempt to offer a blueprint for evaluation. The diversity of provision referred to earlier, the wide range of teaching methods being employed, the variations in experience and expertise of teachers, and the widely different assumptions underpinning social education rule out the possibility of a standard blueprint of this kind.

Figure 2: Comparison of the profiles of two teachers'
use of different types of question in the classroom

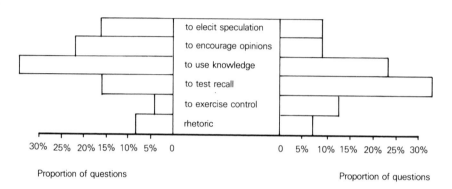

- to elecit speculation
- to encourage opinions
- to use knowledge
- to test recall
- to exercise control
- rhetoric

30% 25% 20% 15% 10% 5% 0   0 5% 10% 15% 20% 25% 30%

Proportion of questions   Proportion of questions

What I have offered instead in figure 3 is a kind of checklist of focal points which could be kept in mind when deciding how best to evaluate one's own teaching.

Uses of Assessment

Three years ago I was evaluating innovations in social and political education in secondary schools. In the course of a visit to one particular school I asked the teacher responsible for coordinating the social education course whether she or her colleagues had considered any form of course assessment. Her reply was: 'How can you pass or fail students on a social education course? What would it mean to be a failure? So many schoolkids are labelled as failures anyway but what label would we be pinning on them here: anti-social, socially inadequate, socially incompetent, or what?' I share that teacher's concern. The very idea of passing or failing students and grading them on some notional scale of success in social education lessons

Figure 3

What is to be Assessed?

* Self-knowledge?
* Knowledge of group behaviour?
* Knowledge of social structures?
* Knowledge of civil, social and economic rights?
* Knowledge of educational and welfare benefits and entitlements?
* Knowledge of trades unions?
* Awareness of job prospects and availability?
* Understanding of interpersonal relations?
* Understanding of social and political issues?
* Understanding of moral dilemmas?
* Understanding of social, political and moral ideas and concepts?
* Understanding of alternative ways of life?
* Understanding of alternative ways of settling disputes?
* Predispositions? (for example, respect for others, tolerance of diversity, non-racist and non-sexist attitudes, willingness to work for social change, identification with the community, etc)
* Procedural values? (open-mindedness, respect for truth and reason, etc)
* Personal qualities and character? (self-confidence, self-esteem, assertiveness, reliability, honesty, initiative, self-reliance, cooperativeness, leadership, etc.)
* Knowing how and where to obtain useful information:
* Knowing how to use information for own ends?
* Social skills? (for example, abilities to relate to others, to perceive accurately how others react to your behaviour, to perceive accurately the state of relationships between others, to put people at ease, to collaborate with others, etc)
* Life skills? (for example, personal problem-solving, job search skills, effective performance at interviews, etc.)
* Communication skills (for example, ability to express feelings, to express information or opinion, to use the appropriate medium in a given situation, to listen to others, to empathize, etc.)
* Political skills? (for example, effectively using different tactics in groups to achieve desired ends, organizing skills, persuasive skills, decision-making skills, etc.)
* Study skills? (for example, abilities to process and weigh evidence and information, to think causally and consequentially, reasoning skills, etc.)
* etc., etc.?

seems difficult to justify on wholly educational grounds. It also raises ethical questions, particularly if social education is concerned with the student's behaviour, values and personal qualities. To say that a student has performed poorly in mathematics lessons is to make a relative statement (i.e. 'poor compared with last year', 'poor compared with the other pupils', etc.). To say that a student has shown himself or herself unreliable, unwilling to take responsibility in a group, uncooperative with fellow students, lacking in initiative and leadership qualities, may also be intended as a relative statement but more often than not such statements will be read by others as 'absolute' judgments about the student's character. In considering the ethics of passing such judgments we cannot divorce the intention from the result.

And yet increasingly there are pressures on teachers to make precisely these kinds of judgments on their students. There is also a risk that assessment of this type becomes, and is perceived as such by students, a form of 'policing'. How else is one to interpret the MSC's guidelines to counsellors on YTS courses? They are asked to appraise and take account of 'any change in work performance against the trainee's norm'; 'signs of alienation in matters of time-keeping, discipline, etc.' and 'any unsatisfactory relationships'. Precisely how the counsellor is expected to assess 'alienation' or 'an unsatisfactory relationship' is not made clear but it is revealing that the MSC assumes that students who are so assessed are in need of counselling. No thought appears to be given to the possibility that the scheme might need to be reappraised in the light of such findings.[7]

This seems to me to get to the heart of the matter regarding assessment in social education. The key question is: assessment for what? Nevertheless, assessment can perform other functions than just grading, passing, failing or even controlling students. Individual assessment can identify any learning difficulties a student may be having (diagnosis); it can provide the teacher with an evaluation of a lesson or course (feedback); it can give students information on their progress and give them encouragement; it can also be an integral element of the learning process itself. I think I can best illustrate this last point by reference to the problem of skills development. Skilled performance requires reflection on past performance and the capacity to adapt to different circumstances. This applies whether we are talking about technical skills or social skills or political skills. But reflection and adaptability depend upon the learner having the ability to assess his or her own capabilities and having the benefit of feedback on his or her performance from others, whether they be teachers or peers, or both.

Techniques of Assessment

My contention is that what is needed in social education and related areas is a form of assessment and feedback which:

> (i)   provides information to the student about performance in all the dimensions of the course and not just those which are easy to assess;
>
> (ii)   does not grade students in inappropriate and misleading ways;
>
> (iii)   would not dominate teaching in the way that the formal examination system tends to dominate other areas of the curriculum but rather contribute to course evaluation and subsequent improvements.

Two assessment strategies seem to fit all three requirements: self-assessment procedures and student profiles.

Self-assessment

This is a term which tends to be used in a rather specific way by those engaged in social skills training. They often restrict its use to the process of finding out 'Who I am'; 'What am I good at and not so good at?'; 'What are my feelings and attitudes?'; 'What are my interests?', etc. But with the growing interest in student profiling the notion of self-assessment has broadened to cover the processes of appraising one's own learning and performance continuously through the duration of a course. The two usages are not mutually exclusive and in social education there is a strong case for encouraging self-assessment in both senses.

Regarding social education I would emphasize four points about self-assessment.

> (i)   It can be a very useful life skill. As Priestley *et al* say, 'We should be teaching young people "take-away" assessment skills for use with future problems and in different social contexts.'[8]
>
> (ii)   It is a learned state of mind as much as a learned skill involving a willingness to question and challenge one's own assumptions about oneself as well as the assumptions of others.
>
> (iii)   Provision for self-assessment needs to be built into learn-

ing activities in social education. It is an integral element in skills-based learning (and I would include academic skills here as well as social, political and problem-solving skills) and experience-based learning.

(iv) it provides highly useful feedback to the teacher for evaluating the aims, content and practice of the course, unit or lesson.

The processes of self-assessment can be encouraged in a number of ways. McGuire and Priestley in their book, *Life After School*, have devised a social skills survey which is a kind of diagnostic device that can be used initially and then later on in the course to give some guidance on the kind of learning activities needed.[9] For my taste it is a bit too formal and the five-point scale is over-elaborate. Some social educators might also quibble with some of the social skills listed or omitted. Nevertheless, it offers a useful model for developing one's own self-assessment schedules.

This particular book, and the other publications by Priestley, McGuire and their colleagues also suggest a wide variety of learning activities, especially in problem-solving, which have built into them some provision for student self-assessment.

Other methods of self-assessment currently used in social education involve diaries and weekly reviews of their work by students as well as informal but regular discussion between teachers and individuals about their work. The 'group critique' approach referred to earlier also has potential for peer assessment. As Rowntree has pointed out, this kind of assessment is formative: 'At the end of a learning assignment or project, the student may be asked to indicate his thoughts and feelings about it. What did he make of it? What did he get out of it? What did it do for him? How interesting was it? How difficult? How worthwhile? What was the best thing about it? What was the worst thing? What other experiences does it connect up with? What would he like to work on next?'[10] He goes on to assert that 'In some cases such assessment will be not only different from but also more "true" than what might arise from the teacher's attempt to gauge the qualities in question'.[11]

Student Profiles

The term 'profile' is used in a variety of ways and can serve very different functions, some of which may be logically incompatible.

For instance, some advocates and critics see profiles as equivalent to school-leaving certificates or structured references for employers or further and higher education. It has even been proposed as a format for court reports. Others see the profiles as a kind of entry qualification for subsequent courses, and yet others (including me) emphasize its value as a learning experience and as a means of providing feedback to learner and teacher alike. Throughout this last section of the chapter I shall be using the term 'student profile' to refer to a means for recording assessment and evaluative data rather than a means of assessment in itself.

Clearly decisions about which categories and items to include in a profile and which to omit can be crucial since it is likely that those omitted will be assumed to be less important even if that were not the teacher's intention. This can raise problems since some categories and items are certainly easier to assess than others, or, to be more precise, we have more experience in assessing them. Nevertheless, if the profile only includes those items which are relatively non-problematical then the danger is that students will assume that only these aspects of the course are important.

The checklist in figure 4 offers just one of many possible lists of items which could be used to construct a student profile for social education.

There are a number of related questions and issues concerning the use of profiles in social education. For example, when deciding which items to include in a profile:

(i) Are there any categories or items which you would not include in a profile because they might be interpreted by parents as a reflection on students' home lives?

(ii) Are there any items here which you would not assess because they might be seen by students as making moral judgments about them?

(iii) Are there any items in the checklist which you would not feel competent to judge and assess?

(iv) Are there any items which, from past experience, you tend to give undue weight to when assessing students?

(v) How comprehensive could the profile be and still remain feasible given constraints of time, access to students, etc.?

(vi) How comprehensive must the profile be in order to be useful to students and to you as feedback?

Figure 4: Focal points in course evaluation

1   For a given learning activity, lesson plan, teaching resource, unit of lessons or course:
    — Is it consistent with the overall course aims?
    — What are we trying to achieve here?
    — Are the methods and materials used appropriate to the course aims?
    — Are they sufficiently varied and adaptable to individual students' needs and preferences?
    — Is the language of materials, handouts, worksheets etc. appropriate for the students?
    — Are the media of communication used the most appropriate ones?
2   Are any of the original aims and intentions of the course proving unrealisable? If so, why? Can this be remedied?
3   Are students responding to the methods, materials and learning activities as expected?
4   Are students unresponsive to any particular teaching methods and learning activities? Do you know why?
5   What difficulties are emerging in the use of specific teaching methods, learning activities or materials? And why?
6   Are any particular topics, lessons, materials proving unsuitable? Why?
7   Is the structure and sequence of the course proving to be appropriate and feasible?
8   Are the opportunities for independent work, group work, remedial work, reflection, skills development sufficient?
9   Is it possibile to detect hitherto hidden and implicit assumptions and values in certain lessons, units, learning activities or materials? (for example, are there implicit racist or sexist or ageist assumptions in a role play, simulation, worksheet, etc.?)
10 Are decisions made about teaching methods and pedagogic style compatible with one's own personality, experience and expertise?
11 Are you pacing the sessions according to the slowest, the quickest, the average or the individual learner?
12 To what extent do students have equal access to the resources being used?
13 Are course intentions being subverted by the institution's hidden curriculum?
14 Is the physical setting suitable for the activities planned for it? If not, are changes feasible?
15 Is progress being constrained by students' misapprehensions and false expectations?
16 Is progress being constrained by factors outside the classroom (for example, the prevailing pedagogic style in other lessons; the negative reactions of senior staff and colleagues; the prevailing climate within the school regarding the status of your course or the methods you adopt?)

There are also operational questions to be considered:

(i)   Who devises the profile? Is it drawn up by the course coordinator or the course team? Is it negotiated with the students? Do outside agencies have a say in it?

(ii) Who completes and comments on the profile?

(iii) Who has access to the completed profile?

(iv) Should the profile represent a consensus on the student's performance and learning or should it highlight discrepancies and disagreements?

(v)   Should the profile indicate the level of the learner's performance by use of grades, labels and descriptors (for example, strong, weak, average, etc.), or should the assessment take the form of 'free comment'?

(vi) If the profile does indicate levels, what kind of evidence will you use: subjective appraisal or objective measurement?

The remaining set of questions to be considered relate to the overall issue of the use to which the profile will be put. The key question here is whether the assessments which appear on the profile are primarily *norm-referenced* (comparing each student's performance with the others); *ipsative*, where a student's level of achievement is compared with her or his past performance; or *criterion-referenced*, where assessment is according to pre-determined standards of performance?

As and when (or if) a profile is developed and the technical and ethical questions are adequately resolved, it may still be necessary to keep two other issues or problems in mind. Firstly, syllabuses, course outlines and rationales for social education are notorious for their predeliction for espousing aims and objectives which look good on paper but are extremely difficult to pursue and even more difficult to assess. For example, empathy, sensitivity, initiative, decision-making, maintaining self-esteem, etc. Essentially what is needed for each item in a profile is a short list of things to look for. Cooper has produced a useful guide for the more academic skills and qualities in this area of the curriculum;[12] and a forthcoming book by the author includes a chapter specifically on what to look for when assessing the political education of students.[13] But a lot more work is needed here.

The second issue which needs to be resolved arises out of the widespread tendency in social education to draw on teachers from different subject specialisms. This undoubtedly can be beneficial but sometimes when profiles are being completed it is apparent that the teacher's own specialism can over-influence his or her appraisal of the student. So there is a strong case for extending the course evaluation process beyond teaching to include assessment itself.

Conclusion

At best end-of-course examinations and formal tests of attainment in social education are highly problematic and of dubious value in judging what the student has learned or in estimating the impact of the course. At worst this kind of assessment is wholly invidious and potentially unethical. As a form of feedback to students to give them some idea of the progress they are making, and to help them identify the learning problems they may be having, assessment can be very useful. It can also help them to see more clearly what the course is all about. As a form of feedback to teachers this kind of assessment is also an essential element of course evaluation and should be planned for and integrated into the course design and development of learning activities. Without monitoring and self-evaluation much potentially good classroom practice is likely to miss the mark and this ultimately will only encourage the detractors and critics, and lower the status of social education in the eyes of many students, parents and colleagues alike.

References

1   See for example Further Education Unit (FEU) (1982) *Profiles*, available from the Further Education Curriculum Review and Development Unit; and BALOGH, J. (1982) *Profile Reports for School-leavers*, London, Longman.
2   MASTERMAN, L. (1980) *Teaching about Television*, London, Macmillan.
3   LUNZER, H. (1971) *Social Education: An Experiment in Four Secondary Schools*, Schools Council Working Paper no 51, London, Evans/Methuen.
4   EISNER, E. (1972) *Educating Artistic Vision*, New York, Macmillan.
5   FEU (1980) *Developing Social and Life Skills.*
6   CRU (1983) *Political Education: An Assessment of Innovations.*
7   SEALE, C. 'FEU and MSC: two curricular philosophies', unpublished mimeo, London, Garnett College.
8   PRIESTLEY, P. *et al* (1978) *Social Skills and Personal Problem Solving*, London, Tavistock Publications.

9 McGuire, J. and Priestley, P. (1981) *Life After School*, Oxford, Pergamon.
10 Rowntree, D (1977) *Assessing Students*, London, Harper and Row.
11 *Ibid*, p. 147.
12 Cooper, K. (1976) *Evaluation, Assessment and Record Keeping in History, Geography and Social Science*, Bristol, Collins ESL for the Schools Council.
13 Stradling, R. (1986) *Political Education: A Handbook for Teachers*, London, Edward Arnold.

The Organization of Social Education

John McBeath

Introduction

If we were to put together a time capsule with the theme 'Education in the 1980s' what kinds of artefacts would we include? One of the essential items would surely have to be a school timetable, since timetables provide revealing insights into, not only the context, but the organization of learning and teaching in schools. For example, what are we to make of the secondary school timetable which includes one period a week of 'education'? or, even more ambitiously, the school in which pupils enjoy 45 minutes every Wednesday of 'life'?

To find 'social education' on the timetable seems, by comparison a quite modest claim. Nonetheless it tells us just as much about the way learning has traditionally been construed and contained in secondary schools. Schools — and universities for that matter — have been very good at making 'subjects' (by which they mean 'objects') out of aspects of human experience and then 'studying' them. So, history or geography, chemistry or biology, or even 'life', are studied from the outside looking in with a detachment that can properly be described as 'academic' or 'disinterested'. It is perhaps, interesting to wonder, by the way, if that large sector of the school population who get nothing out of their school experience are actually interested in being disinterested.

Some people might argue that the 'educations' (physical, moral, religious, or social for example) are essentially different from other aspects of the curriculum since they are concerned as much with the process as with the content of learning, as much with behaviour as with intellectual understanding. Achievement in PE, for instance, has to be assessed, to some extent at least, in terms of physical development. Likewise it is not unreasonable to assume that social, moral, or religious education should be concerned with personal growth and development in their respective areas.

It is this emphasis on the personal development aspect that distinguishes social 'education' from social 'studies'. While, in common with social studies, it is concerned with the social world out there, it is also concerned with the inner work of self, personal feelings, and the immediacy of ongoing relationships. It is concerned with the immediate present and the immediate future of self and self-other relationships as much as with the society as a whole.

Furthermore social 'education' is also necessarily prescriptive. Even in such personal and delicate matters as feelings, attitudes, and behaviour it cannot be dispassionate or objective and cannot take a detached stance to irrationality, gratuitous violence, bigotry, destructiveness, or racism for example. It issues not merely in broader understanding but also presupposes the rejection by the learner of some attitudes and behaviours as inappropriate or unacceptable.

Social Education and Social Learning

To emphasize this prescriptive aspect we might make another kind of distinction — between 'social learning' on the one hand and 'social education' on the other. Social learning is happening all the time informally and unconsciously, as well as formally and consciously. Social learning is a term we could use to describe all the knowledge, attitudes, and skills which people acquire in the course of their development. These may be defined by others as social or anti-social, desirable or undesirable, ill-informed or well-informed but they represent the sum of what that person has learned in the course of growing up in his own social environment. Social *education*, on the other hand, selects from and emphasizes aspects of social learning of which, by definition, educators approve. In other words, social education presupposes some source of authority which has an interest in certain goals and processes over against other goals and processes. It prefers the pro-social to the anti-social, being well-informed to being ill-informed, and choosing what is 'desirable' over what is 'undesirable'.

Recognition of the difficulties inherent in prescribing values and attitudes may lead us to shy away from social education and opt for something 'cooler' and more objective. It might even be argued that attitudes and values should be 'caught' not 'taught' and that if social education is necessarily about imparting *our* values to children it has no place in a school.

By another argument, though, there is as good a case for including social education as a school subject as there is for English, home economics, or health education. Are these subjects not essentially prescriptive as well? Do they not proceed from a set of undeclared assumptions about appropriate personal/social behaviour? Is the goal of learning and teaching in these areas not, inescapably, about the adoption of some stance and attitudes to literature, to health, to people, and to social living?

The Pragmatic Argument

The case for making social education into another school subject can be made on purely pragmatic grounds. That is, it may not be a 'subject' or should not ideally be treated as one, but it has just as good a claim for curriculum space as anything else. Furthermore if we want social education to be taken seriously has it not to be on the same footing and has it not to meet the same kinds of expectations as other mainstays of the curriculum? By the same token it can be argued that social education should have its own forms of assessment, its own criteria of achievement, it own modes of certification, and it should also be possible to 'pass' or 'fail'. To organize social education in this way, the argument concludes, is to recognize the realities of the history and politics of schools. If one wishes to challenge developed conventions or expectations of the school it can most effectively be done from within the security and status of 'real subject'.

Most pupils, whether high achievers or low achievers know what 'real' subjects are. Their judgment is made primarily by reference to the organizational context and conventions of subject teaching and by how others judge those subjects, rather than by any appeal to the content or worth of that subject itself. These are the most obvious criteria to refer to, given that, by and large, the inherent rationale for studying the subjects of the curriculum is something that schools seem reluctant to discuss and tend not to consider as a matter of primary concern.

There is another argument for social education having its own timetable space and teaching time which is less pragmatically based. Because social education reaches into personal feelings and touches on personal values and sensitivities, should it not logically be a matter for both experts and expert treatment? For to treat it seriously surely means treating it systematically and sequentially. Implicit in this argument is the conviction that social education has evolved its own management and methodologies, tending to be less didactic and less teacher-centred than other subjects, less characterized by teacher-talk, more open-ended, more reliant on discussion, more exploratory, more negotiated, and more respecting of personal opinion. So, if not justifying itself by appeals to a distinctive ideological content it may justify itself in terms of a methodological ideology. One example of a 'methodological ideology' is the notion of 'procedural neutrality' — a disciplined pedagogic approach to the humanities refined by Lawrence Stenhouse. Stenhouse's approach required of teachers a scrupulously impartial and Socratic stance in relation to questions of value. For teachers to effectively play this role Stenhouse argued that a quite specific expertise and training was required.

The Twin Curricula

The peculiar quality of social education lies in its being neither subject-centred nor pupil-centred. It has two foci and draws on two sets of understandings. So it requires a pedagogy which reconciles and illuminates these two sets of understandings. On the one hand, like other subjects, it starts by mapping out those areas of skills and knowledge which are seen, from the educator's point of view, as having priority significance. On the other hand, it draws on a set of understandings and attitudes which are not pre-determined but which are brought by individuals and by groups with them into the classroom and become progressively defined in the educational process itself. The peculiar methodological and management skills for the teacher lie in the bringing together of these two sets of insights. The goal is that of helping pupils as far as possible engage their first-hand world of understandings and experience with the second-hand world of understanding and experience which the teacher represents.

So, for example, as part of this pre-determined curriculum the teacher may wish his pupils to gain insights into roles and relationships within families and, as an integral part of this, to become more sensitive and thoughtful in their relationships within their own family. This goal will only be met, though, by a process through which the teacher himself becomes more sensitive and understanding of the pupils' own experience of family life and treats this as the essential content of the curriculum. In other words the teacher must

Figure 1: The twin worlds of social education

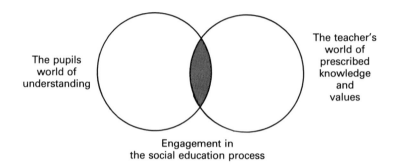

The pupils world of understanding

The teacher's world of prescribed knowledge and values

Engagement in
the social education process

recognize that each pupil is a world expert in terms of his own experience of his family, while holding on to his own greater expertise in helping the pupil to extract from particular experiences general insights and transferable skills. This pedagogic process requires a peculiar expertise and, it might be argued, a peculiar kind of teacher.

The Five Avenues of Social Education

There may be good arguments, then, for giving to social education a space within the curriculum, but is this the only way in which social education may be organized? Another way of seeing the organization of social education is through five different 'avenues' or aspects of school life:

(i)   as separate timetabled periods;
(ii) through extra-curricular activity;
(iii) through residential experience;
(iv) through the ethos and management of the school;
(v)   through mainstream curriculum subjects.

Social Education Through Extra-Curricular Activity

As I have already suggested, the first of these avenues is, perhaps, the most obvious administrative recourse. The second avenue, by contrast, is a much less obvious way of seeing social education. Extra-curricular activities are not normally associated with social education and by their very name have no place in the prescribed curriculum nor have an obvious 'content'. Sometimes a content is suggested since they are, in fact, extensions of school subjects, the history or scientific society for example. Sometimes they are interest-based with an implicit body of skills and expert knowledge — photography, aero-modelling, or judo for instance. Sometimes, though, they appear to have no content at all — for example the Wednesday Society, the rambling, or the hill-walking club. But as far as social education is concerned it is less to the content of these activities that we should look than to the forms of activity they promote and the way they are managed. In pursuit of their various goals (which are not explicitly seen as social education goals) they may, sometimes more successfully than timetabled social education, facilitate the articulation of opinions and feelings, sharing of ideas, listening to and evaluating the experiences of others, assuming and delegating responsibility, taking initiative in making decisions, organizing, planning, budgeting, writing, telephoning, or dealing with authority.

In the Newsom Report, one of the very few sources to deal with the theory of extra-curricular activities, their value was described in the following terms:

> ... we conclude that extra curricular activities ought to be recognized as an integral part of the social education programme ... there is a strengthening effect of bringing together pupils of different ages and abilities who never work together in lessons; and in teachers getting to know their pupils in a different context or form of relationship. The gulf which almost inevitably exists in class between teacher and taught, when the pupil is conscious of his lack of knowledge and skill in, say mathematics, may be bridged when two enthusiasts indulge their hobby in the brass band.

There are some clear advantages in social education through this 'informal curriculum' because it is characterized by a different set of relationships, by high motivation, by enthusiasm and spontaneity, and often by pupil-direction and management. Its shortcomings are that it is low in social education 'content', and cannot be predicted or prescribed. Its virtues are in the social skills and attitudes which may grow from this. Those virtues derive, in great part, from the voluntary character of extra curricular activities, but because of this they tend to be patronized by a minority and by a minority which very often already has some identification with the school and is already getting some rewards from it.

The term 'intra-curricular activities' has been coined to describe the attempt to bring these activities in from the cold and into the mainstream of the school day. While this may seem to be a logical way of capitalizing on the strengths of the informal curriculum it tends to have the effect of moving avenue two into avenue one, in other words, bringing this informal curriculum into direct competition with the formal curriculum. As a consequence 'intra-curricular activities' are almost necessarily seen as an intrusion into the real and valuable things that pupils could and should be doing — 'stealing' good subject time. This perspective may be shared by pupils, parents, and teachers alike.

To cherish the illusion that pupils, or their parents, (or all teachers) will come to grasp the significance of intra-curricular activities for social education and come to value the inherent learning process, is unrealistic in contexts where tangible extrinsic recognition and reward are the real hard currency. And, it is harder still for that value to be grasped when there is little evidence but only pious hope that the process is actually beneficial. There is after all, nothing necessarily positive or constructive in young people discussing things together, working or playing together, going on walks or rock climbing together. It depends on how they go about it, what benefit they get out of it, and in what way those self-defined benefits meet the educator's definitions and criteria.

One teacher who had unquestioningly accepted the value of the games and activities he organized decided to stand back from and study the quality of relationships among pupils. He was shocked to discover that he had, in fact, set up a highly competitive and quite aggressive situation where the need to win and assert oneself had made pupils much less likely to develop the skills that he was after — the cooperation, the sharing and planning together and the investment of personal initiative in group achievement. As a consequence, he ceased to offer these games and began to look for activities which required the skills that he valued — awareness of others, mutual give and take, and joint planning. If social education purposes are to be met through informal activity then the nature of the event has to be both carefully planned and expertly stage-managed to achieve those purposes. That demands a level of expertise that teachers do not normally get as part of their pre-service training.

Social Education Through Residential Experience

The third avenue — residential experience — offers a more extended and comprehensive context than extra-curricular activities for the development of many skills and attitudes that social educators value. The residential setting offers a much less constrained situation for getting the stage-management right. In the first place, going away for the week-end or for a week, tends, from a pupil point of view, to be an attractive and valued activity. It is the one area of school life where pupils are likely to describe the benefits of the experience in terms of the processes rather than extrinsic benefits, for example — 'you get to know teachers better, more like real people', 'you can say things that you wouldn't normally say', 'there is time to discuss things, about yourself like, and people actually listen to you'. In the second place, it offers a more complete alternative to school experience, with a different set of parameters, expectations, and conventions. It may, like school, have its own formal programme and content but scores over school by having more time, more space, greater informality and flexibility.

Like extra-curricular activities, though, residential experience is often optional. It can also be expensive, elitist and divisive. Those who go to Greece or go skiing in the Alps are generally those who can afford to do so, and those who go to Paris or Hamburg may do so by having earned their place because of their achievement in modern languages. Disqualification from these trips can be because of low achievement, bad behaviour, or sometimes simply because the teacher 'doesn't like your face'. Some schools, however, make a residential week an aspect of the compulsory (or at least 'expected') core curriculum, so that virtually all pupils can have the experience.

In one school which has its own cottage, at any given time during the year there are three teachers and a group of pupils in residence there — a demonstrable commitment to the importance of that experience for pupils and teachers alike. In another school the residential week is in the hands of social education teachers who describe their aims for that week in the following terms:

(a)   The development of trust within the group.
(b)   The introduction of new experience and skills.
(c)   The development of responsibility.

One of the main strategies for reaching these objectives lies in the planning and organization of the trip by the pupils themselves. Pupils have to negotiate and come to decisions on planning and timing of their journey, preparing and listing menus, buying food, deciding on rules and policies relative to issues such as smoking and drinking, lights out, duty rotas, supervision, and sanctions.

One outdoor centre which has its own permanent staff and receives schools on a rota basis throughout the year describes its main goals as the following:

> The centre provides an alternative kind of environment to home and to school. It provides the setting in which young people have an extended period of time in which to work out norms of living together in a different context from parents and from teachers. The third year was chosen as the appropriate stage because it represents a critical time in the transition from adherence to adult norms towards the establishment of peer group norms. For example, it is hoped that pupils will learn that idiosyncratic behaviour which may be tolerated in the family will not be tolerated by peers and other adults. Lax personal hygiene, smelly socks, untidy habits, not pulling your weight, all assume more importance in the context where people are expected to live closely together and to share responsibilities. The critical social principle that pupils are required to observe is that they should not expect others to take responsibility for their own lack of responsibility, and that to do so is to infringe on the rights of others.

The incorporation of clearly-defined socially educational goals as an integral part of the structure and process of day-to-day living experience is not apparent to the same extent in the context of the school. If schools really do wish pupils to share and to take responsibility, or if they really want pupils to use more initiative and self determination, why do they appear so often to squash initiative, to create dependence, and to allow so little latitude for the exercise of responsibility? There would seem to be considerable scope within the fourth avenue — through the ethos and management of the whole school — for meeting many social education objectives, or indeed for invalidating them.

Social Education Through the Ethos of the School

Let us assume, for example, that the headteacher and/or his management committee have decided that one of the primary aims of their school ought to be the fostering of tolerance and consideration for others. To attempt to reach these objectives through a social education program or a residential week might actually be counterproductive where the general climate of the school was not conducive to the development of these qualities. In other words, if for one or two periods a week pupils are taught the value of cooperation and tolerance but for the rest of the week learn that what really counts is self-interest and competition, not only are the aims reduced to mere rhetoric but in pupils' eyes may simply come to be seen as some airy ideal with no practical application or validity.

Social education through the ethos of the school implies, on the part of school management, an honest appraisal of school life and routine, consideration of the models that staff present to pupils through their explicit behaviour and their implicit attitude, and examination of the way in which language and humour are used. It implies too an honest appraisal of how rules and sanctions are understood and interpreted, the structure and use of privileges and rewards, and the pressure points in the school for divisiveness and for resentment. In other words, if we are to look at the school as a social system in miniature what are the fundamental lessons that children will, and might, learn through being members of that society?

In many respects, of course, the values the school attempts to pursue or exemplify will be in conflict with what happens in the larger world outside the school gates. Getting on in that larger world might seem to imply the application of a very different set of criteria from those upheld by the school. But it is a central aspect of social education that pupils understand and are helped to work their way through those kinds of questions and conflict of value-systems, and to resolve conflicts of idealism and pragmatism, of self-interest and social interest. It might indeed be argued that pupils who come out of school with the awareness and skill to think their way through contested social and political issues have gained the most singular achievement that an educational system could hope for.

This kind of awareness cannot of itself come through the climate and ethos of the school. There has also to be some systematic process by which pupils are able to build and develop their understanding, as well as their personal beliefs and their attitudes — which brings us to the fifth avenue.

John McBeath

Social Education Through Mainstream Curriculum Subjects

Where, we might ask, if not within the subjects of the day-to-day curriculum should we expect pupils to deal with the central questions about human activity, social organization, and one's own personal relationship to it? If social education does not come centrally through the teaching of English, history, economics, science, art or modern languages, for instance, it is hard to see how any of the other five avenues can effectively compensate for that.

All of these subjects through their content raise issues which have to be addressed at both a general and a personal level — through the discussion of fiction and drama, through examination of historical precedent, through analysis of economic priorities, through comparative culture and language. While all of these subjects serve other objectives one of their central purposes has to be that of developing skills and understanding that are personally and socially relevant for any, or all, pupils.

All subjects are, by definition, concerned with some aspects of personal development. In some subjects, though, that personal development is seen as primarily cognitive and academic, and the implications of the subject content for personal and social behaviour are extremely tenuous. Mathematics, for example, is a discrete symbolic system which requires a detachment from the social world to enter into its internal logic. Attempts to bend it towards social relevance can be a bit strained and not always particularly helpful.

To seek social education within the content of subjects alone is, therefore, partial and limiting. Some subjects do more obviously provide a socially relevant content than others and there is clearly more to discuss about social living in history than in mathematics. But what all subjects do equally provide is a social context, an approach to learning, a set of procedures for objective setting, dialogue among pupils and between pupils and teacher, and implicit or explicit evaluation and criteria for success. Whether it be English, mathematics or music pupils are in a situation where they must work together, in which they must evaluate their work, and in which they can learn with and from one another. Every subject classroom is a stage setting for the whole range of social skills, attitudes and knowledge to come into play.

To return to the earlier distinction between social learning and social education, in every classroom social learning is necessarily taking place. The pupil who spends four years in a mathematics class may learn little or no mathematics but in the process may learn indelible lessons about success and failure, about teachers, about relationships, about power and authority. From the basis of that experience he can come to some firm conclusions about the social system and world in general. While that formative influence is not likely to be a product of his experience in the mathematics class alone, what happens in that one classroom will be fused with what happens elsewhere in the school and may serve to reinforce, to moderate, or to exaggerate the learning that is taking place elsewhere. But it is also possible that the mathematics class itself, totally regardless of its mathematics content, may be remembered by some pupils years later as the most singular and formative experience of their life. If the mathematics classroom or any other classroom is to be a socially educative arena, like the whole school itself, it has to be seen as a behaviour setting which can encourage or discourage the kinds of skills and understanding which are high on the social educator's agenda.

Not all teachers accept this argument. Some complain that they are teachers of mathematics and not social education. They argue that they have neither the responsibility nor the expertise to deal with personal and social development. However, the weakness of this position is that it would appear to assume that teaching is not a social activity. It also ignores the fact that, like it or not, teachers are in that business however they construct and manage their teaching. It ignores too what is perhaps one of the most fundamental and happy of truths, that what makes for good social education is the same as what makes for good subject teaching. In other words, exploiting the dynamics and relations of the social group is not only useful in developing social skills but is a process which makes the subject itself more comprehensible and intelligible at the same time.

This is one of the most significant insights to have been grasped in curriculum development in the last decade. It underpins some of the quite radical shifts in chemistry, mathematics, modern languages, home economics, or English teaching, for example. Two pupils working together on a project in biology may be asked to explain, to question, and to discuss with one another each step of the process as they work through it, and to come to joint decisions about their observations and criteria of judgment. A group of three pupils in a modern languages classroom may each be asked to assume a different role in talking, listening, and evaluating, to rotate these roles and to vary the task three times over, at the end putting together the judgments of the evaluators and assessing their own and each others' performance. A group of four pupils may be working with a set of cards each of which contains a clue to the solution of a mathematical problem which they can only solve by exchanging information, experimenting with combinations of solutions, and making a short written or verbal report on the strategy they used to solve the problem.

Pupil-Pupil Learning

This pupil-pupil learning is a powerful medium. The purposeful absence of the teacher who has chosen not to intervene, not to help, and not to supervise the small group process, can encourage a form of learning which provides for a much greater personal investment and inventiveness on the part of the pupil. It may provide a context which encourages risk-taking since the risk of being wrong or ridiculed in front of the whole class can be the strongest disincentive to learning or creativity. A task which requires pupils to work together in small groups encourages dialogue which is an important generative process for magnifying intellectual power. Real dialogue not only requires a process of active listening to what another person is saying but develops thought by requiring you to articulate your own thinking. 'How do I know what I think until I hear what I say?' is a conundrum with a deep truth. Learning comes not only in silent contemplation but through the act of talking, and we should expect classrooms to be noisy places.

To return to the circles of understanding represented on page 46 what social education in particular, and education in general, requires is the meeting of these two worlds of experience — the experiential world of the learner and the subject world of the teacher. The expertise which the good teacher brings into the learning situation (apart from his own subject knowledge) is a carefully conceived management structure which allows two things. One, it allows, or better still *requires*, of the learners, a set of procedures and behaviour in the pursuance of the task they have been set. Two, it allows, or *requires*, that they bring to bear on that task their own experience, their own opinions, and their own values. The shorthand that may be used to describe this optimum teaching/learning paradigm is 'teacher structure/pupil content'. In other words, the teacher brings the structure and the pupil (as far as possible) brings the content.

As has already been argued, where the content is explicitly social education the application of this is obvious. In many areas of subject teaching too the content is also open enough for this to happen. There are however areas of subject teaching where the content is pretty tightly circumscribed and it could appear difficult to see how pupils would bring their own content rather than being given it. The following are two scenarios, one from a subject where the content is 'open' and the second from a subject where the content would appear to be relatively 'closed'.

The English teacher read to the class a short story taking about six minutes. She then put up on the board a cast of characters that had appeared in that story — seven in all. She then asked pupils to get into groups of five and to come to an agreement on a ranking of those seven characters in order of responsibility for the final outcome of the story. Each group had fifteen minutes in which to do this. Each of the groups reported back by putting up a poster on the wall with the seven characters in rank order. This led to a seven or eight minute class discussion in which the teacher brought out some of the main conflicts of value-judgment among the groups, helping them to interpret some of the criteria they had been using. She then asked them to go back into those small groups and make up their own story. The story could be whatever they liked but it must contain at least five characters each of whom might be seen by others as carrying some responsibility for the final denouement. The final stage of the lesson was for this scenario to be passed from one group to another, each group having a further ten minutes to go through the same ranking process they had already performed, but this time in relation to the story made up by another group of their peers.

The chemistry teacher had split the class into groups of four and each group had conducted an experiment he had set them. Each group was then given a set of cards, each card containing an explanation or observation about the process of the experiment. Groups were given fifteen minutes in which to come to a group decision on the order of priority of these cards using as their criterion of judgment the most accurate to the least accurate statement. Each group wrote its order of priority on a large sheet and these were put up around the wall. This led to seven or eight minutes discussion during which the teacher asked groups to justify their different order of priority. Pupils then went back into their groups with a problem that they had to solve by devising an appropriate experiment. Each experimental design was then passed on to the next group who had to decide whether or not it would work.

In the first example the subject allowed the teacher to construct a situation in which pupils would virtually define the entire content. In the second example where the pupils could not define the content in the same way the teacher had, nonetheless, provided a structure allowing them enough ambiguity and latitude to exercise certain skills and to exchange with one another both chemistry 'information' as well as social information. In the first example there are no right answers but there are preferred strategies for examining value-judgments. In the second example there are right answers, but again negotiable and 'discussable' strategies.

· Jerome Bruner makes much in his educational theory of the value of 'discussability' and ambiguity. The more people are simply given right answers the less room it leaves for their own judgment and their own inventiveness, and by extension the less motivation to engage with the task. What is motivating is the desire to reduce ambiguity, to solve problems, to restore cognitive or social equilibrium. People may shrink from the challenge of doing a whole jigsaw but few can resist the opportunity to put in the last pieces. The entrepreneurs who found a lucrative market in puzzles and problem-solving books have understood and exploited this aspect of individual psychology. Those who have successfully put this into the format of games for a number of players have understood and exploited the social context of games which are motivating. The most recent example of this is the hugely successful marketing of *Trivial Pursuits*, a game which acknowledges by its title that its content (asking and answering questions on aspects of general knowledge) has not much intrinsic value, but understands that the social process which is the by-product of the game is engaging and satisfying. Its magic is, like many good examples of teaching/learning, in the 'hidden' or unwritten curriculum. The value that people derive from an activity is not always consciously recognized and is often not the explicit purpose of the activity. The 'content' that the players bring to the game is not so much in whether or not they know the answers to the questions but in the 'social content' — a set of attitudes and interpersonal skills. What players actually do during the game is anecdotal 'filling in', elaboration, argument and dialogue sometimes either in relation to the immediate purpose of the game sometimes in relation to the social situation which it brings about. The *Trivial Pursuits* formula obviously lends itself to any curriculum subject.

The Achievement Principle

What puzzle-makers and game-makers have also appreciated is that there is satisfaction in an end product, in an answer, and that without achievement of some kind there is no satisfaction. What they ought, perhaps, to appreciate more is the disincentive to play when you are likely to lose, when you have a history of losing, or when the odds seem to be weighted against you before you start. The importance of equal competition and genuine opportunity for achievement is of considerable significance for social education. Personal and social worth are enhanced by achievement and a sense of fairness as much as progress in learning French, chemistry, or Latin, feeds on achievement and possibilities for further achievement.

This is a principle that should underpin each one of the five avenues for social education. The principle is not only relevant to mainstream subjects, to special programmes, or to the informal curriculum but is applicable to the experience of day-to-day life within the school community. The ethos of the school should expect and respect individual initiative and the contribution of individuals to the life of the school as a whole. And it should offer opportunities for achievement in that arena. The corollary to this, of course, is that where avenues are not provided to achieve something that is meaningful pupils will experience frustration and resentment.

There is one principle that is implicit and perhaps obvious but deserves restatement. In every facet of the school's operation the agreed principles and values of social education should be exemplified. If what happens in the five different avenues is conflicting and contradictory rather than complementary there is not the consistency of purpose which a whole school policy for social education requires. Its efficacy is, therefore, seriously compromised.

There is one remaining burning question. Is all this a counsel of perfection? Is it a blue-print for schools in some ideal never never land?

In fact, the theory represented here has developed out of description, analysis and evaluation of 'good practice' in schools. It has been, very typically, developed within the tough arenas of inner-city schools and schools in large peripheral housing estates.

John McBeath

From a standpoint in the early seventies when deschooling seemed, to this writer at least, to be the most logical analysis of a moribund and cliched school system I have, through the experience of working closely with dedicated teachers in honest schools, come to the belief that there is a reschooling movement which is now revitalizing both the theory and practice of teaching and learning. That 'reschooling' must acknowledge that at the very heart of the process lies a commitment to social education.

Social Education As Method

Jean Sames

Introduction

This chapter will attempt to illustrate the process of social education in practice. It draws heavily on the work of Birmingham Young Volunteers (BYV) Social Education Project. The nature of the relationship between a young volunteer organization and secondary schools is in itself interesting; however this chapter will not pursue that relationship — except when essential. It will present the work done in one school as a case study to illustrate one definition of social education.

It is, however, important to trace a little of the history of the BYV Social Education Project in order to understand the development of its commitment to social education as a method.

BYV Social Education Project

Birmingham Young Volunteers often acted as a kind of clearing house for schools who wished to develop community service schemes for fourth and fifth year pupils. Some of these groups were well-motivated high achievers who wished to serve the 'less fortunate', but R.O.S.L.A. precipitated an avalanche of demand for relevant, useful, worthwhile activities for the 'less able', and BYV was pressed more anxiously to provide contacts for community service type courses.

Over the next few years dissatisfaction with the depth, and short-lived nature of the work forced BYV to look critically at its role and to redefine the work it was prepared to undertake. Generally BYV workers felt that many of the community service type courses they served were not 'pupil-centred' — that is, they were not initiated by pupils, took little account of pupils' felt needs and interests, and produced little long-term understanding of the community, nor the motivation or confidence to effect change within it.

It became increasingly clear that the education workers would need to evolve a strategy which would challenge the educational assumptions behind community service and offer something which would either replace or refashion it, putting the needs of the pupils at the centre. It was also apparent that 'education' rather than service was becoming the motivating factor in BYV's reformation, and from that time forward defining and redefining the education of young people and the voluntary projects role vis-à-vis schools was to become a dominant theme. BYV did not rethink its education aims in a vacuum nor in isolation. There were many initiatives during the seventies which addressed themselves to defining Social Education. One which has become well-known was active tutorial work.

Birmingham Education Authority was actively involved in promoting the use of active tutorial work books in tutorial time, and encouraged much-needed training in the use of active learning methods. The Social Education Project became quite directly involved in this training and in some work with pupils in tutorial time.

The attitude of the Social Education Project to active tutorial work (ATW) would need a great deal more unravelling than is possible here. Suffice it to say that there were areas of dislocation, in spite of some very real excitement when the Project first came across active tutorial work. Whatever might have been the original aims of the work, the books, as they appeared to be widely used, gave pupils very little control over what they wanted to learn. Hard-pressed teachers, faced with teaching a 'new area' for which they had received little training were pleased to receive books which offered a structured course, and this structured course was the syllabus. This seemed to the Social Education Project to be one of the major aims of Social Education — that pupils have a genuine say in their own learning. Therefore, the definition of social education finally adopted by the Project was:

Social Education is a process whereby young people are enabled to learn more about themselves, the group of which they are a part, and the society (community) in which they are living. The process fosters critical awareness and is designed to enable pupils to develop skills which make a reasoned and confident participation in society possible. (BYV, 1979)

Although the form of words changed over the years, the project has consistently maintained that social education is a process which fosters:

(i)   an individual's increased consciousness of herself — her values, attitudes and skills;

(ii) an individual's sense of being part of a group, of the role she plays and can play in the group;

(iii) community awareness.

The definition also, and most importantly, answers the 'why social education?' question — to open up the possibility of effecting change.

The general tendency of most schooling is to stress content. The answer to, 'what did you learn in school today?' is likely to be history, or fractions, hardly ever that 'I learned that I or the group can ... or this local area is ...'. The Project has, as one of its primary articles of faith the notion that pupils themselves, the knowledge they bring, the skills they have and the values they hold are a legitimate area of educational enquiry and interest; the pupils themselves were the building blocks on which the educational process was to be built.

Many months were spent negotiating a contract with schools which showed an initial interest in the 'new' ideas of the project. The Project offered experienced teachers, time, contacts and some expertise which schools would tap into.

The Project asked for:

(i)   a teacher who had opted to work with the project;

(ii) a mixed-ability group of fourth or fifth year pupils, who had opted for the course;

(iii) a whole morning or afternoon;

(iv) to meet in a base outside school.

It is obvious from these 'demands' that the Project workers had a genuine critique of schooling itself, not simply of community service. There is no doubt that the development of the project was influenced by the writings of Illich, Freire, John Holt, White and Brockington, and others. The demands made by the project were a genuine attempt to minimize the influence of the compulsory nature of school, the school building, the strange 35 minute blocks of time and streaming. It was a small but brave attempt to show that learning and schooling are not synonymous, and that often traditional schooling gets in the way of true learning. Amazingly in 1976 six Birmingham secondary schools were willing to meet most of those demands.

Jean Sames

A Case Study

What follows is a description of the work of one of these schools. It is a mixed comprehensive school in Birmingham's inner city. Much ground work had been done by the BYV worker, explaining the nature of the 'course', negotiating a base outside school and getting to know the teacher. The work was done with the group from 1979–81. This description is based on a report presented to the head of the school at the end of the first year's work.

Our Aims for the Course

Our definition of social education includes the view that pupils should be encouraged to develop the skills to take an active part in their own society and to enable change to happen in it. We have found that such skills as observation, asking questions, analyzing answers, communication skills and general social skills are fostered best in an atmosphere of cooperation, mutual trust and informality. We have also found that these skills are best developed and practiced in small groups, with adults and pupils learning together. The teacher and BYV worker plan work together, using each session to try to promote this kind of learning. The group consisted of about twenty pupils, mainly girls, fourth year, and of mixed ability.

First Term

The main objectives of the first term were to enable pupils and adults to get to know one another, to work together and to begin to find out about the area in which they lived. Pupils found it hard to talk about themselves — probably because they had not had to do so before, and we had to overcome ... 'But we know one another already' ... when in fact they didn't.

We then asked them to draw the school in its neighbourhood as they saw it. This exercise in 'mental mapping' provided the opportunity for talk, comment, and disagreements — definitely the kind of climate we wanted to foster. The position of the school varied considerably in the drawings — from the very centre of the picture to being a small dot on the horizon! Pupils were then given polaroid cameras, to share, and asked to use up to four photographs, bring them back and mount them. They were simply asked to take photographs of things which interested them in the neighbourhood. The selection of photographs showed:

— old/new buildings
— old people; drunken man
— empty houses/burnt out houses
— Lucas's (employment)
— empty shops

This first session was a kind of model of the approach we wanted to follow. This was not to be a traditional 'lesson'; pupils would offer a great deal from their own observations and insights. We also wanted to show that we trusted pupils with hardware and to go out of school (and the community centre where we met) unsupervised. We also set the pattern for working in small groups around the equipment.

Many of the next sessions were based on the themes identified through the camera exercises. Of particular interest was the local shopping centre (the Community Centre in which we were based is on the edge of that shopping centre). Pupils again worked in small groups; some surveyed the number of empty shops; they produced a graph of their results, and illustrated it with photographs of premises which were either vandalized or empty. Other groups prepared questions, practiced with tape recorders and interviewed shoppers about the facilities available; other groups tried to find out future plans for the modification or development of the Centre; one group tried to interview the Manager of Tescos, who eventually refused! The pupils compared this Centre with another more thriving Centre a few miles away, and with a fairly busy main shopping street. On one memorable occasion a small group was accused of being out of school without permission and of stealing the tape recorder.

These few weeks showed the adults that the pupils were able to organize themselves to work around a topic. After some initial hesitation they grew more confident of finding things out for themselves.

Tape recorders proved to be useful tools for this kind of work. There is ample opportunity to practice, to make mistakes, to start again. Generally it is easier to approach people to ask their opinions because tape recorders are 'formal' tools. Also, and most importantly in a mixed ability group — they overcome literacy problems (for the time being) and allow all pupils to take part fully.

We were left with the problem of how to share the work done. We had gradually evolved a strategy of everyone present sitting down and listening to any group which returned from an interview. We asked questions, and supported their efforts. But the sharing needed to be wider. Did we display the work in school? If so, how? Was it to be beautifully presented — but obviously adult — or should it be the pupils' own presentation. We decided that it should be the pupils' own work, encouraged by the adults. These pupils, embarked on a non-examination course, not rewarded by ticks or marks, needed another kind of recognition. This was truly work — even though quite fun — and we needed to value that work. Some pupils found this kind of work unacceptable — especially after the pressure of exams — so they left to take up more examinable options, but others took their place.

The next few weeks followed a similar pattern, but attempted to move out from the Centre to look at the neighbourhood. We visited voluntary agencies, playschemes, playhouses, the neighbourhood office of Social Services, residents groups, and saw the effects of being described as a housing action area. The whole term's work was summed up by discussion 'How do I see this area?', 'How do I feel about it?', 'Would I want to bring up my children here?'. The ambivalence was obvious — this is home, but it could be improved. A large group discussion made this a difficult session — small group work for part of the time would have improved matters.

The last session was a coffee morning, organized by the pupils, for the adults and other members of staff. We were becoming comfortable together.

Second Term

The pupils had suggested that there were two major areas they wished to tackle in the second term — these were *race* and *crime*. These had been identified in a questionnaire at the end of the autumn term. They also noted that they saw the role of the adult as making it possible for them to interview people and find 'things out'.

Race

The adults felt that a 'gentle' introduction, uncovering the pupils' own experiences and expectations was an appropriate place to start. *Hassle* (produced by CSV) suggested some ideas for role plays. The group produced two very telling role plays. The first explored the difficulties of finding a job — but reversed the 'normal' trend in our society by having some black employers refuse a job to a white applicant.

This provided the opportunity to talk about racism in employment and gave the white members of the group the chance to feel a little of what black job applicants feel. The second role play concerned the situation at home if the young people brought home a girlfiend or boyfriend from a different race. This gave the pupils the opportunity to explore how they felt about 'mixed' relationships and the reactions of their parents. The one Asian girl in the group felt able to contribute at this point (the first spontaneous contribution) about arranged marriages.

Much of the role playing was, as yet, outside pupils' own experience, but not far removed from it. Role playing was a vehicle to explore myths, reality, hearsay and wishful thinking. It was more valuable than facts about black unemployment in the area — at this stage.

The role plays were essentially pessimistic as they uncovered racism, prejudice and misunderstanding. There are many agencies in the area around the school which are actively engaged in combatting these problems at various levels, and we felt that visiting these agencies could be useful. We followed the pattern of working in small groups. Pupils grouped themselves (usually along friendship lines) and prepared themselves for visiting several agencies.

Initial visits were made in order to set up interviews at mutually convenient times. Pupils gave some introductory information at this stage, to signal what they hoped to achieve. Groups varied in the amount of time they were prepared to give to preparation. All the agencies welcomed them; often pupils were more interested in the motivation of the workers than in the work of the agency; generally people answered with surprising openness. Some of the projects visited were AFFOR (All Faiths for One Race); Asian Resource Centre; Black Studies section of the local library.

The model used was very similar to the first term's visit.

Preparation	Visit	Report back
What do we want to know; preparing questions; testing tape recorders.	Length varied according to interest.	Impressions, play tapes, comments, questions for further discussion.

The number of skills employed regularly was impressive; pupils practiced negotiation, asking questions, synthesizing answers; more questions — as well as a high level of general social skills in visiting people and being welcomed back again!

When pupils work in small groups and are out on visits, it is easy for pupils and adults to lose a sense of the overall framework. We decided to have a whole morning together reviewing the questions which the pupils had identified as important to them. The most pressing issue seemed to be the group's attitude to Rastafarianism. Some felt that Rastas 'let down' the whole black community and made it more difficult for others to get jobs and be accepted. Others felt that at least Rastas 'fought back'. The whole group rejected the idea that law could remove prejudice or racism; some pupils felt strong enough to confront people and shame them into behaving with less discrimination. It seemed from the discussion that all their efforts to change society (at this stage in their lives) would be on a personal rather than on a collective or legal level, even though they had visited several agencies who worked at a community level.

School and race

Schools are part of society; their own school was a microcosm of the world. Schools can, in the pupils' opinion, help to create a more genuinely multi-cultural society or hinder that process. One session was spent examining how pupils thought schools could encourage a more genuine understanding and change in areas of race. The technique we used is called the statement card game (Richardson *et al.* 1982).

The statements produced were these:

(i) Pupils — teacher — parent — community relationships. They wanted a 'children's night' when they could talk to teachers about their problems in school.

(ii) More black teachers. Teachers should be given more time to explore the area in which they teach — especially with regard to housing problems etc.

(iii) Three traditional subject areas were chosen for special mention. These subjects should be tackled in more relevant ways
   — History should tackle slavery, immigration and the opportunity to 'share realities' and cultures.
   — Religious education — understanding one anothers' faiths and how that affects lives.
   — Home economics-tasting one anothers' food, learning to cook different things.

(iv) Teacher training — teachers should learn (get an 'O' level in) multicultural things.

The adults were impressed by the statements. They showed an understanding of the schools as they are, and what it might be possible to do. The statements might now give us a sense of deja-vu, but they are still not implemented in many places.

Pupils thought that it would be worthwhile visiting the three departments singled out by the cards. We followed the same model as for the other visits — preparation — interviews — report back. It was more difficult to have flexibility here as members of staff were teaching. It was however dialogue between teachers and pupils and broke down some of the 'traditional barriers'.

The final session on race was a visit by one of the workers from an agency which a small group had visited. We tried an agenda-forming exercise — pupils brainstormed questions which they would like discussed, and we saw this session as a summing up and challenge. However, the agenda and the speaker never really met! It was typical of a session with an expert guest speaker. The speaker's analysis was far removed from the pupils' own; they were silenced rather than challenged. Pupils were left feeling they were not valuable; that their approach was naive. It turned out to be the opposite of learning together.

Crime

We introduced the subject with a visit to the law courts. This sparked off many questions. This was followed by a simulation game called 'Justice' (BYV, 1976) in which pupils take the roles of magistrates and defendants; defendants are tried and magistrates pass sentence. It gives a good indication of power, powerlessness, a sense of fair play or justice and these were explored. After this pupils thought that they would be particularly interested in violence against women. We set up a meeting with Birmingham's Rape Crisis Centre who agreed to come and talk and answer questions. As a preparation we looked at how cartoons depict women; pupils tried their hand at creating their own cartoons. The adults thought that the pupils would make a connection between the portrayal of women as inept, weak, lazy, and women as victims. The connection was rejected. When the visitors came these ideas were further developed, but the group found the concept of rape as power rather than sexuality difficult. The discussion lasted the whole morning and was thoughtful and sensitive.

Lunch

Pupils themselves were very keen to prepare for a West Indian lunch for members of staff as a summing up of our multicultural work.

They saved money, organized the shopping, liaised with the home economics department and finally prepared a splendid lunch. Everyone took part, and staff appreciated the meal, although some did find talking to our pupils about the course rather difficult.

An Evaluation

The work in one particular school has been described at some length in an attempt to give a flavour of the way the project worked, and maybe illustrate the strengths and weakness of the approach. From BYV's perspective the main strength of the year's work was that the course evolved gradually but surely from the pupils' own interests. Many of the starting points were rooted in the pupils' own experience, but there is universality about the themes which gave us courage to believe that a pupil-initiated curriculum would not be frivolous or 'unworthy'.

In terms of fulfilling the aims of social education as defined by the project, the area least covered is 'myself'. All the work was done in small groups; there was ample opportunity to learn the skills of small group work, but probably not enough (although some) for an exploration of personal identity.

Pupils grew in self-confidence. At the beginning of the year some were very noisy, others said nothing. Small group work enabled more cooperation. As the pupils met new people, and new situations, as they prepared their own questions and made many visits they were able to begin to make a confident exploration of their own locality.

The role of the adults is worth exploring. We rarely had to 'police' the young people; relationships of trust and mutual respect grew as the young people realized that they could use our materials, make visits without us and were trusted to come back. It was also obvious that in some areas they knew far more then we did. We had to trust their judgment about the area, about racism, about their school. This enabled a more equitable balance of power than is 'normal' in most schools.

The major drawback of working in this way was made apparent as the year progressed. The management of the school was genuinely interested in the work going on, but it took a considerable amount of energy to keep the school informed of what was being done. Although the school was genuinely pleased with the attendance and enthusiasm of the young people (attendance remained at almost 100 per cent for the two years of the course, even though some pupils only came for our course!), we found that it was possible to pursue a successful course without touching the great mass of schooling. Our efforts in the community centre were marginal to the 'real' work, and might be 'good for the pupils', but hardly able to influence the core of the school's work.

Working with pupils in the way outlined above was exciting but risky. It was not possible to work to a syllabus, nor plan a course well in advance. It is, however, possible to know what skills we would like to practice and how important the exploration of values and attitudes is.

The pressure which BYV felt to influence the 'core curriculum' grew. The Project was able to work within religious education departments, English and social studies where much of the methodology was welcome. Although there is less 'risk' when a syllabus is given, opportunity for 'small scale', almost impromptu, visits outside the classroom grew less, whole mornings or afternoons and mixed ability groups became almost a thing of the past, so the Project lost some of its edge, and its critique of schooling. However, it gained a foothold into more traditional areas of school life; it showed possibility for change in unexpected places. The classroom work was to continue alongside a programme of in-service training for teachers. One area of work continued to influence another.

Conclusion

At present, there seems to be a general move towards valuing social, personal and moral education in schools. Much work has been done exploring the legitimacy and even the necessity of schools being involved in this area of learning. The consensus seems to be that social education is 'a good thing'. However, much of the discussion is still on the level of 'what should we teach in social education?'. The emphasis of the Birmingham Young Volunteers Social Education Project is very much on 'how?'; and contained in its statements of intent are some indications of 'why?'.

References

BIRMINGHAM YOUNG VOLUNTEERS (1976) *Justice*, produced by students of Westhill College for the BYV Social Education Project.
BIRMINGHAM YOUNG VOLUNTEERS (1979) 'What is social education?',

statement to the in-service training course for teachers.

RICHARDSON, R., FLOOD, M. and FISHER, S. (1982) *Debate and Decisions — Schools in a World of Change, World Studies Project*, London (there is in this a detailed example of the statement card game).

Further Reading

The BYV Social Education Project produces reports of work undertaken which are available on request from: BYV Social Education Project, 17 Cannon Street, Birmingham, B2 5EN.

Part II   Social Education:
Curriculum Developments

Development Education

Scott Sinclair

The Nature of Development Education

The first part of this chapter considers the nature of development education and reviews the implications of this for the curriculum. The second part explores practical approaches. Many of those who have written about development education and the school curriculum — not only in Britain — have noted the problem that '. . . There is a real confusion over what development education is' (Thompson, 1982). This confusion is in part a healthy debate common to just about all areas of the curriculum. What is geography? . . . English? . . . multicultural education? . . . etc. If development education aims to function for all ages, across the curriculum and in different subjects (which indeed I argue it should) then clearly it is not any 'one thing'.

It is also the case that the phrase 'development education' has been adopted by a range of people who bring to it very different assumptions about models of development, processes of learning and the function of schooling. Definitions of development education tend to function at such a level of abstraction that they are very limited in the extent to which they mould our plans. Experience has shown that they are easily adapted to a wide ideological interpretation and therefore often reduced to rhetoric. Before considering definitions it is important to review some of the influences which contribute to different ideas about development education.

Initially it is important to reflect on our assumptions about development itself. Reed (1982) suggests that there is a parallel to be drawn between notions of development and models of development education. The traditional idea of development — (which is still widely used!) — is centred on western concepts of progress — and on the transfer of knowledge, technology, finance and institutional structures. Aid has a central role. The belief, whatever the rhetoric, is that we have the answer — indeed that there is an answer. The educational response therefore centres on information/knowledge and transmission models of learning. It is important to note that this approach can be adopted from 'a left' or 'a right' perspective.

Many see, or at least assume, that development education's major function relates to creating a better climate for the support of aid. It is fair to note that its most significant sources of funding may well have that idea as a base line. Hatcher (1982) describes the idea behind setting up of the ODM's (Ministry for Overseas Development) now defunct development education fund. 'To win popular support for Labour's international economic policies' ... in response to the findings of the Slackman Report (1977) on attitudes in Britain to overseas development. Hatcher sharpens up this debate with his own emphasis — 'People did not understand that increased aid was not extravagant charity but an essential strategy for maintaining the profitability of British Imperialism'. To put it another way or as Brandt, for example, might have put it, we live in an interdependent world, concern about development is in our mutual interest. It is also important to note that 'aid' like development is a word with a wide usage. The 'Real Aid Campaign' has done some useful work to influence ideas on what aid could/should be (Elliot *et al*, 1982).

At its worst, the focus on aid alone can lead to an 'African cavalry approach' which the media too often revels in. The powerful image of starvation and malnutrition is used to blast away all our skills in questioning what is happening and why. It reinforces popular misunderstanding by suggesting that the only answer is aid and that the problem is that there is not enough of it. Stradling (1984) relates this approach to the use of guilt and an attempt to approach these issues as if they are apolitical.

Many of the aid agencies, such as *Oxfam* and *War on Want*, are putting more effort into 'campaigning for development' and placing their aid work in the context of the wider issues. For example, their research and that of academic 'development studies' are an invaluable asset to development education. However, if their work is simply used to update knowledge in transmission models of teaching then the main challenge is avoided. The challenge is not one of finding a more enlightened analysis but of using methods which enable pupils to develop skills in exploring the complexity of situations for themselves.

There are those who argue for 'development education' to be a subject in its own right, with space on the timetable and an exam.

There are those that see 'development education' as information about aid — (even a form of fundraising) — or as the soft end of issue campaigning. Braun (1981) explores these tensions more fully.

There is a tendency, which may too often be expedient, to assume that these views are all different views of the same thing. This type of debate is of course a familiar one in other areas of curriculum innovation. There is in fact often more to share between people with similar approaches to learning but primarily interested in social education, multicultural education etc., than between people with different approaches but using the same label. For example, a report on political education (Crick and Porter, 1978) concludes . . . 'political education has as its objective political literacy for all — a blend of skills, attitudes and knowledge'. Political education is therefore seen as an approach to a variety of subjects and not a discipline in its own right. My own view of development education follows similar lines — with the objective being a 'global literacy'. Like that report I also recognize the need for dealing directly with issues, which are too often glossed over.

Hicks (1983) describes 'open' and 'closed' ends of a spectrum of educational thinking. At the 'open' end of the spectrum there is considerable common ground in terms of models of learning, views of the function of education and approaches to curriculum change between those involved in social education, political education and education for a multicultural society, etc. etc. This common ground is centred on the needs of the pupil, the role of attitudes and skills, the questioning of the dominant role of knowledge and active involvement in learning. At the 'closed' end of the spectrum in development education there is an isolated emphasis on the poverty and disadvantage of the poor in the 'third world'. It is vital that curriculum projects in development education give priority to work at the 'open' end of the spectrum.

Another very important influence on development education has evolved from asking questions raised by the leading thinkers of Asia, Africa and South America about the process of development and underdevelopment in the context of our own society — and its education systems. In the early 1970s 'conscientization' was a popular phrase among those attempting to shape development education programmes. It was inspired by the Brazilian educator Paulo Freire (1972) who took 'life situations of learners here and now as the starting point from which to raise consciousness'. He argues that learning should be liberating and that literacy is about organizing ones own experiences and ideas. This type of thinking has also influenced the development education approach to knowledge. He speaks out against what he calls the 'banking system of education' where the teacher holds the knowledge — gives it out — to collect it later by assessment.

Wren (1977) draws on the ideas of Freire to consider learning situations about justice. People learn about justice through experience. Experience of the relationships in the classroom or the school are more influential to that learning than the overt curriculum. A recent review of the role of development education for young children (Grafton, 1984) highlights the importance of the hidden curriculum and the structures of the school. The early experiences of school and its structures are probably a child's first major experience of the social world and how it works — and where (s)he fits in. What does that child learn about the world?

Another South American Ivan Illich is credited by Hargreaves (1982) for raising the awareness of the role of the hidden curriculum in Britain. Development education has to be concerned about this '2nd curriculum' and the evidence that it is dominant over the overt curriculum in terms of the relationship between schooling and society. If we are not concerned with this then development education is in danger of merely being part of the 'classical humanist' (Skilbeck, 1976) tradition of absorbing the fundamental challenges of change by introducing apparent change, and maintain into the traditional function of school viz society's inequalities.

In a similar way we can use Tanzania's education for self-reliance which is described by Williamson (1979) as a 'change of direction in the development of education'. There is a need to ask similar questions to those asked by President Nyerere in our own society. Perhaps we should be seeing recent moves to vocational training, TVEI (Technical and Vocational Education Initiative) and the role of the MSC (Manpower Services Commission) in education policy in this context. Certainly looking at case studies from the 'third world' may help us to ask more effective questions about these ideas in our own society. Davies (1984) provides a useful start in this direction.

Finally, it is important to review these ideas in the context of proposals for a movement towards a 'new international economic order' which involve new strategies for economic and political relationships between countries .... 'such objectives have an education dimension, which entails a drastic revision of orthodox assumptions about the relationship between economic development and education' (Encel, 1980). Too often this change is seen to be about development in 'the south'. It is equally important in 'the north' — in Britain and Europe as a whole for example.

Development education as a process of curriculum innovation has to relate to the current levels of consciousness. It has to operate at the 'open end' of the spectrum and be concerned about the issues raised by other contemporary social change related curriculum innovation. The issues are complex and highly debatable — we don't have any certain answers. They are also confused by our own attitudes and assumptions — and the powerful images of need which the TV can show are very real. Attempts to make this accessible to pupils and to their own personal/social development raises challenges about the very way we teach.

In this context a definition like this one from the United Nations can be very challenging. Development education seeks

> ... to enable people to participate in the development of their community, their nation and the world as a whole. Such participation implies a critical awareness of local, national and international situations based on an understanding of the social, economic and political processes....

As to the content of development education, the UN argued that it is

> ... concerned with issues of human rights, dignity, self-reliance and social justice in both developed and developing countries. It is concerned with the causes of underdevelopment and the promotion of an understanding of what is involved in development, of how different countries go about undertaking development, and of the reasons for and ways of achieving a new international economic and social order.

Practice

This section explores the potential of development education in relation to practice. While larger questions about the organization of schools and their relationship to society are important, it is appropriate here to concentrate on the planned curriculum.

If, as I have already suggested, development education has a role across the curriculum then it may seem important to consider the practical organization of secondary schools, at least to the extent of questioning the current fragmentation of the curriculum into subjects and the lack — (in the majority of cases) — of coordination between these fragments. Clearly development education, like those other areas of innovation in this book, would welcome more real interest in these questions.

I have been involved in different development education curriculum projects relating to home economics, geography, environmental education, English, religious education and, more recently, the early stages of a history project. Clearly it would be a nonsense if this simply involved introducing a specific element into each of these components of the curriculum. Basic questions and challenges need to be considered within the context of each subject. These questions may relate to attitudes and skills or the contribution the subject makes to how the pupil makes sense of change in the modern world.

I will at a later stage return to these specific subject areas. However, before that I would like to focus on four main areas of importance to all those interested in development education:

(i) the implications for the teachers — planning;
(ii) the role of attitudes;
(iii) the development of skills;
(iv) the potential content.

The Implications for Teachers — Planning

In the type of approach I am advocating a key factor is planning both in the long-term and for particular sessions. It is one of the myths about open learning processes — (sometimes referred to as active learning) — that they require less preparation, though it should be noted that an important part of that preparation is for participants to be in a responsive frame of mind.

A vital dimension of planning is finding the opportunity — (as part of your own group or inservice workshops) — to explore your own assumptions about change, about the wider world, to grapple for yourself with some of the complexity of the issues and to review what you are hoping pupils will gain from the course you are designing.

What are we going to 'do' about the 'third world'? Much course planning, however energetic, starts with a rapidly compiled list of content. . . . we don't have time to stop and reflect on our assumptions. Why is it that when it comes to the 'Third World' all too often our content headings are a list of problems? What analysis do we put over to our pupils by approaching 75 per cent of the world's population from that perspective?

In a planning group where this sort of question comes up we turn to reviewing our aims. Aims are clearly important but too often they are presented in a language which does not relate to our actual teaching approaches.

The group of teachers who developed *People Before Places?* (Daniels, 1985) used a 'card game' to facilitate their discussion about aims. This centred on the question:

> What do we hope pupils will gain from a development education approach to geography?

The game, which is described in the book, involves everyone in writing their own cards and then dealing them out for selection. This allows everyone an opportunity to express their views. The procedure identifies areas of consensus and disagreement. These can then be followed up.

As a result of using this game and other similar approaches to teach in-service work such as those in *Debate and Decision* (Richardson, 1982) it is possible for a group to be more creative, to identify their own needs and for the challenges which arise to have a more practical outcome. For example, one group exploring their ideas were able to identify the following points of agreement. From this they were able to take on the question of whether their teaching methods and materials reflected their own ideas:

- (i) Development means different things to different people.
- (ii) Development is about people, not just economics. People are the key factor.
- (iii) Development does not necessarily involve economic development on the model of industrialised countries with advanced technologies.
- (iv) Pupils should be aware of and able to question information and recognize bias.
- (v) Pupils should recognize that development is taking place in their own local environment, not only in other countries.
- (vi) Pupils should gain the idea that development is about choice, and that any choice has both positive and negative aspects.

Too often policy is not seen as a practical issue yet it is quite clear that teachers — (like pupils) — have a range of attitudes, for example to race . . . and to education. So whatever policy an LEA or school develops for 'multicultural education' or 'anti-racist education' for example, it is of little real value unless it is redeveloped as real policy with 'ownership' belonging to the teachers implementing the policy — and indeed the pupils receiving it. 'Open' processes of learning involved in developing staff policy are therefore central to the possible effectiveness of any new policy. It is only through processes such as these that policy can effect, in any real sense, the ethos of the school and the 'hidden curriculum'.

The Role of Attitudes

There is often an assumption that it is a central objective of development education 'to change attitudes'. There is some truth in this at least to the extent that the values and attitudes that contribute to the design of a scheme of work will have an influence beyond the learning structure itself. Procedural values, for example, relating to openmindedness, questioning and human qualities such as empathy are clearly important. It is also clear that such values cannot be introduced by teaching strategies which themselves do not reflect those values. It is, however, a limited view of development education which advocates an attempt to teach particular substantive attitudes about aid or 'the third world'.

Our attitudes and assumptions — however well informed — are a strong influence on our ability to analyze any other information which we receive on a particular subject. If therefore we have a stereotyped view of people in a particular part of the world then this will influence how we perceive their achievements. There is a tendency, for example, to assume and therefore stress the differences between the nature of situations here and in other parts of the world, rather than starting from a recognition of the fundamental similarities between human situations.

There are many examples of school books which attempt a synthesis of the 'third world' pivoted around the idea that population growth and a lack of resources are the key to explaining 'the third world'. There is a need to develop skills in exploring the nature of bias because this skill will then have a wide application.

Activities such as brainstorming are a useful starting point for exploring attitudes. Groups throw out, without reaction, their first ideas they have relating to a theme. Another version of this is to work from expectations. For example before showing a film of . . . you ask groups to brainstorm what they expect to see in the film. This kind of activity not only brings out assumptions about the issue or place but also has the advantage of encouraging more active viewing of the film. *Seeing and Perceiving* (Richardson and Taylor, 1982) suggests a. number of other activities to make more use of films. Sets of photographs can also be a useful stimulus to group work on attitudes. An activity selecting photographs which 'say something to you about development' from a set on Ghana (CWDE, 1980) for example, can enable a very constructive discussion about assumptions which often see development as a process of 'westernization'.

There is a temptation to turn these activities into a judgment of the pupils' attitudes and use it as evidence against them. This is not very constructive. It is important to use them for genuine group exploration and as a starting point for learning more about the issues involved. It is important that pupils can express their assumptions and attitudes freely even when they are far from certain about them. We should also be clear that it is not surprising that pupils have limited views of Africa, for example, when you take into account factors such as:

(i) the 'aid agency' images, used for fundraising, by which they promote important work but all too often in a way which increases popular misunderstanding of that work and the people they work with;

(ii) the fact that media coverage emphasizes periods of crisis and focusses on that crisis in isolation from the other events and lifestyles in the location.

Some pupils may of course use the opportunity — especially if it is one they do not get very often — to express views which quite clearly need challenging. Expressing strongly racist ideas for example. It is important to bring out views from other pupils to provide a challenge or to contribute evidence yourself to enable discussion of different viewpoints. It is also important that in the role of facilitator you maintain the ground rules, for example relating to openmindedness, listening to each other and exploring different perspectives.

The Development of Skills

If we are able to describe development education in terms of skills then they can provide the basis for planning learning strategies and a framework from which to select the detail of content and review the role of attitudes. They can also express the objectives of development education in terms of enabling the development of the skills necessary to participate in the modern world. Skills such as the following are of importance:

(i) Skills of recognizing our own values and the influences on these:

(a) For example using a stimulus like photograph sets — for example *What is a Family?* (Braun, 1985), *Doing Things* (Redknap, 1983) and *The World in Birmingham* (Sinclair, 1982) — to work in groups or organize and share our experiences of a theme. It is possible to use such activities to build up an agenda related to the broad theme of ideas and issues which the group think are important for further study.

(b) Working in groups ... Which ideas do we agree about — which do we want to challenge each other on?

(c) Using a series of quotes about a situation — which do we identify with most ... and least ... why?

(ii) Skills of empathy with people in different situations and with different cultures:

(a) For example using case studies or 'situations' (i.e. brief description of an event illustrating dilemmas of case study). How would you react if you imagine that you are the person described or found yourself in that situation?

(b) Using role cards to argue an issue from a particular perspective, or using simulation games to get deeper into role and grapple with the complexity of an issue.

(c) So ... you are for 'whole foods' and against convenience foods? Brainstorm all the advantages of convenience foods.

(iii) Skills of acquiring information and of critical analysis of such information:

(a) For example, using a collection of newspaper articles on the same event. What is the different emphasis? Pupils developing their own checklist of types of biased image that they identify.

(b) Collect different information about your town — from the tourist board, local campaigning groups etc. What are the contrasts? Design posters about the school to show it in different ways.

      (c) Take a policy statement such as the regional plans published by county councils and underline the main words — arrange items on a large sheet of paper linking with arrows to show the argument ... then add questions to the diagram. Do you agree with the statement? What assumptions does it seem to make?

      (d) Use a grid of 100 dots to sketch on the figures you are dealing with to make them easier to relate to.

  (iv) Skills of recognizing the validity of different points of view:

      (a) For example start by identifying different points of view about a local issue or development project. Build up these skills with more familiar issues before using case study material to do a similar exercise for a development project overseas.

      (b) Use role cards taking different political profiles to stage a debate about an issue.

      (c) The complexity of situations often reflect the existence of a range of subjective views influencing the situation. It is important to develop skills in getting a sense of this collection of subjective views rather than synthesizing a notional objectivity.

      (d) Simulate a government or an aid committee. You have ten projects before you. Which do you give priority and why? What actually happened? Simulations such as Oxfams Aid Committee Game provide a useful format for this approach.

  (v) Skills of forming our own conclusions:

      (a) For example, use activities, especially towards the end of a course, which bring together the major debates. These activities could either be a framework for the pupils to fill in their own ideas (for example, a web or mental map) or be a series of overviews which you provide to be used in ranking-type exercises. Pupils use them to consider their stance in the light of what they have been learning.

There are a number of teachers' handbooks, such as those mentioned at the end of this chapter, which provide a fuller account of ideas such as these. Collectively they provide an approach which has the potential for adoption to fill a wide range of needs in course design.

It is useful to note an assumption that discussion, the use of photographs and similar stimulus, role play, questioning information etc. all make demands on skills in group work. Clearly it is therefore also important to plan to build up experiences of learning in groups.

The Nature of Possible Content

In planning any specific work the content will be influenced more by the curriculum subject area than has been seen to be the case in terms of the role of attitudes or the development of skills. It is useful in terms of content to define development education as a perspective which provides a global context.

Despite the more dominant influence of the subject area there are some important general approaches to content in development education such as the recognition of a local dimension, the need to make the complexity of many development issues more accessible and the need to use other objectives to help choose from the massive amount of possible content.

The local dimension expressed in its most basic form is the idea that the world is here — that we are part of it — it is our everyday experience. Furthermore that processes of change and the tensions of development choices operate in our own community — (and country) — in a similar way to other places. *The World in Birmingham* (Sinclair, 1982) shows how these local choices are not only influenced by local tensions but also the processes of investment from overseas, aid from the government or the EEC. Also events in other parts of the world which effect the price of oil or cocoa, or increase the demand for manufactured goods — such as tanks or guns — all influence developments in Birmingham.

It is important to introduce concepts such as aid, development — (or indeed underdevelopment) in a local context. Starting local is not just a question of building out in concentric circles from you to the world. It is recognizing that the way you teach about your own locality or make use of a pupil's own experiences is introducing both skills and analysis which helps pupils to relate to the issues you wish to tackle in those outer circles — and more importantly to the people who are involved in those issues.

Recently there have been many courses introduced on the theme of 'Understanding British Industry'. Many of them give little or no importance to seeing what is happening in Britain in terms of the international system in which we now function. There is a direct relationship between some of the pressures for particular types of development through industrialization in the 'south' and the deindustrialization in the 'north' — such as for example, that documented in the West Midlands (Gaffikin and Nickson, 1984).

On the global scale the issues are complex and dynamic. We are responding to, and attempting to analyze, events which are happening today, which are changing and which are part of international social economic and political patterns. Even if we give considerable personal energy to it we cannot, without simplistic dogmatism, provide our pupils with answers, we cannot even get hold of a lot of the evidence. It is also the case that we cannot define a specific body of knowledge about the world and change in the world which could be contained in even the most extravagant syllabus. All these factors are a challenge, to conventional models of learning — to our role as a teacher. We have to become aware of our own confusion — and be open about it. *75:25 Ireland in an Unequal World* (Regan, 1984) provides one of the best overviews available with regard to this problem.

We need to make use of teaching techniques which make this complexity, the dilemmas and indeed contradictions of particular situations more accessible. Simulation games or role play, for example, can allow pupils to build up a considerable insight into the factors involved in an issue. We can also use case study material which allows us to relate to the human experience of development tensions.

One final challenge relating to content is worth noting. It is usually the case that those involved in development education put the major proportion of their energy into materials and ideas for teaching about 'the third world' and the disadvantaged in 'the third world' in particular. There is growing interest in the idea of the local dimension already discussed but this too tends to concentrate on the processes of disadvantage. There is a need also to consider the rich. As Simpson (1984) puts it 'in order to understand powerlessness in some groups it is important to focus on the ways in which power is maintained by others'.

The Application of Development Education Approaches to Particular Areas of the Curriculum

There are a number of general handbooks which are useful to producing schemes of work. *The Development Puzzle* (Fyson, 1984) will be helpful to those interested in an overview of different uses of development education in a wide range of subjects, though it does in part make some very different assumptions about development education to those I make here. *Learning about Change* (Richardson, 1976) remains the most useful general introduction and stimulus for developing your own ideas. My main purpose in this section is to offer the reader some starting points to follow up the kind of issues raised in this chapter in the context of their own needs. I will therefore restrict myself to a very limited annotated list.

Geography

People Before Places? (Daniels, 1985) is an ideas book which offers a framework for planning courses in geography. *The Changing World and Geography* (CWDE, 1979) reviews a range of geography text books and their content about development. The journal *Contemporary Issues in Geography and Education* provides a regular package of challenges to geographers.

Social Education, Home Economics, Teaching about the Family

Values Cultures and Kids (Bovey, 1983) is a handbook outlining some basic teaching activities. *What is a Family?* (Braun and Eisenstadt, 1985) is a photopack which complements this.

Environmental Education

The forthcoming materials pack from the World Wildlife Fund Global Environment Education Project will provide a good starting point.

English

There is considerable potential for using literature from other countries and cultures. *A Handbook for Teaching African Literature* (Gunner, 1984) is a useful starting point. *Seeing into Words* (Bridle, 1986) takes a different approach by focussing on language and how it influences our perceptions of the world. The pack is organized round pupil discussion groups — the emphasis is on oral skills. The *World Studies Journal* (5, 3) has recently given over an issue to English teaching. This included a challenging article by Chris Searle.

History

A short paper (Shah, 1982) set the scene for possible work but little to date has been done in History and Development Education. *Half the Lies are True* (Regan and Sinclair, 1985) outlines a history project which is in its early stages.

Structured First Hand Experience

An important influence on the work of the Development Education Centre (Birmingham) and the ideas outlined in this chapter has been the experience of in-service courses which have included structured study visits in different parts of West Africa, India and Colombia. In *Learning about Africa* (Sinclair, 1979) a series of fourteen challenges were identified for these courses. One was titled barriers:

> Could we identify the barriers to our understanding of another country, its culture and its development? Would we be able to relate the way we cross these barriers through first hand experience to methods we could use in our teaching, to enable our pupils to cross similar barriers?

There is considerable practical value in this sort of in-service work especially when the teachers selected are able to lead local workshops for other teachers after the course. The style of preparation work before the visit is also of particular importance (Braun and Sinclair, 1980).

Recent experience of working in cooperation with those involved in development education in Ireland suggests that there is potential to learn about these barriers much closer to home (Regan and Sinclair, 1985). Viewing Britain/Ireland as a microcosm of international understanding (or misunderstanding) does, however, serve to remind us that the principle of introducing the concepts of development/underdevelopment in a local context is not an easy option — the issues are real, controversial and less easy to explain away!

References

BOVEY, M. *et al* (1983) *Values, Cultures and Kids — Approaches and Resources for Teaching Child Development and About the Family*, Birmingham, Development Education Centre.

BRAUN, D. (1981) 'What is development education?', *World Studies Journal*, 3, 2.

BRAUN, D. and EISENSTADT, N. (1985) *What is a Family?*, Birmingham, Development Education Centre.

BRAUN, D. and SINCLAIR, S. (1980) *Birmingham and the Wider World*, Birmingham, Development Education Centre.

BRIDLE, M. (1986) *Seeing into Words*, Birmingham, Development Education Centre.

CRICK, B. and PORTER, A. (Eds) (1978) *Political Education and Political Literacy*, London, Longman.

CWDE (1979) *The Changing World and Geography*, London, CWDE.

CWDE (1980) *Living with the Land*, London, CWDE.

DANIELS, A. *et al* (1985) *People Before Places*, Birmingham, Development Education Centre.

DAVIES, L. (1984) 'Alternatives in education from the third world' in HARBER, C. *et al Alternative Educational Futures*, London, Holt Educational.

ELLIOT, C. *et al* (1982) *Real Aid — A Strategy for Britain*, London, Oxfam, Christian Aid and WDM.

ENCEL, S. (1980) 'The future of education in relation to the new international economic order' in AVAKOV, R.M. (Ed) *The Future of Education and the Education of the Future*, Paris, Institute of Educational Planning.

FREIRE, P. (1972) *Pedagogy of the Oppressed*, Harmondsworth, Penguin.

LUI FYSON, M. (Ed) (1984) *The Development Puzzle*, London, CWDE and Hodder and Stoughton.

GAFFIKIN, F. and NICKSON, A. (1984) *Job Crisis and the Multinationals — The Case of the West Midlands*, Birmingham, TURC.

GRAFTON, T. (Ed) (1984) *Starting Together — Development Education and Young Children,* Birmingham, Developmnet Education Centre.

GUNNER, E. (1984) *A Handbook for Teaching African Literature*, London, Heinemann Educational.

HARGREAVES, D. (1982) *The Challenge for the Comprehensive School — Culture Curriculum and Community*, London, Routledge and Kegan Paul.

HATCHER, R. (1982) 'The construction of world studies', *NAME Journal*, II, I, pp. 23–35.

HICKS, D. (1983) 'Development education' in HUCKLE, J. (Ed) *Geographical Education*, London, Oxford University Press.

REDKNAP, C. *et al* (1983) *Doing Things — In and About the Home*, Maidenhead, Teachers Centre.

REED, S. (1982) *The Impact of DEC on Birmingham Schools*, unpublished thesis, University of Birmingham, Faculty of Education.

REGAN, C. (1984) *75:25 Ireland in an Unequal World*, Dublin, CON-GOOD.

REGAN, C. and SINCLAIR, S. (Eds) (1985) *Half the Lies are True — Ireland/Britain: A Microcosm of International Misunderstanding?*, Birmingham, Development Education Centre.

RICHARDSON, R. (1976) *Learning for Change in World Society — Reflections Activities and Resources*, World Studies Project.

RICHARDSON, R. (1981) *Culture, Race and Peace — Tasks and Tensions in the Classroom*, occasional paper no 2, Lancaster, Centre for Peace Studies.

RICHARDSON, R. *et al* (1982) *Debate and Decision — Schools in a World of Change*, World Studies Project.

RICHARDSON, R. and TAYLOR, A. (1982) *Seeing and Perceiving — Films in a World of Change*, Ipswich, Concord.

SHAH, S. (1982) *The Contribution of History to Development Education*, London, The Historical Association.

SIMPSON, A. (1984) 'The rich as a minority group', *Contemporary Issues in Geography and Education*, 1, 2, pp. 18–21.

SINCLAIR, S. (Ed) (1979) *Learning about Africa — Dilemmas, Approaches, Resources*, Birmingham, Development Education Centre.

SINCLAIR, S. (1982) *The World in Birmingham — Development as a Local Case Study*, Birmingham, Development Education Centre.

SKILBECK, M. (1976) *Culture Ideology and Knowledge*, Milton Keynes, Open University Press.

SLACKMAN RESEARCH ORGANIZATION LTD. (1977) *Survey of Attitudes Towards Overseas Development and Development Education*, London, Central Office of Information.

STRADLING, R. (1984) 'Teaching third world issues' in STRADLING, R. *et al Teaching Controversial Issues*, London, Arnold.

THOMPSON, A.R. (1982) 'World development: A challenge for teacher education', *International Education Review*, Paris, UNESCO.

WILLIAMSON, W. (1979) *Educational Social Structure and Development — A Comparative Analysis*, London, Macmillan.

WORALL, M. (1981) 'Multiracial Britain and the third world: Tensions and approaches in the classroom' in JAMES, A. and JEFFCOATE, R. (Ed) *The School in the Multiracial Society*, Oxford, Oxford University Press.

WREN, D. (1977) *Education for Justice — Pedagogical Principles*, Mary Knoll, N.Y., Orbis.

Political Education and Peace Education

Clive Harber

This chapter, like the other chapters of the book, concentrates on describing the nature and aims of its area of concern before going on to examine practical ideas for classroom method. However, readers interested in the controversial history surrounding the development of political education and peace education should see Brennan (1981, chapters 3 and 4) and Heater (1984, chapter 1).

The Nature of Political Education and Peace Education

There are many different definitions of 'politics'. However, as Porter *et al* suggest (1983, appendix 1), in the debate over political education in Britain the range of such definitions has been limited. The definitions utilized have certain characteristics in common: they all stress that at the basis of politics is conflict and disagreement (usually over the allocation of scarce resources), that choices, and thus decisions, have to be made and that the making of decisions will involve the exercise of power and authority both by those who made the decisions and those that try to influence them.

Politics as thus understood manifests itself at a great variety of levels of human activity — small groups, local communities, nation-states, regional blocs of states and world wide. Unfortunately, however, the subject association which has been most directly concerned with political education, the Politics Association, has had its main professional interest in the teaching of British government and politics (Heater, 1980). The Programme for Political Education, which developed the idea of political literacy, seemed to widen the area of concern to include small group behaviour but was less explicit about global or international political education (Porter, 1979). As a result the global dimension of political education has tended to be considered under the general heading of 'world studies' and has developed a separate tradition. The dominant model of international relations used by those involved in world studies is the 'web', as opposed to the 'billiard ball'. In the billiard ball model '. . . only the outer surface of the balls (states) are in contact. There is surface interaction, even occasional collision, but the internal structure/ relationships of each ball (state) are not significantly affected . . .'. The web model, on the other hand, emphasizes the notion of the 'global village' and the idea of global interdependence i.e. that events in any one part of the world can have significant repercussions in many — possibly all — other parts (Selby, 1984).

How does 'peace education' differ? Like political education it deals with conflict and its resolution but its main area of concern is not with conflict and disagreement per se but in identifying, and thereby eventually removing, the causes of *violent* conflict. Violent conflict is not restricted either to nuclear war or war in general because, it is argued, 'peacelessness' can be found in many situations where acts of overt physical violence do not exist. This is because human relationships can be characterized by 'structural violence' i.e. where people live in conditions of oppression, injustice, domination and exploitation. Curle (1977) uses the following example of peacelessness: '. . . in South Africa, the relatively "peaceful" status quo is maintained by injustice and . . . a masked violence is constantly done to the rights and lives of human beings'. Also like 'the political', peacelessness or structural violence can exist between individuals, groups or nations.

Referring to the content of peace studies Derbyshire LEA has commented that 'in its concern to sharpen pupils' awareness and understanding of conflict and its aim to search for alternative non-violent solutions there is considerable overlap with the aims of political education (1983). This overlap also holds true in the area of skills to be developed through political education/world studies/ peace education. For example, one of the earliest and best known courses in peace education at Atlantic College in South Wales talks of the need to find non-violent solutions to conflict and to develop 'skills necessary for their implementation' (NUT, 1984). More specifically the course wishes to develop the capacity to select evidence, to construct arguments both oral and written, and to modify these in the light of criticism and discussion (Heater, 1980). These relate closely to the skills specified by the Programme for Political Education: interpreting and evaluating political information and evidence, organizing political information, applying reasoning skills and constructing arguments based on evidence, perceiving the consequences of taking or not taking political actions in given contexts, expressing one's viewpoints through an appropriate medium, participating in political discussion, understanding (if not agreeing with) the views of others, exercising empathy, participating in group decision making and effectively influencing political situations (Porter, 1979). When compared with a checklist of skills for world studies (Hicks and Townley, 1982) there is also considerable overlap except that this list rightly includes the skill of enquiry i.e. that students should be able to find and record information from books, maps, statistical tables diagrams, photographs, newspapers, audio-visual materials, and should be able to interview people with specialist personal experience.

However, despite the general description above, it would be mistaken to assume that there is complete agreement about the nature of political education and peace education. What is meant by those terms depends on the ideological stance of the person using the term. Ideologies of political education and world studies have been classified according to various political labels — conservative, liberal, reformist, radical etc. according to aims, content, classroom method, theories of knowledge etc. (Richardson, 1974; Porter *et al*, 1983; Harber, 1984). The same as yet has not been done for peace education but, apart from those who are totally hostile to the whole idea (Cox and Scruton, 1984), there would initially seem to be a similar range of views.

(i) Conservative — This outlook has a narrower focus on peace as the absence of physical violence and a belief that pupils should accept the military status quo, including support for 'deterrent' nuclear weapons as the best defender of peace. An example of this approach is the *Peace and Conflict Studies Syllabus* (British Atlantic Committee, 1983) in which structural violence is dealt with in optional modules while deterrence, defence, disarmament and arms control are part of the core course and which comes out in favouring a reliance on armaments, including nuclear armaments.

(ii) Liberal — This stresses the need to consider a range of arguments and evidence and thus to educate the individual to enable him or her to make up their own minds. Typical of this outlook is this quotation from *Peace Education*

Network Letter (1984). 'If peace education is about anything, it is about putting *all* information before pupils *in
order that they can make their own decisions and come to
their own conclusion*'.

(iii)   Radical — This aims to convince pupils of the need for
change. Heater (1980) describes this outlook as follows:
'Education can thus never be neutral: it must be morally
committed to denouncing structural violence and to preparation for, and incitement to, positive action . . . education
must be a dialogue between teacher and taught to bring the
latter to a realisation of the crucial necessity for change'.

I have argued elsewhere (Harber, 1984) that such conservative
and radical ideologies are aimed at socialization rather than education. This is because they have an 'answer' they wish the pupils to
accept. An approach stressing openminded *educational* values must
permit people to make up their own minds and hence it is to the
'liberal' (for want of a better word) ideology that political/peace
educators should turn if their desire is genuinely to enhance awareness and ability to act politically when necessary.

Practice in Political Education and Peace Education

The aim in this section of the chapter is to direct readers to some of
the methods and materials that exist in this area of social education.
No such chapter can claim to be completely exhaustive though I have
tried to minimize the risk of excluding important ideas and resources
by including references to further bibliographies and resources lists in
the latter part of the chapter. The chapter concentrates primarily on
the key concerns of political education as it tends to manifest itself in
British schools. However, where possible, reference is made to
materials that can be used for peace and world studies and other
sources in these areas are given in the further references mentioned
above. Relevant addresses are provided at the end of the chapter.

Syllabuses

The initial problem is always: 'what to teach'? The answer will, of
course, depend on the resources available and the interests of staff and
pupils. However, syllabuses constructed by others provide a useful

starting point in the development of one's own ideas about what to teach. Existing politics syllabuses at 'O' GCSE and 'A' level can be obtained from the examination boards but an introductory overview for 'A' level is provided by Magee (1983). At BEC and CSE level the Politics Association Resources Bank supplies reviews of syllabuses and examinations.

There is also help and guidance for those who have the freedom to design their own courses and want to draw on the ideas of others. For non-'A' level sixth form courses (see Bright 1979; Edwards 1978; and Davies and Quartermaine, 1983). Below sixth-form level there are model courses in Crick and Porter (1978) and quite a detailed syllabus is suggested in Clayton (1977). The journal *Teaching Politics* has run a series of 'short course' articles and some of these describe courses developed at various schools (Ridge 1980; Booth 1981; Hunt, 1981; Lease 1982). Blackfyne Comprehensive School in Durham has produced a very full political education syllabus for 14–16 year olds which is based on the idea of political literacy and which contains not only suggested topics but also lesson plans and ideas for resources and methods (Smith, *et al*, 1985).

Examples of world and peace studies syllabuses can be found in O'Connor (1980), Heater (1980) and Heard (1983) while the Centre for Peace Studies at the University of Lancaster provides a document containing six brief case studies of peace education. Alternatively there is the syllabus produced by the British Atlantic Committee (1983) referred to above. Finally, Avon County Council (1983) provide a useful checklist of objectives for planning courses and syllabuses in peace education.

Discussion Method and Simulations

A major aim of political education is the exploration of political values, ideas and opinions in the classroom. Many teachers will not simply want to transmit these to the pupils but will want them explored in the classroom through discussion. Hence discussion method is of particular importance to political education and many of the resources detailed in this chapter are geared towards promoting it. A second method of importance is the use of games and simulations. These are increasingly used in political education as a way of removing the distance of 'the political' from young people and creating political situations in the classroom. However, to a large extent simulations are a means to the end of encouraging discussion of the ideas and relationships that have been simulated.

The nature of discussion and its benefits have been fully explored in Bridges (1979). Strategies for handling the discussion of controversial issues in the classroom ('balanced', 'objective', 'devil's advocate', 'committed', 'neutral chairperson' etc.) are described and analyzed in Stradling *et al* (1984) and Brown (1980). The question of how best to organize classroom discussions is comprehensively dealt with in Rudduck (1979) and the Schools Cultural Studies Handbook (1978). One resource that can be used to encourage classroom dialogue is visiting speakers. The various active tutorial work books have good advice on preparing for and receiving a visitor (Baldwin and Wells 1979–81 and 1983) and it is dealt with in O'Connell (1980). Often this works best if the pupils are primed on background issues prior to the visit and have worked out their questions beforehand. It is also possible to use one or two members of the class as (rehearsed) interviewers in the Robin Day mould prior to opening up for the whole class for questions.

Political simulation games will be mentioned in reference to the content of political and peace education. However, general guidance on the use of simulations in political education can be found in Brace (1975), Clarke (1980), Leng and Thomas (1976) and Cohen (1978). Also, some good general points are made in Russell (1976) though the article is actually about teaching sociology. The use of role play and drama in peace education is described in Carey (1982) while at the level of international relations a full discussion is provided in Clarke (1978). Those involved in world studies have increasingly been advocating the use of 'experiential' learning i.e. where the emphasis is less on deducing intellectually what another person's political position might be and more on emotional identification or feeling what its like to be in certain roles (Wolsk, 1975).

One final consideration that ought to be mentioned before looking at resources and methods for teaching the content of politics is the question of assessment. This might be for some sort of examination or simply because a teacher wishes to monitor progress. Those teachers who wish to try to assess the development of political skills as well as knowledge should see Harber (1983a).

Clive Harber

Interpersonal, Small Scale Politics

The problem of relevance in political education is a real one: pupils tend to have a restricted, personalized view of politics and as a result see it as an activity which is solely the concern of adults and which has little to do with their daily existence. Therefore an examination of politics at this level can be used to discuss the idea that the major components of politics — disagreement, choice, power, authority, decision, rules etc — are present in all social groups and organizations and hence in the daily experience of the pupils. This approach is outlined in regard to the family, the schools and gangs in Harber (1980) and by Gomm (1982) with regard to the family. A school book that contains some useful material on the idea of power in everyday experience, including that of unequal power relations between races and sexes, is Beecham *et al* (1982). If it can be obtained, the programme entitled *Anatomy of a Gang* from the BBC *Scene* series is an excellent study of the internal politics of two groups of boys on a council estate in Bristol. Programme 1 of the Yorkshire Television series *People and Politics* uses the context of a football team choosing a new strip to point to the bases of democratic and authoritarian government. As regards classroom activities, Jukes (1985) describes a role play based on a group of boys who go on a camping holiday while further ways of using groups to bring out political ideas are suggested in Birmingham Young Volunteers (1981). The Longman *Interplay* series contains a unit called Authority in which five simulations of everyday situations that involve authority relationships are suggested. A simulation based on solving puzzles in small groups which are organized differently is described by Ellis (1982) as a way of illustrating the concepts of what she terms democracy, dictatorship and Utopia. The active tutorial work books (Baldwin and Wells 1979–81 and 1983) also contain ideas for lessons and activities that can be used to explore themes in this area, especially in relation to school rules. Lessons using small scale contexts to look at conflict and violence — football hooliganism, the generation gap and bullying for example — are described in Avon County Council (1983).

Alternatively teachers can use an imaginary situation where pupils find themselves alone in the world and have to decide what to do. One such situation is the need to survive after being marooned on a desert island (the predicament used by William Golding in *Lord of the Flies*) and Riches (1977) discusses how this context might be used in the classroom. Another possibility is survival after a nuclear attack, perhaps using the stimulus provided by the 'Humanus' tape which consists of a computerized voice informing the class of their position and the choices they must take (address in Ellis, 1982). However, some teachers might feel that the idea of survivors after a nuclear war is stretching the imagination a little too far.

Human Rights

Considerations of the need for decisions and rules in human groups leads directly to the notion of rules and laws existing not only to control behaviour but also to protect rights. (It is also another way of suggesting the relevance of politics in that it is universal and unavoidable because we are all subject to rules and laws.) There are even recent suggestions that a separate 'human rights education' is developing thereby adding even further to the fragmentation in this area (Lister, 1984).

An exploration of what life might be like without laws takes place in the video *No Laws Today* produced by Educational Media International while the book by Rae *et al* (1979) is a useful and interesting introduction to the legal rights of young people. The latter takes various facets of life (family, school, employment, sex, alcohol, police etc.) and looks at the corresponding rights from birth to the age of 21. The 16–19 book in the active tutorial work series (Baldwin and Wells 1983) has ideas for lessons on rights in it and the Audio-Visual Centre produces a relevant set of slides called *Freedom of the Individual*. However, in a period of mounting youth unemployment it could be argued that as important as legal and political rights is knowledge of welfare rights. This is a complex area where straightforward guides to the provision of welfare benefits could be very useful to young people. Stradling *et al* (1984) refers to a number of resources that are useful in dealing with the rights of unemployed people while Birtles and Hewitt (1980) deal with the rights that exist for those who are employed. An example of a very good attempt to provide a handy and readable guide to legal and welfare rights is the pocket book produced by Newcastle-upon-Tyne Education Committee (1984). Wider global issues of rights are taken up in two books written for schools — Richardson (1978) and Selby (1985). Amnesty International has also now produced their own education pack on human rights (Amnesty International, 1983). Finally, issues of laws and rights are taken up in two programmes in BBC series for schools called *Politics and You* which was broadcast for the first time in 1985. The programmes are called *You and the Law* and *Who Benefits?*.

Political Processes, Institutions and Organizations

The following section looks at some of the resources and methods available for teaching political topics which are often found in school syllabuses. References will be made to books and other resources relating to specific topics rather than to general textbooks on government and politics. For the latter see the article by Porter in the *Times Educational Supplement* (17 June 1983) and Hesketh and Vernon (1980). New resources for all levels of teaching are regularly reviewed in *Teaching Politics* and *Social Science Teacher*, the journals of the Politics Association and the Association for the Teaching of Social Sciences respectively. Moreover, each association sells a number of resources relevant to this area through their Resources Bank and Resources Unit. Most of the resources that follow, while geared to the 14–18 age range, are not specifically for 'A' level. Those interested in 'A' level should also see Wilde (1985) while those interested in teaching politics below the age of 14 or through some of the more 'traditional' curriculum subjects (history, geography, English, religious education etc.) should see Harber (1985). At the end of this chapter some comprehensive resource lists are mentioned and these also ought to be consulted. Finally, it ought to be noted that British political institutions and organizations are disproportionately composed of people of certain attributes — white, middle class and male. Many standard politics textbooks deal with social class but gender and political participation is fully analyzed in Reid and Wormald (1982). Race as a political issue is dealt with in a number of textbooks (for example, MacFarlane, 1982) but Reeves and Chevannes (1984) provide interesting material on the alienation of many young black people from conventional British politics.

Local government

Although this is a topic which may not initially sound too stimulating, it is important because it is the level of government which often most directly affects our daily lives and thus is the level of government that people are most likely to come into contact (or conflict) with. The information office of most local authorities will usually provide free material that can be used as it is or adapted for handouts or worksheets by teachers. Community Service Volunteers produce a useful pack entitled *Local Government* as well as two simulations, *Greenwood District Council* and *Greenwood Gypsy Site*, that explore the role of the councillor and consider how local decisions are made. (All three CSV aids were revised in 1984). Suggestions for method are also provided in Baldwin and Wells (1983) and, again via gypsies, in Avon County Council (1983). Ideas for a simulation on officer/councillor relationships can be found in Greenwood and Wilson (1982) and these could be adapted for use in the senior secondary school. The Yorkshire ITV series *People and Politics* has a programme on local government in it and the BBC series *Politics and You* also has such a programme. Finally, teachers might find Brennan (1984) useful while the tried and tested texts are Allsop (1978), Jamieson (1978) and Jones (1975).

Pressure groups

Like local government, a great deal of free material is available on this topic. This is so for two reasons. First because letters to pressure groups requesting information usually provoke a generous response, especially from promotional groups such as Oxfam, Shelter, STOP, NSPCC etc who rely for a lot of their influence on publicity and hence have to have good publicity material. Second, the daily press is full of articles on pressure groups who are trying to influence government policy. Scissors, paste and old newspapers can therefore provide the basis of a lesson. These materials, plus ordinary slides and/or slides that you can write and draw on, and a cassette machine, can be used by teacher and pupils to make a tape/slide sequence tailored to address a particular issue or type of pressure group or to illustrate pressure groups in a particular locality. Baldwin and Wells (1983) have some useful suggestions for classroom method but by far and away the most comprehensive source in terms of developing the potential political skills involved in pressure group activity is Smith (1981). This is a must for any teacher wanting to cover this topic and who wants to include the 'how' as well as the 'what'. The Granada ITV series *Politics — What's it all About?* covered pressure groups in programme 3 as did Yorkshire Television in their series *People and Politics* in programme 7.

Clive Harber

Political parties

Most textbooks deal with the origins, structure and policies of the different parties — Coxall (1981), for example, gives a useful introduction for teachers (and sixth-formers) that covers pressure groups as well. The Yorkshire ITV series *People and Politics* covers the topic in programme 3 and it is also covered in programme 5 of the Mary Glasgow *Power and the People* series of cassette tapes. What was said above about newspapers and letters in reference to pressure groups also applies to political parties and the judicious teacher will also keep hold of electoral material from the different political parties that comes through the post. Local parties will sometimes provide speakers — especially at election time. However, not all teachers will necessarily be happy about dealing with the National Front as if it were just another political party because of its association with racism. Nevertheless, two points ought to be borne in mind. First, there is a difference between analyzing and discussing racism in the classroom as a political phenomenon on the one hand and making racist statements on the other. The latter may not be acceptable but the former is very necessary. Second, in many areas of Britain the pupils themselves will raise the issue of the National Front. These points both suggest that the teacher must be prepared to deal with the issues likely to be raised. Useful in this regard is *So What Are You Going To Do About The National Front?* by the Rev. Tony Holden (AFFOR) especially for its reading list and list of addresses at the back.

Elections

Again, most teachers dealing with government and politics will cover elections and the journals *Teaching Politics* and *Social Science Teacher* regularly have articles which update information in this area. For example, the September 1983 edition of *Teaching Politics* dealt with the performance of the Conservative, Labour, SDP and Liberal parties in relation to the general election of that year while *Social Science Teacher* contained an article by Haslam (1983) updating on voting behaviour. A particularly useful book for teachers (and for sixth-formers) is McLean (1980) while Jones (1982) gives a useful checklist of methods and Thomas (1983) gives advice on how mock elections can be organized in schools. Some interesting ideas for a simulation on gerrymandering are given in Barns (1982) though they would have to be adapted for the 14–16 age range. A summary of some resources relating to electoral reform is given in Harber (1983b) and the House of Commons Education Office has produced a tape/slide sequence called *Fighting an Election* which is obtainable from the Central Film Library. Finally, some classes might well appreciate Monty Python's send up of fringe candidates and television coverage of elections in *Election Night Special*.

The mass media

Most of our information about local and national politics is gained through the television, radio and newspapers. Of course, these are far from being neutral vehicles and as well as being purveyors of information they are also transmitters of values and attitudes. A key aim of political education is the ability to detect bias and hence 'media literacy' is an important part of political literacy. As regards television, Masterman (1980) is a comprehensive text which provides many ideas on methods and resources and which has a section specifically on political education. His more recent book (1984) covers newspapers as well. Practical suggestions for classroom activities are provided in Baldwin and Wells (1979–81 and 1983) and the Granada Television series *Politics — What's it all About?* has three of its programmes devoted to the mass media.

Central institutions

Although these would constitute the sole focus of a traditional 'civics' approach, some consideration of them is necessary in any course concerned with decision-making and conflict resolution. Most textbooks deal with this aspect of politics thoroughly so what follows will concentrate on other aids and resources. Audio-Visual Productions, for example, have *The Development of the British Political System* and *The British Constitution* on slides or filmstrip and cassette tape or video. The House of Commons Education Office has produced tape/slide sequences on *The House of Commons, The Work of an MP, Making a Law* and the *House of Lords* (available from the Central Film Library). The Yorkshire ITV series *People and Politics* has a programme on the work of an MP and the Mary Glasgow set of cassette tapes *Power and the People* has tapes on the Cabinet, the Civil Service, the Commons and the Lords. The Politics Association itself has produced a filmstrip on Parliament called *The British Parliament: A Guided Tour* and Common Ground have a filmstrip called *Britain's Government At Work*. *Teaching Politics* has included simulations in this area that could be adapted for a variety of age groups. Examples are Kemp (1978), Munday (1984), Laver (1978) and Roome (1980). The scripts for the BBC's *Yes Minister* (Lynn and Jay, 1984) provide an unending source of material on the internal relationships of central government. For information on arranging a visit to the Palace of Westminister see Stones (1985).

Terrorism and Northern Ireland

Political conflicts are not always settled peacefully. These two topics have been included together because Northern Ireland is part of the UK and therefore pupils ought to know something about the political problems they see reported in the media and because it is also a significant source of planned political violence and thus a case study of the wider phenomenon of 'terrorism' to build out from. For the teacher a useful introduction is Arthur (1980). There is a helpful chapter on 'Teaching about Northern Ireland' in Stradling *et al* (1984) while Osborne (1978) gives a social science perspective and a peace education approach is provided in Avon County Council (1983). On the broader issue of terrorism Freeman (1981) is designed for CSE/ 'O' level and Educational Audio Visual have a cassette tape/filmstrip set entitled *Terrorism* that includes an incident from Northern Ireland as a case study after examining what is meant by terrorism.

Political issues

One suggestion of the Programme for Political Education was that political education could be organized around the teaching of issues rather than organizations, processes and structures. There are, however, disadvantages as well as advantages to this (Harber, 1981; Brown and Townley, 1981). Moreover, the list is potentially endless, though the 'top ten' issues in schools are reproduced in Stradling *et al* (1984). McFarlane (1982) deals with a wide range of political issues but here I will describe resources for only two issues about which there are fundamental party policy differences which seem unlikely to disappear very quickly and to which the parties give a high public profile — unemployment and nuclear weapons. Audio-Visual Productions have slides or filmstrips or videos covering both these topics (*Social Problems in Britain Today* and The *Nuclear Debate*), while Stradling *et al* (1984) has a chapter covering the teaching of both issues. Issues and methods surrounding education in nuclear matters are discussed in The Bishop of Salisbury *et al* (1984). A strip/slide set called *Nuclear Weapons* is produced by Mary Glasgow Publications and two books for use in schools are Turner (1983) and Cox (1976). Suddaby (1984) has written seven units on nuclear weapons which can be purchased singularly or as a set. A comprehensive introduction to the issue of unemployment is provided in Crick (1981). The Media Production Company produces a filmstrip and cassette tape set simply called *Unemployment* and Community Service Volunteers produce a pack called *Working it Out: The Survival Game* (1983) which attempts to simulate the experience of unemployment and give some understanding of the difficulties unemployed people face. CRAC have also produced two booklets — Dauncey (1983) which offers information and ideas on using your time if you're unemployed and Jamieson (1983) which explains the ideas behind the YTS programme and the rights and responsibilities of 'trainees'. While these last two resources are potentially useful additions, there is a danger that the use of this type of resource alone could help to foster skills of coping with a situation where mass unemployment is accepted as a taken for granted fact of life. Hence discussion of coping with/surviving unemployment should be held in conjunction with discussion of what causes unemployment and what remedies there may be. On this point of the relationship between 'life skills' and critical awareness in social education see Harber and Brown (1983).

Further sources of information

While global or world aspects of politics have occasionally been referred to above this, by definition, is a vast area. For present purposes reference will simply be made to sources that themselves provide information on a wide range of ideas and resources. The DES (1979) has produced a handbook of information on organizations concerned with international understanding. Of these organizations particular attention should perhaps be drawn to the Council of Education in World Citizenship which has been providing resources and speakers for schools for over forty years. Its history, structure and activities have recently been described in Heater (1984). O'Connor (1980), Heater (1980) and Hicks and Townley (1982) all have resource/address lists and bibliographies as does Richardson (1979) which also has many useful ideas on method in it. Selby (1984) provides commentary on sixteen starting points for teachers wanting to learn more about world studies while the best way to keep in touch with developments in this field is by obtaining the *World Studies*

Journal. Avon County Council (1983) has a long section on further reading and resources for peace education while teachers interested in developing political education through the more specifically focussed European studies should see Williams (1977) and Harber (1978). Useful guidance on resources and suggested further reading as regards political education are provided in Ellis (1982), Hesketh and Vernon (1980), Porter *et al* (1983) and Chandler and Hill (1984).

Conclusions

Only a small part of the above discussion of resources and methods refers specifically to peace education. This is so for two reasons. First, at school level it is a very new development. Discussion really only got going with increased fear of nuclear conflict following the advent of Mr. Reagan and Mrs. Thatcher and the Cruise/SS20/Trident debates. Though it is about much more than the nuclear weapons debate, it helps to explain why its opponents find the CND accusation easy to levy. Its recent appearance also means that discussion is largely at the level of rhetoric and there are as yet few examples of practical methods and resources. Second, even where work does exist it is very difficult to see a clear-cut distinction between peace education and political education. The former is perhaps best understood as an emphasis on non-violent solutions to conflicts and a concern for social justice within the broader context of political education. Political education is itself, of course, an emphasis within an education about and for society that should include sociological and economic dimensions. In some ways it is a pity that peace education has arrived to further fragment this area of the curriculum and by using this label to provide a convenient stick for those who are all too ready to beat any area of the curriculum that wishes to encourage critical social education. Tactically those in favour of peace education approaches might have been better advised to work within existing areas of the school curriculum (social studies, social education, humanities, social sciences at 'O' and 'A' level etc.) rather than set themselves up as a visible target. Conversely a change of label to security studies, the new title in the United States (*Times Educational Supplement*, 25 January 1985), might have produced less hostile reaction!

Addresses

AFFOR (All Faiths for One Race)
1 Finch Road
Lozells
Birmingham B19 1HS

Amnesty International
British Section
5 Roberts Place
Bowling Green Lane
London W8 4BN

Association for the Teaching of the
    Social Sciences
3 Battlefield Road
St. Albans
Hertfordshire
(publishes *Social Science Teacher*)

Association for the Teaching of the
    Social Sciences Resources Unit
Department of Sociology
University of York
Heslington
York Y01 5DD

The Audio-Visual Centre
88 Queen Street
Newton Abbot
Devon

Audio-Visual Productions
Hocker Hill House
Chepstow
Gwent NP6 5ER

Birmingham Young Volunteers
Room 17
2nd Floor
17 Cannon Street
Birmingham B2 5EN

British Atlantic Committee
30A St. James's Square
London SW1Y 4JH

BBC
The Langham
Portland Place
London W1A 1AA

Careers Research and Advisory
    Centre (Publications
    Catalogue)
The Publications Department
Hobsons Press
Bateman Street
Cambridge CB2 1LZ

Central Film Library
Chalfont Grove
Gerrards Cross
Bucks SL9 8TN

Comedia
9 Poland Street
London W1V 3DG

Common Ground Filmstrips
Longman Group Ltd
Pinnacles
Harlow
Essex

Community Service Volunteers
237 Pentonville Road
London N1 9NJ

Department of Education and
    Science
Elizabeth House
York Road
London SE1 7PH

Educational Audio Visual
Mary Glasgow Publications Ltd
Brookhampton Lane
Kineton
Warwick CV35 0JB

Educational Media International
25 Boileau Road
London W5 3AL

Granada Television Ltd
Manchester M66 9EA

Yorkshire Television
The Television Centre
Leeds LS3 1JS

ILEA
The History and Social Sciences
   Teachers Centre
377 Clapham Road
London SW9 9BT

Institute for European Defence and
   Strategic Studies
13/14 Golden Square
London W1R 3AG

Longman Resources Unit
62 Hallfield Road
York YO3 7XO

Mary Glasgow Publications Ltd
140 Kensington Church Street
London W8 4BN

Media Production Company
Mary Glasgow Publications
Brookhampton Lane
Kineton
Warwick CV35 0JB

National Association of Youth
   Clubs

30 Peacock Lane
Leicester LE1 5NY

National Council for Civil Liberties
186 Kings Cross Road
London WC1X 9DE

National Union of Teachers
Hamilton House
Mabledon Place
London WC1H 9BD

Newcastle-upon-Tyne City Council
Research Unit
Policy Services Department
Civic Centre
Newcastle

Peace Education Network
33 Churchill Avenue
Kenton
Harrow
Middlesex

Politics Association
16 Gower Street
London WC1E 6DF
(publishes *Teaching Politics*)

Politics Association Resources Bank
5 Parsonage Road
Heaton Moor
Stockport SK4 4JZ

Richardson Institute for Conflict
   and Peace Research
University of Lancaster
Lancaster LA1 4YF

West Sussex Institute of Higher
   Education
Upper Bognor Road
Bognor Regis
West Sussex PO21 1HR

World Studies Project
C/o One World Trust
24 Palace Chambers
Bridge Street
London SW1A 2JT

World Studies Teacher Training
Centre
University of York
Heslington
York YO1 5DD

References

ALLSOP, K. (1978) *Local and Central Government*, London, Hutchinson.

AMNESTY INTERNATIONAL (1983) (British Section) *Education Project.*

ARTHUR, P. (1980) *Government and Politics of Northern Ireland*, Harlow, Longman Political Realities.

AVON COUNTY COUNCIL (1983) *Peace Education Guidelines for Primary and Secondary Schools*, Bristol, Avon County Council.

BALDWIN, J. and WELLS, C. (1979–81 and 1983) *Active Tutorial Work Books, Nos. 1–5 and 16–19*, Oxford, Blackwell.

BARRS, D. (1982) 'The art of the gerrymander: A classroom exercise in political geography', *Teaching Politics* 11, 1.

BEECHAM, Y. *et al* (1982) *Power and Conflict*, London, Harrap.

BIRMINGHAM YOUNG VOLUNTEERS (1981) *Working Together*, Birmingham, BYV.

BIRTLES, B. and HEWITT, P. (1980) *Your Rights at Work*, London, National Council for Civil Liberties.

BISHOP OF SALISBURY *et al* (1984) *Lessons Before Midnight*, Bedford Way Papers, London, University of London Institute of Education.

BOOTH, A. (1981) 'Political eduation at Tile Hill Wood School', *Teaching Politics*, 10, 3.

BRACE, D. (1975) 'The use of educational gaming and simulation in political education' in BRENNAN, T. and BROWN, J.F. (Eds.) *Teaching Politics: Problems and Perspectives*, London, BBC Publications.

BRENNAN, T. (1981) *Political Education and Democracy*, Cambridge, Cambridge University Press.

BRENNAN, T. (1984) *Local Government* London, Longman Political Studies.

BRIDGES, D. (1979) *Education, Democracy and Discussion* Windsor NFER.

BRIGHT, J. (1979) 'Politics in the sixth form — A general studies course', *Social Science Teacher*, 8, 3.

BRITISH ATLANTIC COMMITTEE (1983) *Peace and Conflict Studies*, London, British Atlantic Community.

BROWN, C. and TOWNLEY, C. (1981) 'Theory and content bases of social/political education in Britain' in *Social/Political Education in Three Countries*, Boulder, CO, ERIC Clearing House.

BROWN, J.F. (1980) 'Bias revisited', *Teaching Politics*, 9, 3.

CAREY, J. (1982) 'Peace education through drama — a personal approach', *World Studies Journal*, 3, 3.

CHANANDLER, M. and HILL, D. (1984) *Political Education: A Response to the Thompson Report on Youth Service*, West Sussex Institute of Higher Education.

CLARKE, M. (1978) *Simulations in the Study of International Relations*, Ormskirk, Hesketh and Vernon.

CLARKE, M. (1980) 'Simulating reality' in HESKETH, G. and VERNON, A., *Teaching Methods, Social and Political Education in Practice*, London, Politics Association.

CLAYTON, A. (1977) 'Producing a syllabus', *Teaching Politics*, 6, 2.

COHEN, L. (1978) 'Putting stimulation into simulation, *Teaching Politics*, 7, 1.

COMMUNITY SERVICE VOLUNTEERS (1983) *The Survival Game*, revised edition.

COX, C. and SCRUTON, R. (1984) *Peace Studies: A Critical Survey*, London, Institute for European and Strategic Studies.

COX, J. (1976) *On the Warpath*, Oxford, Oxford University Press.

COXALL, W.N. (1981) *Parties and Pressure Groups*, Longman Political Realities Series.

CRICK, B. (1981) *Unemployment*, London, Methuen, University paperbacks.

CRICK, B. and PORTER, A. (1978) *Political Education and Political Literacy*, London, Longman.

CURLE, A. (1977) 'The scope and dilemmas of peace studies', *Teaching Politics*, 6, 3.

DAUNCEY, G. (1983) *Facing Unemployment*, Cambridge, Careers Research and Advisory Centre.

DAVIES, P. and QUARTERMAINE, T. (1983) 'A foundation course for seventeen plus students', *Teaching Politics*, 12, 1.

DERBYSHIRE L.E.A. (1983) *Personal and Social Education in the Secondary School*, Derby.

DEPARTMENT OF EDUCATION AND SCIENCE (1979) *International Understanding*, London, HMSO.

EDUCATION COMMITTEE, NEWCASTLE-UPON-TYNE COUNCIL (1984) *Pocket Survival Kit and Guide*, Newcastle.

EDWARDS, M. (1978) 'Political education: A course for sixth form general studies', *Cambridge Journal of Education*, 8, 2/3.

ELLIS, V. (1982) 'Resources for political education, *Social Science Teacher*, 11, 2.

FREEMAN, C. (1981) *Terrorism*, London, Batsford.

GOMM, R. (1982) 'Authority within the family' in GOMM, R. and MCNEILL, P., *Handbook for Sociology Teachers*, Heinemann.

GREEN, J.R. and WILSON, D.J. (1982) 'Councillor/officer relationships: case material for simulations', *Teaching Politics*, 11, 3.

HARBER, C. (1978) 'Teaching politics through area studies: The case of European studies', *Teaching Politics*, 7, 1.

Harber, C. (1980) 'Teaching the politics of everyday life', *Social Science Teacher*, 10, 2.

Harber, C. (1981) 'Political education and social studies in the 14–16 core curriculum', *Teaching Politics*, 10, 2.

Harber, C. (1983a) 'Assessing political skills', *Teaching Politics*, 12, 2.

Harber, C. (1983b) 'Resources for teaching electoral reform', *Social Science Teacher*, 12, 3.

Harber, C. (1984) 'Politics and political education in 1984,' *Educational Review*, 36, 2.

Harber, C. (1985) 'Political education: A bibliography of practice by level and subject', *Social Science Teacher*, 14, 2.

Harber, C. and Brown, C. (1983) 'Social education and the social sciences', *Curriculum*, 4, 1.

Haslam, A. (1983) 'Electoral behaviour', *Social Science Teacher*, 12, 3.

Heard, A. (1983) 'The Welsh A/O syllabus in world development', *World Studies Journal*, 4, 3.

Heater, D. (1980) *World Studies*, London, Harrap.

Heater, D. (1984) *Peace Through Education*, Lewes, Falmer Press.

Hesketh, G. and Vernon, A. (1980) 'Choosing and using subject books' in Hesketh, G. and Vernon, A., *Teaching Methods, Social and Political Education in Practice*, London, Politics Association.

Hicks, D. and Townley, C. (1982) *Teaching World Studies*, London, Longman.

Hunt, D.J. (1981) 'Political education at Churchill School', *Teaching Politics*, 10, 2.

ILEA (1982) *Clio* (The History and Social Sciences Teachers' Centre Review), 2, 2 and 3, editions on political education.

Jamieson, A. (1978) *Local Government*, London, Evans.

Jamieson, A. (1983) *The Young Workers Handbook*, Cambridge, Careers Research and Advisory Centre.

Jones, B. (1982) 'Teaching Elections' in Gomm, R. and McNell, P., *Handbook for Sociology Teachers*, London, Heinemann.

Jones, G. (1975) *Local Community*, London, Harrap.

Jukes, A. (1985) 'Teaching politics through the familiar: a play', *Social Science Teacher*, 14, 2.

Kemp, A. (1978) 'The selection of parliamentary candidates: A simulation approach', *Teaching Politics*, 7, 1.

Laver, M. (1978) 'Playing at coalitions', *Teaching Politics*, 7, 3.

Lease, P. (1982) 'Political education as part of social studies', *Teaching Politics*, 11, 1.

Leng, P. and Thomas, C. (1976) 'Simulation — A useful teaching aid?', *Teaching Politics*, 5, 2.

Lister, I. (1984) *Teaching and Learning About Human Rights*, Strasbourg, Council of Europe.

Lynn, J. and Jay, A. (1984) *Yes Minister*, London, BBC Publications.

MacFARLANE, L.J. (1982) *Issues in British Politics Since 1945*, London, Longman Political Realities series.

McLEAN, I. (1980) *Elections*, Longman Political Realities Series.

MAGEE, F.I. (1983) 'Politics at 'A' level: An initial overview', *Teaching Politics*, 12, 1.

MASTERMAN, L. (1980) *Teaching About Television*, MacMillan.

MASTERMAN, L. (1984) *Teaching the Media*, London, Comedia.

MUNDAY, J. (1984) 'Negotiating a constitution: A simulation', *Teaching Politics*, 13. 1.

NATIONAL UNION OF TEACHERS (1984) *Education for Peace*, London, NUT

O'CONNELL, B. (1980) 'Using outsides Speakers' in HESKETH, G. and VERNON, A., *Teaching Methods, Social and Political Education in Practice*, London, (Politics Association).

O'CONNOR, E. (1980) *World Studies in the European Classroom*, Strasbourg, Council of Europe.

OSBORNE, K. (1978) 'Teaching Northern Ireland', *Social Science Teacher*, 7, 5.

PORTER, A. (1979) 'The programme for political education: A guide for beginners', *Social Science Teacher*, 8, 3.

PORTER, A. *et al* (1983) *Teaching Political Literacy*, Bedford Way Papers, London, University of London.

RAE, M. *et al* (1979) *First Rights*, National Council for Civil Liberties.

RATHENOW, H.F. and SMOKER, P. (1983) *Peace Education in Great Britain*, Lancaster, Richardson Institute for Conflict and Peace Research, University of Lancaster

REEVES, F. and CHEVANNES, M. (1984) 'The political education of young blacks in Britain', *Educational Review*, 36, 2.

REID, I. and WORMALD, E. (Eds) (1982) *Sex Differences in Britain*, London, Grant McIntyre.

RICHARDSON, R. (1974) 'Tensions in world and school' in HAAVELSRUD, M. and RICHARDSON, *Bulletin of Peace*, 5.

RICHARDSON, R. (1978) *Fighting for Freedom*, Sunbury-on-Thames, Nelson.

RICHARDSON, R. (Ed) (1979) *Learning for Change in World Society*, London, World Studies Project.

RICHES, J. (1977) 'Political education for the nine to thirteens? An experiment', *Social Science Teacher*, 6, 3.

RIDGES, B. (1980) 'Political education and general studies', *Teaching Politics*, 9, 3.

ROOME, S. (1980) 'The Cabinet Game: A simulation', *Teaching Politics*. 9, 2.

RUDDUCK, J. (1979) *Learning to Teach Through Discussion*, Norwich, University of East Anglia, Centre for Applied Research in Education.

RUSSELL, A. (1976) 'Simulation and the teaching of sociology', *Social Science Teacher*, 6, 1.

SCHOOLS CULTURAL STUDIES HANDBOOK, No. 4 (1978) *Discussion as a Teaching Strategy*, Education Centre, New University of Ulster.

SELBY, D. (1984) 'World studies: Towards a global perspective in the school curriculum', *Social Science Teacher*, 13, 2.

SELBY, D. (1985) *Human Rights*, Cambridge, Cambridge University Press.

SMITH, J. *et al* (Eds) (1985) *A Course in Political Education for 14–18 Year Olds*, York, Longman Resources Unit.

SMITH, M. (1981) *Organise!* Leicester, National Association of Youth Clubs.

STONES, L. (1985) 'The role of education officer at the House of Commons', *Social Science Teacher*, 14, 2.

STRADLING, R. *et al* (1984) *Teaching Controversial Issues*, London, Edward Arnold.

SUDDABY, A. (1984) *Nuclear Weapons and Warfare*, York, Longman Resources Unit.

THOMAS, H. (1983) 'A general election in school', *Social Science Teacher*, 12, 3.

TURNER, J. (1983) *The Arms Race*, Cambridge, Cambridge University Press.

WILDE, A. (1985) 'Resources and methods for teaching politics at 'A' level', *Social Science Teacher*, 14, 2.

WILLIAMS, M. (1977) *Teaching European Studies*, London, Heinemann.

WOLSK, D. (1975) *An Experience-Centred Curriculum*, Paris, UNESCO.

Teaching Media Studies

Tim O'Sullivan, Holly Goulden and
John Hartley

Why Media Studies?

Media studies is usually justified on two related grounds. First, as an area of *public concern*; second as an area of *private experience*. The media constantly give rise to issues of public concern and controversy. For example, media coverage of world events, from strikes to wars, is always controversial — not just because it may be fair or unfair to a particular person, group or government but because that coverage can itself influence the course of events. The ways in which the media represent different people, groups and ideas are also controversial — and their portrayal of women, workers, ethnic and linguistic minorities has been justifiably criticized.

Of course there are also those who are constantly irritated by the media's use of 'bad' language, violence and sexuality; by their alleged celebration of conspicuous consumption, consumerism and the cult of personality; by their perceived tendency towards sensationalism, trivialization and stereotyping. For some, the media are the cause of moral decline, of bad behaviour, of undermining traditional educational standards. The media have been blamed for apparent declines in standards of literacy, respect for authority, discipline and the pursuit of 'worthwhile' interests (Lusted, 1985; Masterman, 1980).

On this basis, it might seem that a course in media studies should have one of the original aims that mass education set itself in the nineteenth century — the aim of inculcating in people the virtues and duties of a *good citizen*. The question of what constitutes 'good citizenship' is by no means as clear now as it appeared to the sponsors of the 1870 Education Act. In their terms education was itself a medium, 'good' citizenship would be achieved by educators if they could persuade the 'individual in the mob' to use his or her 'political influence' not to disrupt but instead to reinforce the established institutions and hierarchies of the nation.

An important strand of thinking within formal education is influenced by this ideology and it has played its part in the development of media education. It is still not uncommon for teachers to regard the media as partly responsible for the direction society as a whole appears to be taking. Popular culture in general, and the media in particular, are threatening because they are perceived as pandering to 'the mob's' worst instincts and often dangerously beyond the control of 'responsible' sections of society. Thus, media education has been regarded *negatively*, as an antidote to the media and to peoples' experience of them. The danger in this approach, however, is that if we are formed, individually and collectively, partly by our continuing encounters and relations with the media, teaching students to despise the media can result in encouraging them to despise themselves.

For those who accept the media as a *positive* part of our individual and social lives, media studies is not simply a means of celebrating the pleasures of the media. Behind every screen and speaker there is an array of social, economic and political forces which play a major part in determining not only our entertainments but also our knowledge of the world and ourselves. As a result media studies can be the focus for a totally different view of what constitutes 'good citizenship'. Rather than the inculcation of moral values and standards to enable people to resist the temptations of popular culture, it is an attempt to recover and 'place' popular culture as a progressive and challenging social force in its own right. From this point of view, the structure of the media is modelled far too closely on the structure of capitalist corporations. The different media are owned and controlled by a remarkably small number of people. Much of what we see on television and read in newspapers is produced by a minority of specialists. The production of media output is hedged about by social, professional, legal and other restrictions which make access to production very difficult for outsiders — the very public that the media ostensibly serve. A 'good citizen' in this context is one whose criticism of the media leads not to a negative dismissal but to a positive attempt to achieve change.

Studying the media is a good way of studying contemporary society because they are part of it, both institutionally and in terms of the social and political relations that exist between cultural producers and consumers. Beyond this they also represent society in general, in the images, sounds and words that are their stock-in-trade. In this way, studying the media leads inexorably to examining society's norms and beliefs, contradictions and forms of resistance, opposition or alternatives. It is the very fact that studying the media can result in awareness, discussion and debate of such issues that makes media studies worthwhile. That is 'why' media studies.

What is Media Studies?

At this point we turn to the *what* of media studies: what are the media under study, and what should a course in media studies be teaching about them? As yet there is no definitive answer to either of these questions. Not only is there little agreement over what constitutes 'the media', but also there is no *essential* definition that will do for all time and any purpose. Here for example, is a list of characteristics which, through discussion, might be agreed to separate *mass* media from other means of communication:

> mass media: reach large numbers of people; employ high technology; are modern; involve large-scale commercial corporations and finance; are state controlled or regulated; are centrally produced but privately consumed; are co-operative not individual forms of communication; are popular.

Once such a set of characteristics has been introduced however, it is quite easy to think of things that fulfil these criteria but that are not conventionally understood as mass media — religion and education being clear examples. Further, there are things like music, photography, pictures, drama, speech, and printing that appear in more than one of the mass media — are these *forms* of communication or media in their own right?

Beyond showing that there's no *single* definition of the media, this also illustrates that despite their diversity, and the differences between them, the media are *socially recognized*. Everyone agrees that they include television, radio, cinema and the press. After discussion, most will agree that music and publishing should be included, as well as advertising. Often people will express their recognition of mass media most easily by reference to a *technological apparatus* (Williams, 1974), but people are less used to thinking of the media as *social institutions*.

With these points in mind, it's not surprising that different syllabuses focus on different media — although the majority foreground the press, cinema and TV. Such disparity is less surprising given the absence of an 'agreed' set of issues or concerns at the 'heart' of media studies — what you study depends very much on what you are looking for. In recent years this has led to the development of a range of syllabuses that were heavily orientated towards the concerns and methodologies of established school disciplines. Teachers of English drew up one kind of agenda, general and liberal studies another, art and drama teachers entirely different courses again. More recent developments however, are characterized by the emergence of a set of syllabuses that establish media studies as a discipline in its own right. The aims, objectives and analytical approaches demanded by these syllabuses are in part founded on the recent developments of media study in the higher education sector and can be expected increasingly to become the 'what' of school media studies in the future.

In considering the content of a media studies course, we draw on the example set by the Welsh Joint Education Committee's 16+ syllabus, which was piloted in September 1985. It's a syllabus that we have been directly involved in developing and it promises to be typical of others currently under development. Its agenda has emerged from the various experiences of earlier school courses, developments in media study in the higher educational sector, including a Postgraduate, In-Service Diploma in Teaching Media Studies, validated by the Polytechnic of Wales.

The media specified by this syllabus are television, radio, cinema and the press as major focal area's of study, but it also recommends that attention should be given to advertising, photography, music, and video. Each of these media, drawing on their own distinctive 'languages', codes and conventions, offer us 'a window on the world'. In media studies there are two main issues at stake in this metaphor. First, *What is the world that is shown through the media window like*? How does it, for example, differ from the world as we perceive it outside the media? Are there any views that cannot be seen through the window? The media window may appear to show the whole world but from whose point of view? Second, *what is the nature of the window itself*? What is it made of? Under what conditions? How is it made and who makes it?

The conceptual framework of the course falls into three broad areas of enquiry: representations, industries and institutions, and audiences and identities. To show how these relate to and organize the questions outlined above, its useful to provide a brief map of each of them in turn.

Representations

To begin the course it is important to establish that the media 'window' is not *transparent* but *constructed* and that the view of the world and of the people and events in it is *mediated*. In short, a distinction needs to be introduced between events, people, issues and ideas as they occur in the world at large and their *representation* in the media (Dyer, 1985). One way to introduce the general concept of representation is to select a range of simple examples of visual, graphic and aural forms, and to examine the ways in which they offer us particular viewpoints of their subject. This work can be usefully developed by using photographs, pictures and photocopies which can be cut and cropped in different ways to produce a variety of meanings. Such exercises can be extended by devizing headlines applicable to the whole or different component parts of the images under study (Greenhill, *et al*, 1977; Evans, 1978; BFI and SEFT packs). In a similar way, work on advertising imagery can be used to encourage an analytic and practical familiarity with visual construction and representation (Dyer, 1982; Fiske, 1982; Williamson, 1978). Ferguson (1981) outlines a range of practical exercises using video or film which explore the ways in which meanings can be constructed by manipulating the basic elements of visual texts. The variations produced through these kinds of exercises should illustrate that every view of the world presented by the media is only *one* of many potential 'ways of seeing' and representing it.

Once it has been established that representations are constructed, attention can move to a detailed analysis of how the media represent different aspects of the world to us. Perhaps the best way of tackling this is by initially selecting one theme and examining how this is represented across a range of media and genres of output. Modern societies are characterized by divisions of different kinds between groups, and some of the most fundamental social divisions provide productive themes to concentrate on. These are some examples of possible themes, with suggestions for the different media contexts in which they could be studied:

Age: Images of youth in popular newspapers, teenage magazines and selected films; equally images of old-age or childhood (Gillis, 1974; Muncie, 1984; Pearson, 1983).
Social Class: Representations of working class and middle class life in, for example, soap operas and serials on television (Woolacott, 1982; Dyer, *et al*, 1981). Also media

representations which rarely access the dimension of social class — in news coverage of industrial disputes, for example (Hartley, 1982; Brunsden and Morley, 1978).

Gender: The separation of the world into different domains and the construction of gender stereotypes of feminity and masculinity. Representations of men's and women's roles in adolescent and adults magazines, news and sports coverage, advertisements and soap operas (McRobbie, 1981 and 1982; Stott and King, 1977; Hobson, 1982; TUC, 1984).

Family: Representations of domestic culture, chosen from TV sit-coms, advertising etc. Coverage of the Royal Family in newspapers (Woollacott, 1982; Dyer *et al* 1981; Ellis, 1982; Brunsden and Morley, 1978).

Nation: Images of national stereotypes. The construction and identification around the separation of 'us' from 'them', both in terms of the difference between 'home' and 'foreign' attributes, and in terms of 'alien' characteristics attributed to deviant or dissident groups (McArthur, 1980; Cohen and Young, 1981; Cohen, 1980; Hartley, *et al* 1985).

Race: Images of ethnicity — representations of race as a 'problem' and attempts to represent multicultural society (Hartmann and Husband, 1974; Hall, *et al* 1978; Husband, 1982).

People: Individual people, for example, politicians and performers. Groups of people, for example, professionals and experts, law enforcers, deviants etc (Langer, 1981; Gardner and Young, 1981; Hurd, 1981; Schlesinger *et al* 1983).

Places: Media representations of the local area, of London, of regions, holiday resorts, the countryside etc.

Ideas: Media images of science, medicine, ecology, history and the past, war, industry etc. (Gardner and Young, 1981; Hartley *et al* 1985).

Important aims for this kind of work are to discover, first, how these social divisions and themes are made sense of in the media; second, to show how similar representations of gender, for example, occur across a variety of different media and genres. The advantage of this thematic rather than 'media map' approach (which studies each chosen medium in turn, focussing primarily on distinctive characteristics) is that it encourages pupils to recognize not only the differences *between* media but also focusses their attention on important, often less immediately apparent *similarities*. Simultaneously, the approach raises questions about the relationship between the world of the media and the world in general. If, for example you choose to look at representations of gender, questions raised might include how far the media are simply reflecting the facts of existing gender differences and how far they are constructing and regulating these gender differences in particular ways. To take this a step further, how far are our own individual perceptions and assumptions concerning gender differences and gender identity the result of constructions and representations circulated by the media. This is a fundamental question which can be asked of all the other taken-for-granted social relationships that 'we' inhabit as part of our own selves. In other words, our sense of belonging, or not, to a particular gender, class, nation, race, family or age group will depend, at least to some extent, on the ways in which particular senses of those relationships are made available to us (*or not*) through the media. In fact, it is difficult to think of any aspect of ourselves which is not in some way determined or mediated by media representations.

To bring out these points, it's important to consider at least two of the social divisions outlined above, and to move on to more situated analysis of other kinds of representations such as 'people', 'places', 'ideas' and 'events'. Often, a widening of focus occurs naturally, for example in studying representations of men and women in advertisements there will clearly be other representations in the image which can be taken up — age, class, places etc. When structuring a programme of work, it's worth selecting examples which encourage this gradual extension of concern. It's also important to draw on examples taken from all kinds of popular culture. The concept of representation, includes the notion that both the media and their audiences are socially and culturally situated and that representations are produced and circulated within the sphere of popular culture which extends beyond the media alone. In these terms, its important to stress that popular culture is central to the experience of producers and consumers alike. Since we all partake of and are represented in popular culture, it cannot be understood as merely the 'unimaginative', 'trivial' or 'mass' that is left over when the 'high' culture has been identified. Such an approach does not get us very far, as such negative value judgments do not provide an appropriate or adequate framework for the analysis of the media in particular, or popular culture in general.

As we've already suggested, media studies involves analyzing not only media representations themselves, but also how representations and their meanings are produced. The very familiarity of the images and their taken-for-grantedness can make this aspect of study difficult to open up; analytical devices are needed to disrupt the familiar and to isolate the ways in which various *forms* and *conventions* are used in the selection and combination of words, sounds and images to produce meanings. Two kinds of analysis are appropriate for this section of the course. The most basic is content analysis, a method for examining the manifest content of media output (Fiske, 1982; McQuail, 1983). It is a statistical method, generally employed to compare the frequencies of key units of content as the basis for inference. For example, in comparing representations of gender in boys and girls comics and magazines, content analysis can be used to examine the range of character types, locations or situations found in a sample of publications. A survey of locations, for instance, would involve the construction of categories into which all locations represented can then be recorded, as in the example below:

Setting[1]	Girls Stories	Boys Stories
Home	54	16
School	54	16
Local community	38	32
National community	4	0
International community	0	53
Fantasy world	4	5

Content analysis can produce some revealing results, and its useful to employ it to put particular hypotheses to the test. Not only can it be applied in the analysis and comparison of contemporary media texts (for example one days or weeks newspapers), but it can also be used to make comparisons historically — for example, womens' magazines from the 1940s to the present. (Ferguson, 1983)

The second type of analysis is derived from semiotics — the study of signs and sign systems. Semiotic analysis draws attention to the *distinctive features* of a given image or text in order to show *how* it works. It is concerned with the way in which the basic elements of an image or sequence of words, sounds and images are selected and combined into *codes* — the informal grammars that we use in interpreting and making sense of images. Semiotics also pinpoints how images do more than denote their subject, they also connote cultural values, qualities and knowledges that we recognise from more general contexts. So a picture of a person can, by the way it is lit, vary in its connotations as nostalgia, Britishness, fantasy etc. Thus semiotics resembles linguistics (from which it is derived); it is used for *structural* rather than qualitative analysis.

With any work on semiotics, its best to begin with simple visual images and then progress to the more complex moving images of film and television. It can be taught, either in the course of work described earlier, in examining how different aspects of the world are represented in the media or in conjunction with initial practical exercises on construction and representation (Hartley, *et al* 1985; Fiske, 1982; Hartley, 1982). However you choose to introduce it, there are two other forms and conventions which demand attention. First the concept of *realism* — the distinction between reality and realism. The product of realism is an impression that the sounds, words and images from which it is constructed are a direct, unmediated *reflection* of reality and conventions are selected and combined to produce their realistic effect (see Bennett, *et al* 1981; Donald and Mercer 1982). Second, the concept of fictional and factual *narrative*. This demands attention to the ways in which both fictional and factual representations are constructed into stories, and into the general narrative flow of media output. Such a focus entails consideration of *characterization* and *stereotyping* within the development of a plot, and to the succession of narrative moments — from initial tension, through conflict, to eventual resolution and the restoration of normality. Examples here may be taken from news stories (Hartley, 1982), soap operas (Dyer *et al*, 1981), cinema and television (Ellis, 1982).

Studying the ways in which the media represent the social world to their audiences by means of particular signs, codes and conventions, forms an important basis for teaching media studies. This is a central focus, and one which serves to introduce a series of concepts, debates and issues which need to be developed in a number of ways.

Industries and Institutions

As we've outlined, the idea of representation is predicated upon the notion that media images and texts — despite often powerful appeals to the contrary — are social constructions and cultural products. In short, newspapers, magazines, radio and television programmes clearly do not just 'drop from the skies', they are all made in certain ways, they are the results of organized practices and occupations. Our position as everyday consumers of media output does, in some respects, take this into account, but it also tends to mean that many of the organized processes of production are masked from us. Stuart Hood, (1983) for example, argues in his discussion of television:

In the most highly developed countries television is as easily available as water, gas or electricity. We can switch all of them on or off at will. Just as we do not wonder where the water, the gas or the electricity came from, how they get to us, or what processes they go through, so we do not generally wonder how television pictures reach our screens. Television pictures tend to be unquestioned; they are accepted as being as 'natural' as gas, water or electricity.

An important component of media studies involves unmasking and understanding the processes and practices of production, and it is useful initially to place an emphasis on *how* various media forms are produced, constructed and circulated, on *who* and *what* are involved in their production processes. One strategy for opening up this area of work is by examining the credit lists or 'trademarks' of a newspaper, magazine, film or TV programme. Such material provides an accessible starting point for examining the 'raw materials', the personnel, roles, hierarchies, technologies and so on involved in production.

From such a starting point, analysis can move to more detailed consideration of the *contexts* in which media production is situated. Such contexts not only facilitate, but also shape, guide and constrain the practices and orientations of media producers and professionals in important ways. In short, this is to introduce the ideas of *regulation* and *determination*, to suggest that all media output is subject to a range of constraints and routines — certain *conditions of production*. Perhaps the best way to approach this is by concentrating initially on relatively restricted contexts — the studio, the newsroom, the advertising agency etc. — in order to identify the particular practices, sequences and hierarchies involved in instances of cultural production. Two important directions for work should also be explored here. The first involves groups taking part in their own actual or simulated practical productions — making their own school or community news-sheets or magazines, devizing and producing their own radio or video programmes (Hartley *et al*, 1985.). In addition, such practical work can be usefully extended by developing contacts with media organizations themselves — visiting local media organizations, or receiving visits from media professionals willing to talk about their work. Independent film and video workshops, for example, are also useful contacts for such work.

Crucially, such study cannot be approached uncritically. It is not enough simply to be able to watch a news bulletin, for example, and recount verbatim who does what, when and how. It is also important to encourage an awareness of the implications of such production processes — for those being represented, for the kind of 'product' produced, and for audiences. In this way knowledge of quite specific production contexts and practices has to be placed within its wider context — as part of quite specific *industrialized* and *institutionalized* structures and systems. Beginning with the notion of industrialized production, it can be helpful to draw on the metaphor of the media as factories, sharing many of the characteristics of any other intensive production unit. In this sense, production implies a sequence of operations and processes which organize and coordinate the gathering together of certain 'raw' materials, their processing, assembly and packaging into a required product or form, and their distribution and circulation within markets for consumption. These stages and sequences involve different, often specialized practices and technologies, divisions of labour with divisions of power, control and orientation. There are a range of useful production studies available here. These include studies of news organizations and news production (Schlesinger, 1978; Glasgow University Media Group, 1976, 1978, and 1980; Tunstall, 1971; Chibnall, 1977); studies of television production (Elliott, 1974; Alvarado and Buscombe, 1978; Ellis, 1982; Alvarado and Steward, 1985; Hood, 1983); records and popular music (Frith, 1983; Elliott, 1982); magazines (Ferguson, 1983) and film (Ellis, 1982; Fisher, 1970, Pirie, 1977). As many of these studies suggest, media production is not just a matter of technical skills and equipment. The people employed as professionals also have their own ideals, commitments, routines and values. These in turn have an important bearing on the finished item, which is the product not only of individual professionals, but also corporate professionalism (Elliott, 1977; Schlesinger, 1978).

Implicit in this, is a broader notion of the media as industries, which recognizes that media organizations constitute a significant part of 'big business' within a capitalist market economy. As Murdock (1982) has argued:

> The communications industries produce peculiar commodities. At one level they are goods and services like any others: cans of fruit, automobiles or insurance. But they are also something more. By providing accounts of the contemporary world and images of the 'good life', they play a pivotal role in shaping social consciousness, and it is this 'special rela-

tionship' between economic and cultural power that has made
the issue of their control a continuing focus of academic and
political concern.

In a direct sense then, media organizations are in business to produce
their 'peculiar' commodities to be sold and distributed subject to the
logics of commercial profitability, loss and viability. Under specific
market conditions, they operate to both cultivate and convert forms
of cultural demand into commercially profitable forms of cultural
supply. The changing commercial structures and development of
successive media organizations have provided a rich and often volatile
source for a set of historical debates. Two recurrent and inter-linked
themes are especially pronounced. The first finds its expression in a
qualitative concern for the impact of commerce upon cultural values
and creativity within changing modes of cultural production and
consumption. Such a focus has found its most vigorous expression
in the critical dismay exhibited by those writers and critics who have
tended to condemn 'commercialism' de facto. Here, cultural 'consumerism' and the implications of market organization have been
framed and opposed on the grounds of 'popularization' and 'vulgar-
ization' — their claimed tendency to produce a detrimental 'levelling
downwards' of traditional cultural forms, values and pursuits. Variations on this qualitative theme have had, and continue to exert, not
inconsiderable influence over the framing and assessment of media
policy in Britain.

The second related dimension at issue here concerns the political
implications of the structures of commercial power and interest that
characterize private sector media enterprises. Here, instances of direct
or 'crude' market manipulation — consumer persuasion or political
propagandizing 'pure and simple' have often been foregrounded.
Other commentators, have however, argued that such overt examples
lead to partial and oversimplified and inadequate accounts of what is,
in fact, a more fundamental set of issues. These concern the extent to
which the private and corporate power of media ownership serves as
a basis for major and decisive forms of political and cultural
regulation and control, on behalf of both the dominant owning
groups and their class (Murdock and Golding, 1977; Curran and
Seaton, 1981.) In the British context, such issues and debates have
sharpened as the patterns of private ownership and control have
become increasingly concentrated into large multi-national con-
glomerates. One way to illustrate this point is through local media
research, taking, for example, local cinemas, radio and TV stations,

newspapers etc. and tracing their ownership — often from the local outlet, to national and multi-national owning groups together with their often diverse interests across a range of industries and share-holding companies. From this basis, discussions and simulated exercises can be used to introduce the debates concerning the amount of power that owning groups can actually wield over production and decision-making. A good deal of research has pinpointed the complexity of the relationship between financial owners and professional managers or producers, who have access to considerable specialized knowledge and authority in everyday production (Gallagher, 1982; Murdock, 1977).

From here, consideration can be turned towards a broader perspective, the production, circulation and consumption of a specific media industry; the popular music/record industry (Frith, 1983; Elliott, 1982; Hustwitt, 1984), the press (Curran and Seaton, 1981; Morley and Whitaker, 1984), cinema or television (Tunstall, 1983; Hood, 1983.) One way to approach cinema, for example, entails tracing the different aspects of production — from the initial submission of a film script, through stages of financing, production, promotion and distribution to eventual consumption in local cinema (and possibly) video outlets.[2] It also perhaps worth identifying the record industry as a particularly useful focus for such work, not only because of its immediate interest to most pupils, but also because so many other media (radio, television and magazines) play a significant role in what is produced and how it is circulated and consumed (Hartley, *et al*, 1985; Instrell, 1985).

During the course of such work, the kinds of qualitative and political debates outlined earlier are likely to find a natural place in discussion; it should also become clear that media industries provide salient instances of certain key features of capitalist production and development in general — including, for example, the imperative towards profit, the tendency to monopoly, and the concentration of ownership into more extensive and powerful corporate organizations. On an international scale, this has led towards the cultural domination of some modes of media production — and hence forms of media output — at the expense of others (Matterlart, *et al* 1984; Tunstall, 1977).

A final aspect of such project work might move towards analysis of the independent sectors of cultural production. In financial terms, it is increasingly difficult to establish alternatives to the large scale corporations and to initiate and sustain 'independence' or alternative forms of media provision. As a consequence, many have argued that the commercial structures and relations which regulate media production set fundamental limits on the 'freedom' and autonomy of media organizations, and furthermore, systematically contradict the ideals of democratic control and access to the media. Once again, local independent initiatives can often provide a useful source of information.

The study of the industrial contexts and commercial conditions of media production can begin to answer and develop some of the key questions posed by work done on representations, extending a critical awareness of how, and in what and whose terms, 'the world' is constructed and mediated to audiences. However, the media are not just organized and regulated as industries; they are also socially and politically organized as *institutions*. As Branston (1984), has argued, there are a range of important and valuable pedagogic possibilities involved in teaching the media as institutions. Such a focus is concerned centrally to situate media institutions within relations of social power, and this presents at least two interrelated directions for teaching. The first involves analysis of the historical development of selected media institutions; the second, the exploration of relationships between the media, government and the state in different contexts. Clearly, these two approaches cannot, and should not be entirely separated, as the development of media institutions is simultaneously a history of the relationships between them and various other forces, including the state. Conversely, the relationships between the media and the state — especially in times of national and social crisis — have had a determining influence on the development of media institutions themselves.

In teaching these areas of work, its useful to begin by examining the development of different media institutions in different historical periods — the establishment and control of printing in the sixteenth and seventeenth centuries for example, the emergence of the popular newspaper in the nineteenth century (Boyce, *et al* 1978); selected moments from cinema and broadcasting history in the twentieth century (Curran and Porter, 1983; Dickinson and Street, 1985; Hood, 1983; Tunstall, 1983). Clearly, the differences between these historical epochs mean that the conditions for the development of various media change. But there are also remarkable similarities to be found in the kind of issues that need to be raised if the development and institutionalization of any medium in any period is to be understood. Indeed, some of the political, cultural and commercial factors that influenced the development of printing are still to be found in broadcasting and the development of new media technologies (Hood, 1983; Tunstall, 1983; Aubrey and Chilton 1983). In fact, sometimes, the controversies surrounding these media are debated in language which has hardly changed from the seventeenth century to the present day.

Underlying the development of media institutions are a set of long standing conflicts between those who have by various means appropriated the control of the social apparatus of sense-making, and those who seek to represent or speak for themselves, but lack the power to do so. This is an abiding theme of media development and such tensions are frequently given their clearest articulation during moments of national crisis — the General Strike for example, the Suez Crisis of the 1950s and, more recently, the Falklands Crisis. It is also evident in situations of crisis sparked off directly by controversial media output itself — well documented examples being *The War Game, Yesterdays Men* and *Death of a Princess* (Tracey, 1977; Harris, 1982; Greenberg and Smith, 1983; Curtis, 1984; Patley, 1983; Jones, *et al*, 1985.) Such incidents are particularly useful for the analysis of media relations with the state, political parties and government because when routine assumptions and practices are disrupted by extraordinary events, it is possible to see the disposition of forces that underlie those routines much more clearly (May and Rowan, 1982; Schlesinger, *et al* 1983). Such moments of institutional history can be analyzed by means of structured role play exercises — either built around the actual events of crises or analogous simulations (Branston, 1984.) Whichever approach is adopted however, the crucial aims of such work are to foreground and interrogate the complex legal, political and statutory structures which regulate and inform media production. This demands attention, not simply to the official codes and statutes themselves, but also to their implications 'in action', as parts of institutional and historical process. Some of the key issues here relate to the terms under which these structures, principles and practices exert control over cultural production. The degrees to which they constrain the autonomy of media institutions and producers, most obviously in the form of direct censorship and formal legislation, less overtly, but no less effectively, in the forms of self-censorship and informal convention.

Taken as a whole, the study of media industries and insitutions is quite extensive, drawing together analysis of media products, producers and consumers within the wider social, political and cultural forces that govern them. The important point to bear in mind is that the media cannot be studied in isolation, they are explained by their historical context as much as by their own self-image. Further, the historical context in which they develop is not a bland progression of events ('one damned thing after another'), but a continuing struggle between different interests, factions, policies, social and commercial forces, which are often beyond the control of the participants.

Audiences and Identities

> Audience is not a satisfactory term. Even its everyday use has overtones of passivity: to be a member of an audience is to be a non-contributory recipient. (Tudor, 1974)

Implicit in our discussion of the forms and processes of media representation and the media as industries and institutions are a set of questions concerning audiences. To complete the circuit of the course, we turn to a range of approaches and strategies for studying the listeners, viewers and readers who collectively make up the audiences for media forms. A useful starting point here is to conduct a survey of pupils' own media use. This can be a diary of their own media use during one week, or can be broadened to include the media habits of different members of their family. Such surveys can be used as a useful starting point for a consideration of what is meant by the term '*audience*'. The idea of 'an audience' carries a set of implicit assumptions, such as passive reception, size, 'sameness' and so on, and its meaning has changed within shifting historical contexts. In other words, our ideas of what an audience is are historically and culturally relative; they have been changed over time, in part by the range and nature of available media of communication. At this initial stage it can be productive to develop project and discussion work by examining the historical development of different audiences, from pre-literacy to print, from print to electronic media. In this sense, audiences are placed firmly within a set of changing social, institutional and historical relations — they are defined as specific features of wider social and cultural formations, rather than as abstracted one-dimensional phenomena. In the crudest terms for example, the audiences encompassed within Roman amphitheatres had very different characteristics to a television audience, but the term 'audience' tends often to suppress the distinctions.

It is also important to recognize how thinking about audiences has been powerfully shaped by a set of recurrent themes and concerns which have themselves been born out of specific historical and institutional preoccupations (McQuail, 1983; Tudor, 1979). A useful division can for example, be made here between *measuring* audiences and *researching* audiences. An early stimulant to audience research stemmed from within media organizations themselves. Within commercial contexts of production and distribution, the need to know 'how many?' was given considerable impetus with the development of advertising. This in turn prompted the questions 'who?' and 'what type?'. Subsequently, a predominant way of thinking about audiences has been in terms of *numbers*, statistical profiles or percentages of readership, attendance, sales or ratings (Tunstall, 1983). This data may provide useful resources for certain kinds of insight, but tends to be open to a range of interpretations and can be misleading. As Tunstall (1983) has suggested:

> The national mass media audience in Britain is one of the most heavily researched in the world ... Nevertheless, there is always something in the assertion that the more data we have, the less we know.

Interpreting the significance of such data, given the selective ways in which it is collected for advertisers or media policy makers, is a starting point for discussion. Generally speaking a great deal of statistical information about audiences is derived from analyzing responses to what are fairly simple and direct questions. Such methods may give us a reasonably accurate estimate of the size and, in limited terms, the composition of certain audiences. It is however, much more difficult to give comparable accounts of the different patterns and ranges of interpretation, orientation and interaction that characterise the many sub-groups and sub-cultures encompassed within audiences.

Rather different attempts to measure media audiences have also played an important role in a series of debates concerning media 'effects'. There is a long and recurrent history to the question 'What do the media do to people?' — a history that has been especially pronounced in the context of negative, anti-social phenomena such as violence, delinquency, promiscuity and claimed moral decline (Murdock and McCron, 1979). Such concerns, perhaps especially in terms of their contemporary manifestation (Barker 1984), clearly fall within the orbit of media studies, and it is important to critically evaluate both the basis of the claims, and the strengths and weaknesses of evidence presented. One of the most widely circulating ideas here is the notion that the media *cause* direct *effects*, a model sometimes referred to as the 'hypodermic needle' view of media-audience relations. Such a perspective sees a direct, causal relationship between media, individuals and society, whereby the media 'inject' attitudes and dispositions into the audience with specific, usually anti-social consequences. Despite the fact that the measurement of effects has proved both elusive and inconclusive, the debates go on. They continue to occupy a visible place with regard to media policy and censorship. Such issues should be approached through discussion, especially as young people have been the subject of much 'effects' research, pupils' own attitudes towards violence on television can be usefully compared with relevant studies (Noble, 1975; Gunter, 1985; DES 1983). In all probability, the kinds of conclusion reached in discussion, will provide a useful precursor to more recent work on audiences, discussed below.

Consideration of media 'effects' moves us from a concern with measuring audiences, towards attempts to understand and to *research* audiences in other terms — especially to situate them within their wider social and cultural determinants and contexts. Here, audiences are no longer conceptualized as an undifferentiated 'mass' of passive, gullible consumers. Instead, the focus is on the contexts and relations which structure and mediate the relationships between audience members and a repertoire of media forms. The emphasis here has been placed on audiences as active 'makers' of meanings. Different people in the same audience not only use the media to obtain different types of gratifications (Fiske, 1982; McQuail, 1983; Katz, *et al* 1975; Morley, 1980), but the key to understanding both the similarities and differences between individuals and groups is seen to lie in the specific social, cultural and political discourses and positions that they occupy.

One of the implications of this approach, is that the media themselves can only be understood as instances of larger cultural processes and are just as subject to prevailing social and economic forces as are individuals. Thus some recent analyses of media-audience relations begin by placing the media within the context of capitalist, patriarchal cultures, and the social relations (notably of class and gender) associated with them (Morley, 1980 and 1982; Hall, 1980; Hobson, 1982). In this sense, audiences are not just the sum total of individuals who happened to watch *Eastenders* last night, but are in part identities that media texts themselves specify and close in various ways. Of course, in the act of consumption it is open to viewers and readers to accept, modify, reject or ignore the identities encouraged by the particular programme or media form. However, it remains the case that the ways in which media texts and output are organized does propose certain relations between them and their viewers or readers, and does encourage certain identifications at the expense of others. The concepts which have been used to open up some of these organizing relations include: genre, audience positioning and mode of address (Ellis, 1982; Neale, 1983).

As far as audiences themselves are concerned, the establishment of recognized genres has two consequences. First it allows for selection, towards a definite set of preferences without sampling indiscriminately; second, part of the pleasure of watching or reading can consist in knowing the genre conventions, and identifying with the characterizations, stereotypes, plots and narratives. This pleasure can be increased, of course by genre shifts and hybrids which play with such conventions or subvert them. Thus genre has come to be seen as one of the mechanisms by which textual plurality and potential meanings and experiences are limited, regulated and ordered in a mass market. Genres position audiences by specifying what kinds of pleasures and entertainments are on offer, at the same time limiting the commercial risk of the producer corporations by channeling the production of output into regulated and familiar lines that are known to be marketable to any particular audience type. One consequence of this contractual notion of genre is that it challenges the 'massness' of media output, since it recognizes clear differentiations between potential members of the 'mass' audience.

Relations between audiences and media are also structured through mode of address. Every programme, film, text etc is produced with a given audience in mind, but what is at issue here is an argument about what image producers have fixed on as the image to address. Frequently the audience is addressed as *individuals*, grouped into *families*, which are part of *the nation* (Brunsden and Morley, 1978; Patterson, 1980). In other cases 'we' are addressed ('us'), in a way that, in fact, is appropriate only to a male audience; or a white British audience, or a heterosexual audience and so on. In considering these concepts, it is useful to develop projects which try to pinpoint *what identity* is being addressed or mobilized in a given instance, and to then compare that with others from different genres to see what similarities of position may be found. For example, it is useful to look not only at images or representations of, say, young people, but also at the way young people are addressed *as such* in different types of output (as well as taking note of those categories that exclude or ignore young people as addressees.) Fundamentally, such approaches reconnect us with our starting point — the study of media representations — and raise important directions for ongoing discussion and practical work. Perhaps the key issue here concerns the social and cultural determinations in play as people in audiences produce meanings, experiences and identities (Green, 1985.).

Teaching Media Studies

Media studies in schools has not always paid attention to the kinds of issues outlined above. Until the late 1970s the subject tended to be confined to individual schools scattered around the country whose motives for introducing the subject varied considerably. Such a hybrid form and range of objectives carried their own educational and pedagogic implications:

> In an attempt to bring the consideration of the mass media onto the educational agenda, teaching strategies were adopted which removed the possibility of incisive analysis or the structured development of cognitive and intellectual skills. Paradoxically, this happened when there was a serious concern that the education which students received should be more 'relevant to their needs'. In practice, film and media studies became a potential means of keeping recalcitrant, apathetic or bored students occupied. When the work was more successful it was possible to involve students in discussion about the social and moral relevance of particular narratives and documentary films. In the justifiable enthusiasm which such work aroused it was often unnoticed that discussion of films, though valuable and interesting as a component part of media studies, was substituting for the notion of teaching and learning. Invisibile pedagogies were legitimising the retention of ignorance and establishing work and enjoyment as polarities in the educational system and coming down in favour of the latter. (Ferguson, 1981)

Ferguson goes on to argue that, in the absence of intellectual demand, practical work became structured through the notion of *creativity*, inherited particularly from English teaching. The same pedagogic strategy often continues to characterize other aspects of media study. From this perspective, media studies tends simply to transfer the agenda and analytical techniques well established in English, to texts that move and speak. Thus selected texts might be used to spark general debate on a social issue, literary appreciation skills developed on media output and practical projects used as an opportunity for pupils to express views and emotions by drawing on different media

Tim O'Sullivan, Holly Goulden and John Hartley

forms. Crucially such an emphasis is apt to sweep study of the media themselves off the agenda; the media *message* becomes all important and the way in which that message is constructed, circulated, regulated and consumed is liable to be ignored or marginalized.

If the syllabus that we have outlined sets out with different aims — concentrating instead on what Masterman (1981) terms a 'de-mythologizing' process this will reveal:

> the selective practices by which images reach the television screen, emphasise the constructed nature of representations projected and make explicit their suppressed ideological function.

This does not mean that 'creativity' or personal expression have no place in the pedagogy of media studies. In fact for many this is precisely the place where:

> ... the circle of conformity, deference and passivity can be broken through an active and participatory programme structured around intellectual processes rather than the depositing of enormous quantities of information, and in which emerges a group activity and dialogue, and the teacher can work alongside the students as an older and more experienced member of the group rather than as an omniscient expert. ... A methodology with pupil experience at its centre, is an essential methodology ... (*ibid*)

Personal experience is a crucial starting point for Williamson (1981) too, her particular concern being the problems in exposing the ideological work of the media:

> ... I would say that students learn best to 'see' the 'invisible' ideology, when it becomes in their own interest to — when they are actually caught in a contradiction, believing in things which are directly hindering their own well-being or wishes, or which conflict with a change in experience. I don't think people learn in the abstract, nor through moral purpose — like when some boys try to be feminist. I was asked to speak in a video some third years were making about violence to women; they were discussing violence in films and sexist representations — but it meant nothing to *them*, it didn't *affect* them. ... They were 'doing' images of women as an

132

English student might 'do' medieval poetry, or a history student 'The Tudors'.

Others have expressed concern for a pedagogy that at all times forefronts personal experience. Alvarado (1981), for example argues that personal experience carries strong and educationally dangerous limitations:

> The problem is, for example, an experience of racism doesn't necessarily help one to understand, explain or fight it — and it is vital that people learn how to analyze, understand and explain in order to fight things of which they have no personal experience. ... Thus it is necessary to construct a pedagogy that precisely does not depend upon personal experience and, in certain ways critiques it.

Underlying this concern is a deeper one; that a pedagogy based *purely* on personal experience and 'learning by doing' can lead to the exclusion of areas of work which are vital to an understanding of the media, but which do not lend themselves easily to group discussion and/or 'active' work projects (Masterman, 1980 and 1985; Connell, 1983).

It should be clear then, that the pedagogy of media studies is no less controversial an area than the subject matter itself. Both are arenas for lively debate, both are subject to, and must be responsive to constant updating and development. If it is this contemporaneity and refusal to be 'pinned down' unequivocally that make media studies a challenging subject to teach, it is also these qualities that make it such a worthwhile and rewarding one.

Notes

1　Our thanks to David Brownstein, a graduate of the Teaching Media Studies Diploma course at the Polytechnic of Wales, for the use of his work.
2　For useful resources here contact Ian Wall, Education Officer, British Film Year, 20 Great Pultney Street, London, WIR 30B

Tim O'Sullivan, Holly Goulden and John Hartley

Useful Addresses

Association for Media Education in
  Scotland (AMES)
Department of Film and Television
  Studies
University of Stirling
Stirling

British Film Institute (Education
  Department)
81 Dean Street
London

Centre for Contemporary Cultural
  Studies
University of Birmingham
PO Box 363
Edgbaston
Birmingham
B15 2TT

Comedia
9 Poland Street
London
W1V 3DG

Media Education Development
  Project (SCET)
Dowanhill
74 Victoria Crescent
Glasgow
G12 9JN

Society for Education in Film and
  Television
29 Old Compton Street
London
W1V 5PL

Teaching Media Studies in Wales
The Polytechnic of Wales
Treforest
Pontypridd
Mid-Glamorgan
CF37 1DL

Television Studies
University of Stirling
Stirling

Working Papers in 16+ Media
  Studies
Clywd Media Studies Unit
Clywd Centre for Educational
  Technology
County Civic Centre
Mold
Clywd
CH7 1YA

For information on media studies
  syllabuses:

Centre for Educational Technology
Herrick Road
Leicester

Centre for Learning Resources
275 Kennington Lane
London

SCET
Dowanhill
74 Victoria Crescent
Glasgow
G12 9JN

Welsh Joint Education Committee
245 Western Avenue
Cardiff
South Glamorgan

References

ALVARADO, M. (1981) 'Television studies and pedagogy', *Screen Education* 38 Spring 1981.

ALVARADO, M. and BUSCOMBE, E. (1978) *Hazell: The Making of a TV Series*, BFI/Latimer.

ALVARADO, M. and STEWART, J. (1985) *Made for Television: Euston Films Ltd*, BFI/Methuen.

AUBREY, C. and CHILTON, P. (Eds) (1983) *Nineteen Eighty-Four in 1984*, Comedia.

BARKER, M. (Ed) (1984) *The Video Nasties*, Pluto.

BENNETT, T. *et al* (Eds) (1981) *Popular Television and Film*, BFI.

BOYCE, G. *et al* (Eds) (1978) *Newspaper History: From the 17th Century to the Present Day*, Sage/Constable.

BRANSTON, G. 'TV as Institution: Strategies for Teaching', *Screen*, 25, 2 1984.

BRUNSDEN, C. and MORLEY, D. (1978) *Everyday Television: Nationwide*, BFI.

CHIBNALL, S. (1977) *Law and Order News*, Tavistock.

COHEN, S. (1980) *Folk Devils and Moral Panics*, Martin Robertson.

COHEN, S. and YOUNG, J. (Eds) (1981) *The Manufacture of News*, Constable.

CONNELL, I. 'Progressive Pedagogy?', *Screen*, 24, 3. 1983.

CURRAN, J. and PORTER, V. (Eds) (1983) *British Cinema History*, Weidenfeld

CURRAN, J. and SEATON, J. (1981) *Power without Responsibility*, Fontana.

CURTIS, L. (1984) *Ireland the Propaganda War*, Pluto.

D.E.S. (1983) *Popular TV and Schooling*.

DICKINSON, M. and STREET, S. (1985) *Cinema and State: The film Industry and the British Government 1927–84*, BFI.

DONALD, J. and MERCER, C. (1982) *Reading and Realism Unit 15, U203 Popular Culture*, O.U.

DYER, G. (1982) *Advertising as Communication*, Methuen.

DYER, R. *et al* (1981) *Coronation St*, BFI.

ELLIOTT, D. (1982) *The Rock Music Industry*, unit 24, U203, Popular Culture, OU.

ELLIOTT, P. (1974) *The Making of a Television Series*, Constable.

ELLIOTT, P. (1977) 'Media organisations and occupations: An overview', ch. 6 in CURRAN, J. *et al* (Eds) *Mass Communication and Society*, Edward Arnold.

ELLIS, J. (1982) *Visible Fictions*, Routledge and Kegan Paul.

EVANS, H. (1978) *Pictures on a Page*, Heinemann.

FISKE, J. (1982) *Introduction to Communication Studies*, Methuen.

FERGUSON, B. (1981) 'Practical work and Pedagogy', *Screen Education*, 38. spring.

FERGUSON, M. (1983) *Forever Feminine*, Heinemann.

FISHER, J. (1970) *The Craft of Film*, Attic Publishing.

FRITH, S. (1983) *Sound Effects: Youth, Leisure and the Politics of Rock-'n'Roll*, Constable.

GALLAGHER, M. 'Negotiation of Control in Media Organisations and Occupations', ch. 6 in GUREVITCH, M. *et al* (Eds) (1982) *Culture, Society and the Media*, Methuen.

GARDNER, C. and YOUNG, R. 'Science on TV: A Critique', in BENNETT, T. *et al* (Eds) (1981) *op cit.*

GILLIS, J. (1974) *Youth and History: Traditions and Change in European Age Relations 1770 to the Present*, Academic Press.

GLASGOW UNIVERSITY MEDIA GROUP (1976) *Bad News*, Routledge and Kegan Paul.

GLASGOW UNIVERSITY MEDIA GROUP (1978) *More Bad News*, Routledge and Kegan Paul.

GLASGOW UNIVERSITY MEDIA GROUP (1982) *Really Bad News*, Writers and Readers.

GREEN, M. 'The Audience as Issue and Problem', in *Working Papers in 16+ Media Studies*.

GREENBERG, S. and SMITH, G. (1983) *'Rejoice': Media Freedom and the Falklands*, Campaign for Press and Broadcast Freedom.

GREENHILL, R. MURRAY, M. and SPENCE, J. (1977) *Photography*, Macdonald Guidelines.

GUNTER, B. (1985) *Dimensions of Television Violence*, Gower.

HALL, S. *et al* (1978) *Policing the Crisis: The State and Law and Order*, Macmillan.

HARRIS, R. (1983) *Gotcha! The Media, The Government and the Falklands Crisis*, Faber.

HARTLEY, J. (1982) *Understanding News*, Methuen.

HARTLEY, J., GOULDEN, H. and O'SULLIVAN, T. (1985) *Making Sense: A Course in Media Studies*, Comedia.

HARTMANN, P. and HUSBAND, C. (1974) *Racism and the Mass Media*, Davis Poynter.

HOBSON, D. (1982) *Crossroads: The Drama of a Soap Opera*, Methuen.

HOOD, S. (1983) *On Television*, Pluto.

HURD, G. (1981) 'The Television Presentation of the Police', in BENNETT, T. *et al* (Eds) *op cit.*

HUSBAND, C. (Ed) (1982) *Race in Britain: Continuity and Change*, Hutchinson.

HUSTWITT, M. (1984) 'Rocker Boy Blues', in *Screen*, 25, 3.

INSTRELL, R. (1985) 'Rock School', in *The A.M.E.S. Journal*, 2.

JONES, D. *et al* (1985) *Media Hits the Pits*, Campaign for Press and Broadcast Freedom.

KATZ, E. and BLUMLER, J.G. (Eds) (1974) *The Uses Of Mass Communication*, Sage.

LANGER, J. (1981) 'Televisions Personality System', in *Media Culture and Society*, 4.

LUSTED, D. (1985) 'A History of Suspicion: Educational Attitudes to Television', ch. 1 in LUSTED, D. and DRUMMOND, P. (Eds) *TV and Schooling*, BFI.

MCARTHUR, C. (1980) *Scotch Reels: Scotland in Cinema and Television*, BFI.

MCQUAIL, D. (1983) *Mass Communication Theory: An Introduction*, Sage.

MCROBBIE, A. 'Jackie: An Ideology of Adolescent Feminity', in WAITES, B. *et al* (Eds) (1981) *Popular Culture: Past and Present*, Croom Helm.

MCROBBIE, A. (1982) 'Just Like a Jackie Story', in MCROBBIE, A. and MCCABE, T. (Eds) *Feminism for Girls: An Adventure Story*, Routledge and Kegan Paul.

MASTERMAN, L. (1980) *Teaching About Television*, Macmillan.

MASTERMAN, L. (1981) 'TV Pedagogy', in *Screen Education*, 40.

MASTERMAN, L. (1985) 'Future Developments in TV and Media Studies', ch. 11 in LUSTED, D. and DRUMMOND, P. (Eds) *TV and Schooling*, BFI.

MATTELART, A. *et al* (1984) *International Image Markets*, Comedia.

MAY, A. and ROWAN, K. (Eds) (1982) *Inside Information: British Government and the Media*, Constable.

MORLEY, D. (1980) *The 'Nationwide' Audience*, BFI.

MORLEY, D. (1982) 'Interpreting Television', unit 12, U203 *Popular Culture*, Open University.

MORLEY, D. and WHITAKER, B. (Eds) (1984) *The Press, Radio and Television*, Comedia.

MUNCIE, J. (1984) *The Trouble with Kids Today*, Hutchinson.

MURDOCK, G. (1977) Patterns Of Ownership; Questions of Control, unit 10, DE 353 *Mass Communication and Society*, Open University.

MURDOCK, G. (1982) 'Large Corporations and the Control of the Communications Industries', ch. 5 in GUREVITCH, M. *et al* (Eds) *Culture, Society and the Media*, Methuen.

MURDOCK, G. and GOLDING, P. (1977) 'Capitalism, Communication and Class Relations', in CURRAN, J. *et al* (Eds) *Mass Communication and Society*, Arnold.

MURDOCK, G. and MCCRON, R. (1979) 'The Television and Delinquency Debate', *Screen Education*, 30.

NEALE, S. (1983) *Genre*, BFI.

NOBLE, G. (1975) *Children in Front of the Small Screen*, Constable.

PATERSON, R. (1980) 'Planning the Family: The Art of the Schedule', in *Screen Education*, 35.

PATLEY, J. (1983) Parliament, the Press and Death of a Princess, in *Drama Documentary*, BFI Dossier no. 19, BFI.

PEARSON, G. (1983) *Hooligan: A History of Respectable Fears*, Macmillan.

PIRIE, D. (1977) *Anatomy of the Movies*, Windward Press.

SCHLESINGER, P. (1978) *Putting Reality Together: BBC News*, Constable.

SCHLESINGER, P., MURDOCK, G. and ELLIOTT, P. (1983) *Televising Terrorism*, Comedia.

STOTT, J. and KING, M. (Eds) (1977) *Is This Your Life?* Virago.

TRACEY, M. (1977) *The Production of Political Television*, Routledge and Kegan Paul.

T.U.C. (1984) *Images of Inequality*, T.U.C.

TUDOR, A. (1974) *Image and Influence*, Allen and Unwin.

TUDOR, A. (1979) 'On Alcohol and the Mystique of Media Effects', ch. 1 in COOK, J. and LEWINGTON, M. (Eds) *Images of Alcoholism*, BFI.

TUNSTALL, J. (1971) *Journalists at Work*, Constable.

TUNSTALL, J. (1977) *The Media are American*, Constable.

TUNSTALL, J. (1983) *The Media in Britain*, Constable.

WILLIAMS, R. (1974) *Television: Technology and Cultural Form*, Fontana.

WILLIAMSON, J. (1978) *Decoding Advertisements*, Marion Boyards.

WILLIAMSON, J. (1981) 'How does Girl Number Twenty understand Ideology', in *Screen Education*, 40.

WOOLLACOTT, J. (1982) 'Class, Sex and the Family in Situation Comedy', unit 23, U203, *Popular Culture*, Open University.

Tensions and Trends in School Health Education

Charles Wise

There appears to be little agreement as to what constitutes school health education, but there remains the vestiges of a belief that it may be to do with 'nits and dirty bits' or 'sex, drugs and 'rock n' roll'. This view may indicate the relative importance of certain emotive or high profile health issues, as well as perceiving health education in terms of content. In this chapter, although not wishing to underestimate the importance of a body of knowledge, the writer concentrates upon some of the administrative, curricular, methodological, organizational, pedagogical and social implications of health education in schools.

Expectations and Concerns

Even though the term 'health education' may mean different things to different people, it has received considerable attention within education circles in recent years. A number of government department and independent agency reports have emphasized its importance within the school curriculum (DES, 1977, 1979 and 1981; DES/HMI, 1979 and 1980; HMI, 1978, 1985a and 1985b; Schools Council, 1976 and 1981; SED, 1974; Warnock, 1978) and some major curriculum development projects have focussed upon health education (McNaughton, 1983; Schools Council, 1977, 1982 and 1984). However, in spite of this enthusiasm, within a decentralized education system there is no mandatory obligation on the part of schools to respond to these publications. Teachers may feel that health education poses yet more demands from a society which expects them to be alleviators of major social ills, so what can be reasonably expected of a school's planned intervention?

Charles Wise

Some statements relating to the expectations of a school's health education programme may make particular references to 'health', for example:

1 We can expect school health education to increase understandings about the philosophy and science of individual and societal health.
2 We can expect school health education programmes to increase competencies of individuals to make decisions about personal behaviours that influence their own health.
3 We can expect school health education programmes to increase the skills required by individuals to engage in behaviours that are conducive to health.
4 We can expect school health education programmes to contribute to eliciting healthy behaviours.
5 We can expect schools to increase the skills of individuals to maintain and improve the health of their families and the communities in which they reside.
(Kolbe, 1984, pages 12 and 13)

whereas other sources may cite 'health' as one amongst other foci for personal and social development concerns, for example:

giving young people a basic health knowledge and understanding of human development;

helping young people to adapt to change in themselves and their environment;

helping young people to explore and understand the feelings, attitudes and values of themselves and others;

helping young people to determine where they have control over their health and where they can, by conscious choices, determine their future health and lifestyles.
(Schools Council, 1982)

The traditional approach to school health education has focused upon health topics, with particular attention to those related to personal hygiene, drugs, smoking and sex. The reason for their prominence in programmes may be a particular response to the fears and anxieties expressed by adults. At the extreme, the selection of topics may have been based upon the occurrence or anticipation of a problem or crisis. Whilst not denying their importance, the topics need to be set within the context of healthy development rather than apart from it. Local variation apart, the majority of young people do not sniff glue, use cocaine or become mothers and fathers under the age of 16 and therefore a programme should not be formulated on such a basis.

The focus upon prevention is an attractive one in economic, political and social terms and since much of the western world's ill health is the product of unhealthy life style, it appears to present an attainable goal. However, one has to consider the contribution of health education within the framework of the school as a health-promoting institution.

The Location of Health Education

At the outset, it is important to acknowledge that the formal curriculum is only one source of a young person's health education and not necessarily the most influential one. For the school to intervene in the provision of planned health education, it is necessary to consider the many and varied contexts in which young people's health-related behaviour occurs. If one accepts Green's definition (1979) of health education as being any combination of learning experiences designed to facilitate voluntary adaptations of behaviour (in individuals, groups or communities) conducive to health, then one needs to ask 'how and in what ways does the school assist in this process?'. The statement infers that health education is a deliberate, planned process and whilst this may be true in some instances, it provides an incomplete view of how people are 'health-educated'. The messages of the hidden curriculum may support or counteract the activities within the formal curriculum. In the latter case, the sale of confectionery at the school tuck shop may undermine the work conducted within a dental health programme and the billowing clouds of the staff room may provide mixed messages as to the advisability of smoking!

Health education may not appear within the syllabuses of specific subject areas or as a discretely labelled course or programme, but may result from accidental or incidental occurrences as a by-product of other curricular activities. For example, the treatment of a nose bleed within a mathematics lesson may provide an unplanned yet spontaneous piece of health education.

Since the teaching of health education may be undertaken by a number of subject departments and/or through the school's tutorial provision and given that teachers tend to operate in the isolation of their own classrooms, there is a danger that pupils may fall victims to omission and undue repetition. In a school which attempts to coordinate the planned provision, there appears to be a greater likelihood that where duplication does occur, it takes the form of reinforcement and reiteration within a spiral curriculum.

Although the need for coordination has been supported in numerous publications (Brierley, 1983; Evans, 1981; HMI, 1978; Schools Council, 1976, 1981, 1982 and 1984; Wilcox and Gillies, 1983), the notion remains problematic. The coordination of health education, however, may be justified in terms of the more effective use of manpower, time and other scarce resources, the removal of 'one-off' crisis interventions based upon problems or crises in favour of a programme responsive to the developmental needs and interests of individuals and groups, and accountability to a range of interested parties, for example, parents, pupils and the community beyond the school.

The Target of Health Education

Whilst some headteachers may be eager to express their commitment to 'health education for all', there is sometimes a discrepancy between the rhetoric and the action they support. Scrutiny of the formal curriculum may reveal differential provision in terms of ability, age and gender where, for example, the least able senior girls receive an 'overdose' of health education due to their choice of, or allocation to, a particular combination of subjects within the school's option scheme. In the absence of a core programme, a young person's selection of subjects may have a profound effect upon his/her exposure to health education. In some schools, there is the implication that bright children do not need health education. Using a coded grid system where health issues are set against particular year groups, it is possible to gain a composite view of the school's formal curricular provision in terms of health education (Schools Council, 1984).

Links with Other 'Educations'

Williams and Williams (1980) believe that health education has no well-established educational model over which there is a consensus of opinion and that the same view may be expressed for careers, moral, political and social education. Although their enthusiasts may make claims of clear boundaries between each of these aspects of education, in reality they may be arbitrary, provisional and tentative. There is likely to be considerable overlap in terms of content, methods and purposes, where they share a common focus upon the promotion of personal and social development of young people.

Within the formal curriculum, the 'educations' may appear as a conglomerate under a generic title or be expressed through such mnemonics as OAP (Outlooks and Prospects), TASK (Towards a Survival Kit) or SHARE (Social Health and Religious Education); the latter case is an example of where a school has accommodated religious education within a broader personal and social education framework. The interrelationship of health education with other aspects of education has received considerable attention (Bolam and Medlock, 1985; David, 1983; McPhail, 1982; Pring, 1984; Wakeman, 1984) and many local authorities have expressed their views on such links (Bedfordshire, 1981; Devon, 1978; Gloucestershire, 1971; Lancashire, 1972; Nottinghamshire, 1981; SCEA, 1981; Stockport, 1983; Surrey, 1985; Wiltshire, 1982).

Designing a Health Education Programme

Using Pupil Experience

One of the richest resources which young people bring to school is themselves. Therefore, it may be possible to gain access to this resource to the mutual benefit of the teachers and the taught. A teacher's lack of familiarity with the existing knowledge of young people may lead to a situation where (s)he provides answers to questions that they have not asked. The resultant boredom or disaffection could have a demotivating effect upon their learning and build resistance to future dialogue.

The importance of the daily experience of the young person as (s)he goes through the school may provide some of the raw materials for a health education programme. Too often, teachers plan programmes without reference to their pupils and in so doing, overlook the immediacy of the situation in which young people find themselves. Critical incidents (Hamblin, 1978) such as the induction of new pupils joining the secondary school, examinations, course choices, bullying and a range of decision-making situations have effects on a person's health. The assumption that '(s)he will get over it' is not only callous but ignores some behaviours beyond the school gates that may have their roots in the school and have a detrimental effect upon one's mental, physical and social health, for example, bed wetting, school refusal and tantrums.

Balding (1979) found that in a survey of forty secondary schools in Exeter there were mis-matches between what boys and girls of various ages considered to be of interest and what their teachers and parents considered to be important in a list of twenty-eight health education topics. His work has been repeated in other areas with similar findings and this raises the issue of whose opinions dictate the identification of an appropriate health education programme.

If one is to gain access to the young person's world, it may be through direct approach in which the person discloses his or her views or through the completion of an anonymous questionnaire. The importance of a baseline prevalence study cannot be overemphasized and Balding (1984a and 1984b) has developed a health-related behaviour questionnaire which has been used with over 40,000 pupils in the 11–16 age range. Its purpose is to reveal a pupil profile which embraces aspects of life, at home and with friends (Muirden, 1985). Such information provides useful data to assist in the formulation of a programme and though accepting some weaknesses inherent in self-reporting, provides more accurate indicators than hunch or conventional wisdom.

Such a direct involvement fosters the belief that (i) health education should be something done 'by' and 'with' pupils rather than 'to' or 'for' them; (ii) parents may make a valuable contribution to curriculum design and implementation; (iii) teachers may make inaccurate judgments about pupil interests; and (iv) health education may provide an excellent opportunity for a negotiated curriculum amongst a range of interested parties.

The involvement of pupils may be extended to their role as 'peer leaders' and some recent smoking programmes have emphasized their centrality in this respect (Murray, 1984; SED 1974).

On emotive issues, such as those related to human sexuality, the divide between acceptable and unacceptable teacher-influence may be critical, yet at times, unclear until an infringement occurs. The activities of local, regional and national pressure groups provide a continual challenge to teachers and their loco-parentis role. They may find themselves in a 'Catch 22' situation if, on the one hand through their influence on pupils' health-related behaviour, their actions are considered to impinge upon the ethnic, moral, political and religious integrity/autonomy of the pupil, and on the other, they fail through their influence to transform negative into positive behaviours. For example, Clarke (1982) believes that careful monitoring of teenagers' views and opinions could lead to more effective sex education. However, one should be mindful that sex education within a multicultural society highlights the importance of respecting the views of families in any school-based work (Bunting, 1984). To 'mass- medicate' children is to deny their uniqueness and dignity, and to ignore their personal perspective which is so valuable if others are to learn and grow from the shared experience.

Teachers may by the way they behave within and outside the school, influence pupils more than by the words they utter. However, their curricular activities vis-à-vis health education may become the target for the concern of pupils, parents and pressure groups, in a way unlike the scrutiny afforded to mathematics, modern languages and music.

Influences on Health-Related Behaviour

The complexity of the nature and scope of certain health behaviours may be such that school health education programmes provide a blunt tool. No single influence may adequately describe this complexity. For example, 'peers' may not represent a unitary influence but as Newman (1984) states, peer pressure is a combination of forces which though they appear singular in effect may include the pressure to appear independent, gain recognition, appear to be grown up and have fun. Furthermore, it may not be possible to identify the single most potent influence but one may be able to recognize clusters that are particularly influential on young people. Evans *et al* (1978), for example, identified parents, peers and the media as major influences perceived by young people on smoking behaviour. It may be that certain factors are more influential than others at particular times within one's 'health career' (Dorn and Nortoft, 1982) and this realization may inform the teacher as to the stage(s) at which certain facets are considered. Environmental factors may militate against educational initiatives and be so powerful as to render them ineffectual.

As a way of identifying influences upon a specific behaviour, teachers may wish to undertake the following exercise (Schools Council, 1984):

Figure 1:

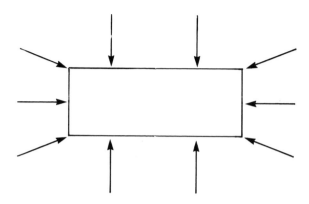

The behaviour under consideration is entered in the box, for example, eating behaviour and influences are noted (figure 2).

Although the responses do not represent an exhaustive list and may require future addition, amplification, clarification and interpretation, they serve as an initial form.

If each topic in the syllabus is considered in terms of a behaviour, then a similar procedure may be adopted for all proposed content areas. It is interesting to note that in spite of the diversity of behaviours, such as cycling, drinking, sexual activity and smoking, there appear to be many common influences (in figure 2, try a number of behaviours in turn).

From a sample of over 17,500 pupils in four years of secondary schools throughout the United Kingdom, Balding (1985a) identified a very positive connection between drinking frequency and the smoking habit. He reported that

> Of the 'non-drinking' boys and girls, 11 per cent and 13.6 per cent respectively are smokers, compared with 33.3 per cent and 63.3 per cent for the '4 + days' group who would like to stop smoking.

This relationship between alcohol and smoking behaviour may lead to asking one or two questions, for example:

(i) What other health-related behaviours may be linked?
(ii) Is a health education programme based upon individual health topics likely to assist in the development or support of positive health behaviours?

Furthermore, if there are relationships should one attempt to develop an 'influences' rather than a 'topic-based' approach to health

Figure 2:

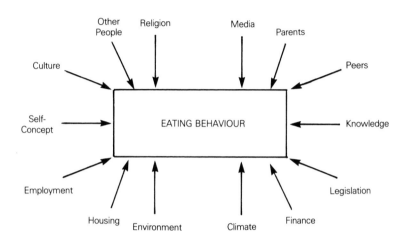

education? The teacher may decide to consider a cluster of influences and how these apply multi-pressure on pupil behaviour. Through such an approach one may focus upon relationships between road accidents (in terms of car driving, cycling, motor cycling and pedestrian behaviour) and the consumption of alcohol (leisure and drinking behaviour).

Knowing and Doing

Newman (1984) states that

> Knowledge alone is insufficient to ensure appropriate action, but it is a vital component of any program to enhance health and counteract social pressure.

The traditional model of health education teaching appears to have been based on the assumption that through the provision of factual information, a person would be persuaded towards positive health behaviour. This simplistic view, whilst it may adequately

Figure 3:

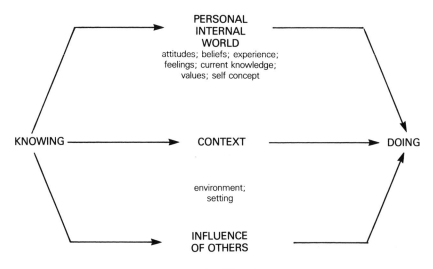

describe the response of some people, fails to cater for the actions of many people. For example, John knows that smoking may damage his health but he smokes. So why does he behave in this way?

One answer may be found in considering the intervening elements of the conversion process of knowledge into action.

In this model (figure 3), it is suggested that acquired knowledge is subjected to scrutiny within the person in terms of his/her personal view of the world; the context in which the new knowledge is to be used may or may not be perceived as relevant or appropriate; and the influence of others may or may not effect the conversion of knowledge into appropriate health action. For example, Jane has learned about birth control methods during sex education lessons, but is persuaded by her boy friend that they should have intercourse. They have both been drinking at the disco and feel that they are not taking an undue risk. Reid (1982), whilst acknowledging the importance of accurate information, suggests that unintended teenage pregnancies are probably caused more by lack of anticipation than by simple ignorance. And contrary to some beliefs, the young person may not be a 'free agent' to choose what (s)he believes to be the most appropriate health choice in view of the influence of others. This situation illustrates the complexity of personal decision-making and should influence the way in which health education is taught in the classroom.

Methods, Materials and Media

The range of learning and teaching strategies used or available for use is considerable and at least nine major approaches have been witnessed. These include:

(i) *Shock/Horror* — When one sees an accident on a motorway the tendency may be to (a) leave at the next exit; (b) travel slowly for the next few miles but then revert to one's high speed driving; or (c) be so upset by the scene that one's driving performance disintegrates. This analogy serves to describe what may occur in lessons where a health education issue is portrayed in terms of self-destructive behaviour; for example, the abuse of drugs by young people. This health 'video-nasty' approach may (a) frighten some from using the drug anymore; (b) lead to a short-term cessation but return to the original behaviour within days or months; and (c) create anxieties which in themselves have a destructive effect upon one's personal health. There are also those who remain untouched by shock/horror tactics. What one can never be sure of is the effect they are likely to have upon a range of individuals who having received the same message, react differently.

Many of the health education films of the seventies and before relating to drugs and sexually-transmitted diseases use fear arousal as a stimulus for primary prevention. There is evidence that 'shock-horror' may have limited influence upon health-related behaviour (Balding 1985b; de Haes and Schuurman, 1971).

(ii) *Information-Giving* has for many years been the predominant approach to school health education through the lecture, film, tape recording, handout, wall chart and the book. One of their primary weaknesses is that they do not provide in themselves an interactive medium, irrespective of the quality and truth of the message. However, these media are not to be discounted if the teacher uses them sparingly so that they do not become 'just another lesson', but are used within other approaches. For example, the trigger film may provide stimulus for discussion which may lead to further action, and the excellent range of schools television and radio programmes can provide a rich resource, as it brings the community into the classroom. The use of video recordings increases editing possibilities. Reid (1985) cites research which indicates that information-giving on its own may have little influence upon smoking behaviour, but its inclusion within other approaches may be more effective. In the case of smoking, peers, siblings and parents may be more influential upon smoking behaviour than any amount of factual information!

(iii) *Conditioning* is used with the very young and with some children in special education schools with particular reference to aspects of safety and personal hygiene. Through task analysis, teachers are able to identify components and teach them sequentially. The cooperation of parents outside school time assists considerably in the reinforcement process.

(iv) *Individual and group counselling* may be particularly relevant to situations where persons are experiencing particular difficulties and where close support and monitoring is necessary; also in cases where health problems are specific to one or more people and where confidentiality is vital if self-confidence is to be boosted.

(v) *Appeals and demands* particularly by those in authority may prove counter-productive though there have been many notable occasions where school assemblies have been used to influence health behaviour. Summoning girls into the hall to hear a lecture on the virtues of not having premarital intercourse since a fourth year girl has recently become pregnant, may have little effect upon the sexual behaviour of others. However, the person making the appeal or demand may have a considerable influence upon the behavioural outcome, irrespective of the apparent logic of the argument being presented. Perhaps the young may respond positively, but some teenagers may perceive 'nagging' as the prime motive.

(vi) *Modelling* may be used where influential people, who demonstrate the positive behaviour, are used as promoters of appropriate health-behaviour(s). The use of senior pupils, who are held in high-esteem, perhaps on the sports field, may have a positive influence on the behaviour of younger ones.

(vii) *The use of experts* as disseminators of information may be counter-productive where their image could be negatively perceived by young people, for example, the police talking about drugs. Even if health professionals have the appropriate knowledge they may be unfamiliar with working with young people in small or large groups and thus their potential effectiveness is undermined by their own lack of confidence and competence in the classroom situation. Doctors, health visitors, environmental health officers and other members of voluntary and statutory bodies may be best taken into school to act as consultants to teachers or to be used for the 'visitor technique'. This technique involves the young people deciding upon whom to invite to school in order to respond to their agenda (Button, 1982; Lancashire, 1980).

(viii) *Reference to consequences* — To suggest to a teenager that her eating of school lunches which consist of 'chips with everything' is likely to affect her health in twenty years' time, may do little to influence her diet. The 'here and now' attitude of adolescents may not be amenable to an adult belief in the virtue of deferred gratification!

(ix) *Coping with Pressure* — If young people are to feel that they have control of their own destiny, their ability to *resist social pressures* needs to be enhanced. Through the use of role play and simulation, opportunities to rehearse coping strategies may be offered.

The mobilization of awareness in young people of the important effect of a range of groups and organizations upon their decisions may in itself be a vital first step towards self-empowerment and a pro-active life style. The local community should provide for young people a rich learning resource; a programme of health education should emphasize their part within it. School health education should not be a passive, information-based experience but should operate on the basis that young people are members of many groups and as such have rights and responsibilities for their own personal, social and mental health and that of others.

Although opportunities for work in the community may be limited during the working day, it may be brought into the school in many different direct and indirect forms. The following examples illustrate some possibilities:

action research	personal experiences
advertisements	media presentations
archives	photographs
art work	posters
community projects	questionnaires
diaries	reports
field work	surveys
film	taped interviews
musical work	visitors
observation	

Within the classroom, one may be able to use these resources and develop them through the use of:

brainstorming	model construction
buzz groups	pattern notes
card sorts/ranking exercises	role play
cartoons	self-perception scales
case studies	sentence completion
collage	simulation
data analysis	slide presentations
debate	story telling
discussion	work shops
drama	writing
games	

Neither list is exhaustive but indicates the range of methods, materials and media available to the teacher who wishes to involve young people in participative learning experiences. Whilst financial support may impede the undertaking of some of these activities, a far greater restriction may be the way in which the teacher perceives his or her role in terms of teaching style.

Teaching Style

Didactic teacher approaches may provide a useful mode of knowledge transmission but have little influence upon health behaviour. Pupils need time and space to reflect and consider their own knowledge, attitudes, beliefs and behaviour, both individually and in groups. The composition of these groups, be they self-selected or teacher-selected, may have a bearing upon young people's willingness to share their views with others. Not all their views are for public scrutiny, no more than are those of the teachers, and the boundaries of one's private and public world may either be infringed or respected by the situation in which one places young people. It is for the teacher to provide an opportunity for discussion within a trusting environment and to monitor that the issue under consideration remains in focus; the teacher acts as a facilitator and not as a chairperson. It is not his/her role to ensure that young people always have to make public pronouncements about their personal stances, or to provide the right answer. Experience suggests that young people will share and exchange opinions when they consider the atmosphere to be supportive and free of fear of punitive action or breaches of confidentiality.

Even the committed teacher may be required to change from a didactic to a less didactic teaching style if the stated aims and expectations are to be realized, but one is reminded that there is no way to teach health education (HMI, 1985).

The movement towards less didactic teaching approaches has been encouraged and supported by the Health Education Council and the Schools Council through their funding of curriculum development projects. The work of the Teachers' Advisory Council on Alcohol and Drug Education (TACADE) has made a substantial contribution to the field and two of their recent teaching packs *Free to Choose* and *Alcohol Syllabus, 11–19* provide pupils with an opportunity to use their existing knowledge and experience as the building blocks for the consideration of their current and future behaviour.

Not only may the materials present pupils with a different classroom learning experience, but they may challenge the teaching style of teachers. The emphasis on participative group activities may be dismissed by some teachers as time-wasting or the latest bandwagon, but the range of possibilities under the broad banner of 'group work' is considerable and offers greater opportunities for the realization of aims and objectives which encapsulate the rhetoric of informed decision-making, personal autonomy, the promotion of self-esteem and health choices.

Thus the teacher may need to reflect upon questions relating to the realization of implicit and/or explicit aims and objectives; for example:

(i) Is the teacher an *instructor* or an *enabler*?

(ii) Is the teacher concerned primarily with the achievement of behavioural change, attitudinal change or knowledge gain in his/her students?

(iii) Is the teacher's style conducive to the realization of one or more of the objectives, indicated in item (ii)?

(iv) Does the teacher have a repertoire of teaching approaches?

(v) Is the teacher aware of the preferred learning style of the pupils?

(vi) To what extent can the teacher be a health educator?

At least, more participative methods signal to young people that it is acceptable for them to discuss health issues and that, however temporarily within a predominantly academic curriculum, 'health' deserves our attention.

Whilst the aims and objectives may be well-articulated within a seemingly convincing declaration of intent, their enactment may be impeded by those who are recruited to teach health education. Some courses or units are staffed with teachers who are members of the 'Remainder Factor', i.e. those colleagues who have a surplus of 'free' periods after the main body of the timetable has been written. Therefore, their competence and confidence cannot be guaranteed. The criticism of their inability and/or reluctance to participate should not be the subject of ridicule or scorn but should be redirected towards the senior management who place colleagues in a vulnerable situation.

The Future

There is evidence that factors beyond the control of children have a profound effect upon their health (DHSS, 1980; Grossman, 1979; Kolbe, 1984b; Newberger *et al*, 1976) for example, education and employment opportunities, ethnic groupings, family size and structure, health behaviour of parents, parental income, social class, medical care and support facilities, housing and regulation of environmental risks. With such a catalogue of seemingly insurmountable barriers to effective school health education, one may be tempted to abdicate one's responsibility to those outside the school. I believe that to do so would be in error, if only because the school population will be the next parent population and will influence its offspring.

Such a proposition shifts the emphasis from solely the 'here and now' to a future date when young people armed with their franchise may have the determination to demand appropriate economic, environmental, fiscal and legal measures to further enhance individual, group and community health. This belief shows the ethical, moral, political and social implications of teaching health education in schools and the pressures upon those who embark on this course.

An increasing number of teachers have become involved with health education in classrooms, by attending courses and through involvement with local, regional and national projects (Brierley, 1983), yet the school's contribution represents a small part of the total range of the nation's possible health promotion activities. Whilst acknowledging this situation, one should strive to find a place for planned health education interventions that provide regular opportunities to reinforce positive health-related behaviour. Health education which does not contribute to health promotion is not a worthy pursuit, particularly in schools who are faced with decisions relating to competing priorities drawn from an ever-increasing agenda.

At a minimum, through highlighting the importance of a healthy life-style, the school may stimulate an interest in our next parental generation to use the economic, legal and political machinery to translate the welter of health knowledge into action.

References

BALDING, J. (1979) 'Health education topics: Their relative importance to parents, pupils and teacher', *Monitor*, 52, Autumn.

BALDING, (1985a) 'Some fourth year alcohol-related behaviour', *Education and Health*, 2, 3, March.

BALDING, J. (1985b) 'A shock-horror debate', *Education and Health*, 1, 3, January.

BEDFORDSHIRE EDUCATION SERVICE (1981) *Health Education: Discussion Paper 8*, Bedford, Bedfordshire Education Service.

BOLAM, R. and MEDLOCK, P. (1985) *Active Tutorial Work: Training and Dissemination: An Evaluation*, Oxford, Basil Blackwell for the Health Education Council.

BRIERLEY, J. (1983) 'Health education in secondary schools', *Health Education Journal*, 2, 42.

BUNTING, A. (1984) 'Sex education for pupils from Asian ethnic minority groups', *Health Education Journal*, 4, 43.

BUTTON, L. (1982) *Group Tutoring for the Form Teacher: Books 1 and 2*, London, Hodder and Stoughton.

CLARKE, L. (1982) 'Teenage views of sex education', *Health Education Journal*, 2, 41.

David, K. (1983) *Personal and Social Education in Secondary Schools*, London, Longman for the Schools Council.

de Haes, W. and Schuurmain, J. (1975) 'Results of an evaluation study of three drug education methods', *International Journal of Health Education*, 4, 18.

Department of Education and Science (1977) *Health Education in Schools*, London, HMSO.

Department of Education and Science (1979) *A Framework for the School Curriculum*, London, HMSO.

Department of Education and Science (1981) *The School Curriculum*, London, HMSO.

Department of Education and Science/Her Majesty's Inspectors (1979) *Education in England*, London, HMSO.

Department of Education and Science/Her Majesty's Inspectors (1980) *A View of the Curriculum*, London, HMSO.

Department of Health and Social Security (1980) *Inequalities in Health, The Black Report*, London, HMSO.

Devon Education Department (1978) *Health and the School*, Exeter, Devon County Council.

Dorn, N. and Nortoft, A. (1982) *Health Careers: Teacher's Manual*, London, Institute for the Study of Drug Dependence.

Evans, M. (1981) *Health Education in Secondary Schools: Ten Case Studies*, Manchester, TACADE.

Evans, R. *et al* (1970) 'Deterring the onset of smoking in children', *Journal of Applied Social Psychology*, 8.

Gloucestershire Education Committee (1971) *The Gloucestershire Scheme for Education in Personal Relationships and Family Life: A Third Report and Handbook*, Gloucester, Gloucestershire Education Committee.

Green, L. (1979) 'National policy in the promotion of health', *International Journal of Health Education*, 22, 3, pp. 161–8.

Grossman, A. (1977) 'Children of working mothers', *Special Labour Force Report 217*, Washington, DC, USGPO, Bureau of Labour Statistics, March.

Hamblin, D. (1978) *The Teacher and Pastoral Care*, Oxford, Basil Blackwell.

Her Majesty's Inspectors (1978) *Curriculum 11–16: Health Education in the Secondary School Curriculum*, London, HMSO.

Her Majesty's Inspectors (1985a) *The Curriculum from 5 to 16: Curriculum Matters 2*, London, HMSO.

Her Majesty's Inspectors (1985b) *Health Education 5 to 16: Curriculum Matters 4*, London, HMSO.

Kolbe, L. (1984a) 'Improving the health of children and youth: Frameworks for behavioural research and development' in Campbell, G. (Ed) *Health Education and Youth*, Lewes, Falmer Press.

KOLBE, L. (1984b) 'Improving the health status of children; an epidemiological approach to establishing priorities for behavioural research' in CAMPBELL, G. (Ed) *Health Education and Youth*, Lewes, Falmer Press.

LANCASHIRE COUNTY COUNCIL (1972) *Pastoral Work, and Education in Personal Relationships in Lancashire Secondary Schools*, Lancashire County Council.

McNAUGHTON, J. (1983) *Fit for Life*, Basingstoke, Macmillan Education.

McPHAIL, P., UNGOED-THOMAS, J. and CHAPMAN, H. (1972) *Moral Education in the Secondary Schools*, York, Longman for the Schools Council.

MUIRDEN, J. (1985) *Editorial to Education and Health*, HEC Schools Health Education Unit, University of Exeter.

MURRAY, D. (1984) 'Towards an effective smoking prevention programme' in CAMPBELL, G. (Ed) *Health Education and Youth*, Lewes, Falmer Press.

NEWBERGER, E., NEWBERGER, C. and RICHMOND, J. (1976) 'Child health in America: Towards a rational public policy', *Milbank Memorial Fund Quarterly*, 3, 54.

NEWMAN, I.M. (1984) 'Pressures affecting teenage health behaviour' in CAMPBELL, G. (Ed) *Health Education and Youth*, Lewes, Falmer Press.

NOTTINGHAMSHIRE COUNTY COUNCIL (1981) *Guidelines for the Teaching of Health Education in Secondary Schools: A Document for Discussion*, Nottingham, Nottinghamshire County Council.

PRING, R. (1984) *Personal and Social Education in the Curriculum*, London, Hodder and Stoughton.

REID, D. (1982) 'School sex education and causes of unintended teenage pregnancies — a review', *Health Education Journal*, 1, 41.

REID, D. (1985) 'Prevention of smoking among school children: Recommendations for policy development', *Health Education Journal*, 1, 44.

SCHOOLS COUNCIL (1976) *Health Education in Secondary Schools: Working Paper 57*, London, Methuen.

SCHOOLS COUNCIL (1977) *Schools Council Health Education Project 5–13*, 'Think Well' and 'All About Me', Sunbury, Nelson.

SCHOOLS COUNCIL (1981) *The Practical Curriculum: Working Paper 70*, London, Methuen.

SCHOOLS COUNCIL (1982) *Health Education 13–18: Teaching Pack*, London, Forkes Publications.

SCHOOLS COUNCIL (1984) *Developing Health Education*, London, Forkes Publications.

SCOTTISH EDUCATION DEPARTMENT (1974) *Curriculum Paper 14: Health Education in Schools*, Edinburgh, HMSO.

SERVICE CHILDREN'S EDUCATION AUTHORITY (1981) *Curricular Guidelines: Health Education*, London.

STOCKPORT, METROPOLITAN BOROUGH of (1983) *Guidelines for Personal and Social Education*, Stockport, Metropolitan Borough of Stockport.

Surrey Inspectorate (1985) *Personal and Social Education: Curriculum Guidelines*, Kingston-upon-Thames, Surrey County Council.

Tacade (1981) *Free to Choose* Manchester, TACADE.

Tacade/Hec (1984) *Alcohol Syllabus 11–19* Manchester, TACADE.

Wakeman, B. (1984) *Personal, Social and Moral Education*, Tring, Lion Publishing plc.

Warnock Report (1978) *Special Educational Needs* London, H.M.S.O.

Wilcox, B. and Gillies, P. (1983) 'The coordination of secondary school health education', *Educational Research*, 2, 25, June.

Williams, N. and Williams, T. (1980) *Coordinator's Guide*, Health Education Project 13–18, University of Southampton, Schools Council.

Wiltshire Education Committee (1982) *Social and Personal Education*, Trowbridge, Wiltshire County Council.

Moral Education and the Curriculum

Janet Strivens

Introduction

In a book dealing with social education it is difficult to write about moral education as a distinct area. Issues of value, obligation and choice permeate every area and topic discussed, so that it would be no exaggeration to say that every aspect of social education contains a moral dimension. Nevertheless, there is an extensive literature and range of curriculum material which take these value-issues as their pre-eminent concern. They offer a rich source of ideas to the school or teacher who wishes to tackle moral issues 'head-on', with time set aside for this purpose, but equally they provide useful guidance for those who prefer a more indirect approach, dealing with the values dimension as it arises in any part of the curriculum or the day-to-day life of the school.

Whichever approach to moral education is taken, however, demands will be made on the teacher to think through his or her own understanding of the nature of morality. Writers on moral education display wide differences in orientation which reflect the lack of consensus over what constitutes the defining features of morality (a debate which promises to keep philosophers in work for many centuries to come). Initially the teacher may find these differences frustrating and irritating. One approach emphasizes rational discussion, another interpersonal sensitivity; in one the teacher is expected to 'diagnose' the moral maturity of the pupil's thought, in another the skills required are similar to those of a counsellor. This chapter takes the view that the teacher prepared to put thought and effort into developing the moral education of pupils will ultimately find that these differences help to clarify a personal understanding of morality and an approach best suited to the particular pupils being taught, the school context and the teacher's own personality.

With this in mind, the following section discusses conceptions of morality and the different components which make up the moral person. This is followed by an overview of curriculum materials and approaches to moral education. Finally some general implications for the teacher's role and classroom organization are drawn out.

The Nature of Morality

Arguments over the nature of morality, like so many philosophical arguments, arise from different conceptions of human nature. One is fundamentally optimistic, believing in an inherent, universal human impulse towards good and the predisposition to be loving and sympathetic. At the other end of the spectrum is the pessimism of the doctrine of original sin. In everyday life many of us swing between these views according to our most recent experiences and the stories in the daily news. Nevertheless, we would probably accept the importance of all the following features or components of morality, the development of which might constitute a process of moral education.

Judgment and Reasoning

An important feature of morality is the ability to reflect upon the rights and wrongs of situations, to work out the values and principles involved and to arrive at a reasoned judgment about the morally correct course of action, which could be defended in debate against a conflicting view. This dimension has a strong appeal to many teachers, since it is primarily a *cognitive* ability, the ability to abstract, analyze and synthesize which is so highly prized in all its forms within our educational system. To develop this feature means to assist pupils in thinking more clearly, constructing 'good' (in the sense of logical) arguments and respecting counter-argument, tasks which fit comfortably into the teacher's role. As we mature intellectually, we become capable of handling considerations both greater in number and more impersonal, and of seeing further implications and consequences of our decisions; thus our judgments become more *universalisable*. The universalisability of the moral principles we hold is for some approaches a crucial criterion in assessing moral maturity.

Sensitivity and Empathy

From a different philosophical tradition comes an emphasis on the feelings associated with morality, what some have called moral dispositions, of which the most important is altruism, the feeling of care and concern for others. An altruistic disposition provides the motivation for much moral behaviour, thus its development would appear to be a major concern for the moral educator. However, a prerequisite of altruistic action is the ability to recognize other people's feelings and in some cases, to enter imaginatively into their experience. Although there is some evidence (Hoffman, 1976) that recognition of another person's emotional state occurs spontaneously at an early age, there is strong support for the view that the quality of our sensitivity can be improved through training ourselves to be more observant and receptive. This again provides a clear task for the educator, though one which many teachers may feel uncertain about handling. It is likely to make emotional demands on both teacher and pupils.

The Content of Moral Knowledge

Content is in many ways the most problematic feature of morality. This is despite the fact that, when people are asked to say what morality is, the great majority will begin by listing right or wrong behaviour. Thus for most people morality consists of a very specific content of moral rules. These may be a combination of what philosophers would call 'formal' principles — general prescriptions like the value of truth, respect for life and acting fairly — and 'substantive' principles — the interpretation of a general rule into a specific context where a moral decision must be made. Clearly, without an awareness of and commitment to such principles, rational thought and interpersonal sensitivity will not necessarily lead to the making of a moral decision. Yet, in real life there is often a conflict between the claims of different moral principles, leading to uncertainty over their application in practice. For this reason, many moral educators are chary of the explicit teaching of principles and rules, preferring to lay emphasis upon the processes of feeling, reflection and decision-making. Underlying this preference is the confidence that certain principles will emerge, to which the pupil will have a real commitment because they have acquired personal meaning. Any teacher tackling the problem of moral education needs to reflect on this tension between encouraging personal choice and presenting general principles, in the light of his or her own beliefs.

Moral Action

Finally we come to the most important aspect of morality, behaviour. To regard the way we behave as an 'aspect' of morality may well seem ludicrous to some: surely 'good' behaviour is the essence of morality and the proper aim of moral education? Yet the relationship between the other components (especially moral judgment) and the resulting actions has been a philosophical battleground since the problem of morality was first pondered. Some have taken it as axiomatic that human beings naturally act on what they know to be right and good; moral failure is the result of uncertainty, misinformation or lack of knowledge. Others believe that such a view flies in the face of our common-sense experience of 'lack of willpower' or moral weakness, and regard the failure to translate principled judgment into action as the central problem of moral behaviour. Straughan (1982, chapter 2) offers a clear and concise account of the opposing philosophical arguments for the possibility of moral weakness.

The philosophical debate is not purely academic, since it has important implications for the way society conceives of morality. Consider how our understanding of morality is embodied within the judiciary system. People are held accountable for the consequences of their behaviour, but whether or not they acted with *intent* often influences the courts' decisions. And undoubtedly the controversies which rage around the question of 'diminished responsibility' in particularly horrific crimes stem from the difficulty we have in comprehending how a 'normal' person could knowingly commit such acts.

This discussion appears to offer two choices to the moral educator; either to assume that morally desirable behaviour will follow naturally from the development of sounder judgments and greater sensitivity; or to grapple with the problem of moral weakness and seek strategies to combat it. This second choice might well lead one to concentrate on training good behaviour, perhaps through an external structure of reward and punishment which gradually becomes internalized[1]. Without going into the arguments at great length, it can be said that the advantage of this approach is that good *habits* are formed, that is, people learn to behave well without reflection or hesitation. The great danger is that in fostering conformity and obedience rather than autonomy, people come to accept great evils in the name of authority (Milgram, 1974). As a society we have learned to prize independence of judgment as well as socially acceptable behaviour, and achieving a balance between the two could be seen as moral education's most important task.

Methods and Materials of Moral Education

Schools Council Project in Moral Education

We shall start with the major British curriculum development project in this area, the Schools Council Project in Moral Education 13–16 undertaken by McPhail, Ungoed-Thomas and Chapman in the late 60s[2]. The project gave rise to a programme of moral education called *Lifeline* which consists of sets of curriculum materials, a handbook on school organization and a book setting out the justification for the approach taken and guidance on methods (McPhail *et al*, 1972).

In terms of the previous discussion of the nature of morality, *Lifeline* is quite clear in its attitude to both content and the priority of certain moral components over others in the developmental process. The major principle to be presented is care and consideration for others, and this remains the priority throughout the increasingly complex ideas and information the pupils must learn to handle. Since this principle is paramount, it is not surprising that the development of interpersonal sensitivity is the first aim and starting point of the programme. The first set of materials is called *In Other People's Shoes*, and is in three parts, entitled 'Sensitivity', 'Consequences' and 'Points of View'. It is also very much in line with this emphasis on *moral feeling* and the ability to recognize emotion in others that *role-play* acquires great importance as a method of utilizing the materials. The materials themselves start with a number of brief descriptions of interpersonal situations, which pupils are invited to empathize with. While writing of various kinds, drawing and discussion are perfectly valid forms of response to these materials, the use of dramatic techniques is particularly encouraged. For a confident teacher, this may be the most fruitful way of encouraging awareness of one's own and others' feelings.

The emphasis on concern for others and sensitivity may be the guiding principle and starting point of the *Lifeline* materials, but the scope of moral education is extended as one progresses through the materials to bring in a stronger dimension of thought and reasoning.

The second set of materials is called *Proving the Rule?* It is intended not only to broaden the context in which moral issues are considered, by setting the 'stimulus' problems in a social context rather than a purely interpersonal one, but also to invite consideration of the way a society handles conflicts of interests and imposes demands on its members. Again, stress is laid on methods of use which involve children emotionally in the search for solutions. The final set of materials, *What would you have done?* continues the developing complexity of the issues presented by describing a number of real incidents but from a context unfamiliar to the pupils (for example, South Africa in 1904, the arrest of Ann Frank in Holland in 1944 and South Vietnam in 1966). The principle of care and consideration is widened to an international context and the moral problems presented are correspondingly more complex and difficult to engage with.

As a programme of moral education, the work of McPhail and his associates has some definite strengths. The authors are quite clear about their priorities, and their objectives are well-supported by the written materials and detailed suggestions for use. Their work has however been subjected to some sharp criticism (Peters, 1973; Hersh, Miller and Fielding, 1980; Pring, 1984). There are two main complaints. One is that McPhail and his colleagues have an incoherent view of moral motivation. Although tending towards the optimistic view of human nature being naturally attracted to the good, they fudge the issue by recognizing a long list of other possible motivations, including external, concrete rewards. The second objection concerns the moral principles implicit in the project materials. As well as consideration, great stress is laid on the values already held by adolescents, as revealed through an initial survey carried out by the project team. This may appear to be taking a view of morality which equates the right with the majority opinion, a morality of convention rather than autonomy. Since there is also a strong suspicion of middle-class bias in the sample of young people who responded to the survey, possible conflicts between the dominant values of adolescents and those of the project team could have been concealed. Nevertheless the critics themselves admit that these weaknesses do not destroy the usefulness of the materials. Some further support comes from a review of teaching materials for disadvantaged children (Gulliford and Widlake, 1975) which suggests that the *Lifeline* materials may be particularly valuable for slow-learning children.

Values Clarification

As a contrast, let us turn to an influential American approach to moral education. Values clarification is not so much a programme as a set of strategies around a general philosophy. The main source of the philosophy is *Values and Teaching* (Raths *et al*, 1966) and of the strategies, *Values Clarification: A Handbook of Practical Strategies for Teachers* (Simon *et al*, 1972)[3]. This body of work is about a process, and methods of encouraging that process. The process is to arrive at a clearer awareness of the values one holds, so that a course of action is chosen in full consciousness of the alternatives and consequences, and the motivations involved in choosing. Thus there is again a major moral principle involved, although it is not stated so explicitly as the principle underlying *Lifeline*: one should have freedom to choose courses of action, but as a consequence, one must take responsibility for that choice. Other than this, no specifications are made as to content, or what action is moral and what not. For this reason some commentators take the view that values clarification should not be regarded as a model of moral education but merely as a relevant strategy.[4]

According to this approach, there are seven aspects of the valuing process:

CHOOSING	1	Choosing freely
	2	Choosing from alternatives
	3	Choosing after thoughtful consideration of the consequences
PRIZING	4	Prizing and cherishing the values chosen
	5	Affirming them publicly
ACTING	6	Acting on the values held
	7	Acting repeatedly and persistently

While moral *knowledge* appears to play a small part in this approach, there is a very strong emphasis on the development of skills. Values clarification has an important cognitive component, in the pressure it puts on the individual to think out alternatives and consequences and to be able to defend the choices made on rational grounds. Much weight is also given to the feeling component, since becoming more aware of *one's own* feelings is a crucial part of clarification. There is no special emphasis on the development of sensitivity to others and the skills involved in this. There is, however, a strong concern for action; repeated, public action in accordance with a stated belief is presented as a necessary criterion for saying that a person 'holds a value'.

How can the teacher make use of this work? We have noted that values clarification is about methods for encouraging a process of choice, and many of these methods require very specific skills from the teacher, most particularly when in dialogue with the individual pupil. First, he or she must be sensitive to an appropriate opportunity to clarify values, picking up on a comment or statement from a pupil with an underlying, unstated purpose, belief or feeling. According to Raths and his colleagues, the 'clarifying response' from the teacher must set an emotional climate 'conducive to thoughtfulness' by 'a respectful, accepting adult attitude ... stimulating but not insistent', brief and clearly but courteously brought to a conclusion. The teacher's own values should not intrude and a particular answer should not be expected.

The teacher's role in this interchange has similarities to that of the non-directive counsellor, and developing the necessary skills takes practice. One advantage is that the approach can be used throughout the curriculum, capitalizing on opportunities which arise in ordinary conversation with pupils. Making it apparent to pupils that their thoughts and feelings are being respected can cause a dramatic change in the relationship between teacher and pupil, with consequences beyond the immediate situation for the pupil's involvement and motivation.

The major criticisms of the values clarification approach arise out of the combination of its emphasis on free choice and its lack of prescriptiveness about moral conduct. A stinging article by Stewart (1975) also accuses it of being coercive and judgmental in practice (in contrast to its claims) because of the emphasis on public statement and action. There is undoubtedly some confusion in the writings of Raths, Simon and their colleagues as to the relativity of values, since they do clearly recognize certain virtues as desirable goals. But a basic optimism about human nature, similar to that of the *Lifeline* team, allows them to believe that the content of morality can be safely left to develop its own course provided the valuing process is encouraged.

Kohlberg's Moral Development Approach

Lawrence Kohlberg is an American psychologist who has devoted himself to the study of the development of moral judgment. He is concerned to understand how judgments change as people mature intellectually, and to uncover universal trends in moral reasoning across different cultures. His methodology involves the presentation of a hypothetical dilemma concerning a man, Heinz, whose wife is dying from cancer. There is a drug that might save her, but the druggist who developed it is selling it at a greatly inflated price which he refuses to reduce. Heinz is unable to borrow the money, and, becoming desperate, wonders whether to steal the drug. It is the reasons which people offer in response to the question, 'Should Heinz steal the drug?' which interest Kohlberg. A clear explanation of his research work, the stages of moral growth and their implications for educators can be found in *Promoting Moral Growth* (Hersh, Paolitto and Reimer, 1979).

It is helpful to consider Kohlberg's approach to moral education in conjunction with values clarification, to highlight important differences and similarities. Kohlberg's work is primarily concerned with the development of moral judgment and the stages through which this development proceeds. It is the cognitive approach par excellence, emphasizing even more strongly than Simon and Raths' work the importance of clear thinking and reasoning about moral issues. The important difference lies in the structure of reasons used in making moral judgments. Kohlberg's claim is that as a person matures intellectually, the values or principles he or she appeals to in making moral judgments become increasingly consistent, objective and universally applicable. He is centrally concerned therefore with the *quality* of reasoning employed.

Like values clarification, Kohlberg appears to be little concerned with the content of the moral reasoning process, in terms of the course of action decided upon. However, the stress on structure gives only a partial picture of Kohlberg's work, since he does in fact hold very definite views on content. His claim is that the research carried out by himself and many colleagues into the development of moral judgment in many different cultures shows a universal tendency towards recognizing justice as the overriding moral principle.[5] In younger, less morally mature individuals, the reasons offered for decisions may be instrumental, egocentric, conformist, legalistic or an inconsistent mixture of these and more. But the importance of 'fair treatment' eventually becomes paramount unless the developmental process is somehow halted. In fact, few individuals appear to reach the higher stages of principled judgment in Kohlberg's model. Most are arrested at the level of conventional morality, a finding of considerable significance for educators.

Development through the stages is thought to be stimulated by open discussion, which highlights inconsistencies in the individual's thinking as alternative viewpoints are presented. In terms of the teacher's role, this creates one important difference between Kohlberg and values clarification. Teachers wishing to adopt Kohlberg's approach are trained to probe pupils' reasoning by asking them why they put certain views forward, and being prepared to offer a counter-argument embodying a more general application of the principle of justice — but only at one stage more general than the pupils' own reasoning, lest they completely fail to comprehend. This strategy requires a teacher to perform rapid analyses of children's thinking, be thoroughly familiar with the stages of complexity through which they develop and apply this knowledge equally rapidly to the formulation of a counter-argument at the appropriate level of complexity. In contrast, Simon and Raths recommend the avoidance of 'why' questions in case these arouse defensiveness; it is more important for the teacher to convey sincere interest.

One other difference is worth noting. Kohlberg's approach is based on a set of materials containing hypothetical dilemmas to stimulate moral conflict.[6] In theory, the teacher who becomes skilled at moral discussion using these dilemmas should be able to utilize 'naturally-occurring' dilemmas within a subject-area or in general conversation. Values clarification also makes use of material from subjects throughout the curriculum but there is an emphasis, as with the *Lifeline* materials, on the real-life situations which boys and girls encounter and the values they personally hold. This provides more of an opportunity for the teacher to encourage appropriate behavioural outcomes as a result of the clarifying process.

Wilson's Moral Components

One of the most prolific British writers on moral education is the philosopher John Wilson. His work has been an attempt to define the nature of moral education through the identification of moral features or components, the combination of which make up the morally educated person. Since his scheme tries to encompass all aspects of morality, the list of moral components he offers contains all the elements mentioned in the previous section in a more detailed and refined form. In *Practical Methods of Moral Education* (1972) he suggests how the scheme can be used to devize a classroom pro-gramme, with the following aims:

1 To make our pupils understand that moral thinking, like scientific and other kinds of thinking, is a serious subject of study in its own right, and can result in right or wrong answers to moral questions; that there is a rational methodology; and thereby to provide them with the right reasons for moral action and feeling.

2 To give them (as it were) a psychological resource when confronted with moral situations in everyday life ...

3 To induce by constant practice the actual *habit* of using this methodology ...

4 To wean them away from false methodologies (reliance on peer-group, on authority or 'anti-authorities', on false ego-ideals and so on).

5 By clarifying the logic of the moral components ... to give them insight into which *particular* components are lacking, both in themselves and other people, in particular cases.

6 Hence, by making them aware of these deficiencies, to give them at least the chance of developing the components for themselves ...

In terms of practical suggestions for the classroom teacher, Wilson's remarks are mainly concerned with developing competence in thinking clearly (but without the understanding of the developmental dimension in cognitive skills which Kohlberg's work demonstrates). However, it is not insignificant that in the book intended to contain the most practical advice to teachers, he spends far more time in discussing the social environment of the school as a source of values education, than in recommending teaching strategies. The value of his work lies more in the attempt at a comprehensive description of the moral person than in the development of educational practice, though his work has moved increasingly in this direction.

Moral Education and Classroom Practice

Despite their differences of emphasis most approaches to moral education will make reference to the classroom 'conditions' which further the aims of moral education. Sometimes certain conditions are presented as a *sine qua non*; without a climate of trust and acceptance and a belief in fairness, no real engagement with moral issues can take place. Classroom practice involves the teacher's role, the organization of the classroom and selection of methods, and these will be treated separately.

The Teacher's Role

A recurrent observation from the many teachers who have written about their own attempts to implement moral education is the challenge presented to their own values and beliefs in the course of moral discussions. With an approach to moral education which stresses conflict of principles and rational decision-making, the teacher is not immune to the process of challenging currently-held value positions. A teacher unprepared for the challenge may be disturbed to find that his or her views and opinions have not been thoroughly thought out and are difficult to support in the face of opposing argument. The temptation is to assert the authority of the teacher over the pupils' opinions and close the discussion, but such action is certain to undermine the very principles of fair-mindedness and reason which the teacher is intending to establish, and is likely to discourage if not stifle future debate. Teachers who feel insecure in their classroom role either through youth, inexperience or a personal ambivalence about the nature of authority, may find such open debate too threatening, and their own needs for personal and moral growth interfere with the process of moral education for their pupils.

Given that the teacher has the emotional security to face value conflicts openly and honestly, she needs certain interactional skills, common to all teaching but particularly important in the handling of moral education. She must be a sensitive interpreter of the emotional climate of the classroom, aware of the signals from individual pupils which might indicate excitement, distress, sudden insight, internal conflict or defensive obstinacy. On a verbal level she needs to be able to analyze and assess pupils' comments rapidly, and to formulate responses at a level of intellectual and emotional challenge that the pupil can handle. The intellectual or cognitive analysis of moral content is especially important in those approaches which stress cognitive conflict as a prerequisite to the development of higher-order moral judgment. However, even the process of 'clarifying' value statements in a value-neutral manner requires interpretive skills of a high order, both to assist the individual pupil offering a contribution and to involve the whole class in sharing view-points.

Finally (though perhaps it goes without saying) the teachers' own commitment to moral principles must underlie her practice. In particular her handling of the class should demonstrate respect for persons and the democratic process. This consideration leads us to the organization of classrooms for moral education.

Classroom Organization

The term 'democratic' is much bandied about in discussions on moral education. In the context of classroom practice, it is taken to mean, above all, a fair hearing for the different points of view of all participants in the situation, with protection for minority views. In this restricted sense, it implies that the classroom is organized (both physically and in terms of group dynamics) to allow the expression of individual views. The teacher has the task, not only of monitoring the effects of her own position of authority, but also of remaining aware of the balance of power within the class. It may be argued that the purposes of democracy are served by providing the opportunity for each individual's view to be presented. However, a classroom is by definition a place to learn, and part of that learning is the ability to avail oneself of such an opportunity. The teacher has an important part to play in the pupils' learning of democratic procedures, since she is in a position to encourage the reticent, check a domineering voice and provide a model of 'active listening'.

A broader understanding of democracy will take pupils beyond the ability to give a fair hearing for different viewpoints, difficult though this is. It will lead them towards negotiation, compromise and attempts at reconciliation, in the search for creative resolutions to problems. To take this broader understanding as an objective has repercussions outside of the classroom. It suggests action springing from moral decision-making and the chance for pupils to shoulder responsibilities resulting from their decisions. As an approach to moral education it implies the involvement of the whole school in providing pupils with the chance to participate in decisions and experience the consequences for the whole community. A few schools provide an explicit institutional procedure to develop their pupils' capacities in this direction, though sometimes the aims are couched in terms of the development of political skills rather than moral education. If a distinction can be made between the different orientations it is in the terminology offered to pupils to handle the issues raised.[8]

Choice of Methods and Materials

In the review of curriculum materials, some comments on the different approaches have already been made with the intention of aiding the teacher to assess their suitability for her own particular situation. However, for the teacher who prefers to develop her own material, some more general observations are offered here. It is convenient to categorize material into four types:

(i) hypothetical dilemmas;
(ii) fictional dilemmas presented through novels, short stories, plays or films;
(iii) real-life dilemmas occurring in history, or currently in the news;
(iv) personal dilemmas.

Hypothetical dilemmas usually present a situation of moral conflict involving contradictory principles. The context of the dilemma is given in the minimum detail, supposedly in order to promote discussion of principles unclouded by 'non-moral' considerations. After the principles have been thoroughly aired, the teacher may then lead or encourage the discussion in the direction of their application to other situations, or these may arise naturally if the pupils become engaged in the dilemma and begin to think and feel their way through it.

On the other hand, pupils may be resistant to involvement in such an abstract exercise where their imagination and sense of reality is artificially constrained. Younger and less-able pupils may be puzzled and frustrated by a distinction between what one *would* do and what one *should* do in the situation. The task being set requires the capacity for what Donaldson (1978) calls 'disembedded thought'; the ability to sustain attention on an isolated aspect of a problem, unsupported by a meaningful context. Schools place a high value on this capacity and the alienated pupil is likely to reject a task which requires it. Moral education curricula on the whole recognize a problem in this demand for abstraction, and some explicitly suggest working from 'would' towards 'should'.

Fictional dilemmas have the advantage of a meaningful context, with the possibility that pupils have already been drawn into the drama of the situation and are emotionally engaged with the characters. Unless the teacher artificially interrupts the flow of the narrative, most stories provide their own conclusion, with the consequences of the decision made clear. It is sadly the case that the quality of fictional writing often suffers when the author's intention is most didactically moral, therefore care is needed in the selection of examples. The teacher needs to be aware of the level of language skills required, of the power of fiction to persuade and thereby to inhibit the consideration of alternative possibilities. On the other hand the complexities of fictional treatment can help children to consider a problem through multiple perspectives by engaging with different characters.

History lessons provide a rich variety of *real-life dilemmas*, offering much scope to the teacher wishing to draw out moral issues for discussion. In particular, abundant opportunities arise for an exploration of the interpenetration of moral considerations with political and economic arguments, leading pupils to a better appreciation of the slippery nature of political argument. Clearly the teacher's judgment must decide on the amount of information required by the pupils in order to engage with the problem, and whether to personalize the situation through simulation and role-play.

The distance created by history can also be useful as a way into current issues which need sensitive handling. Racism, trade unionism and the role of women all lend themselves to introduction in a historical context, whether the purpose be to avoid the rapid adoption of entrenched positions or to arouse initial interest in the apparently apathetic.

Personal dilemmas are likely to arise in a rather different context, perhaps in lessons on health or child care or more informally outside class time. Warnings about the importance of sensitive handling of such personal material abound in the literature, as do arguments for the centrality of personal values and decisions in the moral education process. Teachers may find useful the study of adolescent values in *Disclosures to a Stranger* (Kitwood, 1980). This study draws on long interviews with young people in the setting of a youth club, talking freely about personal experiences which for them embodied values conflicts. The material is introduced by a sensitive discussion of the ethics of drawing such confidences out of young people, for whatever purposes, by adults in a position of authority.

The problem of morality continues to exercise a fascination over people with a curiosity about human behaviour, the different forms of human society and the limits to its perfectability. This chapter has tried to present moral education as a rich and varied field to explore, in the hope that this will prove a rewarding experience for the teacher as well as adding an important dimension to the education of the pupils.

Notes

1 Some readers will recognize this as a behavioural approach to the problem of morality. See especially SKINNER (1971), BANDURA and WALTERS (1965), ARONFREED (1968).

2 The project also produces a curriculum package for younger pupils, called *Startline* (McPhail, Middleton and Ingram, 1978).

3 The Schools Cultural Studies Project, based at the New University of Ulster, Coleraine, Northern Ireland, has made use of values clarification in developing a programme of cultural studies for secondary schools in Northern Ireland. For more information write to the project team at the New University of Ulster, or see MCKERNAN (1983a and 1983b).

4 Exponents of the Kohlbergian approach tend to view values clarification as insufficiently clear about the specifically *moral* as opposed to other sorts of value issues. COLBY (1975) comments:

> Simon is interested in clarifying a broad range of values of which moral values are only a small part. Self-knowledge and self-esteem are essential goals in his program . . . the failure of values clarification to treat moral and non-moral questions as fundamentally different obscures such philosophical issues as ethical relativity (the view that validity of a moral judgment is relative to the values or needs of the individual or culture) and adequacy of justification.

PRING (1984), commenting in a similar vein, concludes that 'to identify values clarification, therefore, with moral education would be wrong' despite the important part that personal growth and the achievement of autonomy play in moral development.

5 As Kohlberg acknowledges, this view of morality draws heavily on the work of the philosopheer JOHN RAWLS (See RAWLS 1971).

6 See for example COLBY *et al* (1973) and FENTON *et al* (1974). These are obtainable through the Centre for Moral Education, ROY, E. Larsen Hall, Harvard University, Appian Way, Cambridge, Mass. 02138, U.S.A.

7 See for example LADENBURG (1977) on moral reasoning and the teaching of history, LADENBURG and LADENBURG (1977) on the social sciences; also HERSH, PAOLITTO and REIMER (1979) chs 5 and 6.

8 For a disucssion of school organization as an explicit means towards the inculcation of values and development of political skills, see STRIVENS (1986).

References.

ARONFREED, J. (1969) *Conduct and Conscience: the Socialization of Internalized Control over Behaviour*, New York, Academic Press.

BANDURA, A. and WALTERS, R. (1963) *Social Learning and Personality Development*, New York, Holt, Rinehart and Winston.

COLBY, A., (1975) Review of *Values and Teaching* and *Values Clarification* in *Harvard Educational Review*, 45, 1, pp. 134–43.

COLBY, A., SPEICHER, B. and BLATT, M. (1973) *Hypothetical Dilemmas for use in Moral Discussions*, mimeo.

DONALDSON, M. (1978) *Children's Minds*, Glasgow, Fontana.

FENTON, E., COLBY, A. and SPEICHER, B. (1974) *Developing Moral Dilemmas for Social Studies Classes*, mimeo.

GULLIFORD, R. and WIDLAKE, P. (1975) *Teaching Materials for Disadvantaged Children*, Schools Council Curriculum Bulletin No. 5, Evans-Methuen Educational.

HERSH, R.H., MILLER, J.P. and FIELDING, G.D. (1980) *Models of Moral Education: An Appraisal*, New York; Longman Inc.

HERSH, R.H., PAOLITTO, D.P. and REIMER, J. (1979) *Promoting Moral Growth*, New York, Longman Inc.

HOFFMAN, M.L. (1976) 'Empathy, role-taking, guilt and the development of altruistic sympathies', in LICKONA T. (Ed), *Moral Development and Behaviour: Theory, Research and Social Issues*, New York, Holt, Rinehart and Winston.

KITWOOD, T. (1980) *Disclosures to a Stranger: Adolescent Values in an Advanced Industrial Society*, London, Routledge and Kegan Paul.

LADENBURG, T. (1977) 'Cognitive development and moral reasoning in the teaching of history', *History Teacher*, 10, 2, pp. 183–98.

LADENBURG, T. and LADENBURG, M. (1977) 'Moral reasoning and social studies', *Theory into Practice*, 16, pp. 112–7.

MCKERNAN, J. (1983a) 'Clarifying values in the classroom: some teaching strategies', *Social Science Teacher*, 6, 1, pp. i–iv.

MCKERNAN, J. (1983b) 'Cultural studies and values education: the role of the teacher', *Social Science Teacher*, 6, 2, pp. 12–15.

MCPHAIL, P., MIDDLETON, D. and INGRAM, D. (1978) *Startline: Moral Education in the Middle Years*, Schools Council Project Moral Education 8 to 13, Harlow, Longman.

MCPHAIL, P., UNGOED-THOMAS, J.R. and CHAPMAN, H. (1972) *Moral Education in the Secondary School*, Harlow, Longman.

MILGRAM, S. (1974) *Obedience to Authority*, London, Tavistock.

PETERS, R.S. (1973) Review of *Moral Education in the Secondary School* in *Journal of Moral Education*, 3, 1, pp. 413–5.

PRING, R. (1984) *Personal and Social Education in the Curriculum*, Guildford, Hodder and Stoughton.

RATHS, L.E., HARMIN, M. and SIMON, S.B. (1966) *Values and Teaching*

Columbus, OH, Charles Merrill Inc.

RAWLS, J. (1971) *A Theory of Justice*, Cambridge, MA, Harvard University Press.

SIMON, S.B., HOWE, L. and KIRSCHENBAUM, H. (1972) *Values Clarification: A Handbook of Practical Strategies for Teachers and Students*, New York, Hart.

SKINNER, B.F. (1971) *Beyond Freedom and Dignity*, Harmondsworth, Penguin Books.

STEWART, J.S. (1975) 'Clarifying values clarification: a critique', *Phi Delta Kappan*, 56, 10, pp. 684–8.

STRAUGHAN, R. (1982) *I Ought to But ...* Windsor, NFER-Nelson.

STRIVENS, J. (1986) 'Values and the social organization of schooling', in TOMLINSON P. (Ed), *Values Across the Curriculum*, Lewes, Falmer Press.

WILSON, J. (1972) *Practical Methods of Moral Education*, London, Heinemann.

Education for Family Life

Dorit Braun and Kate Torkington

The Context

Family life education in schools in Britain has evolved over the last twenty-five years in response to demands from a variety of government and other committees that schools should prepare young people for parenthood and family life.[1] The curriculum areas which contain elements of family life education will be reviewed in detail later in the chapter but the major curriculum area associated with family life education is personal, social and moral education (PSME). There is some interest in noting when and for what apparent reasons the term 'family life/parenthood education' began to be used explicitly in the context of the curriculum. PSME established itself in the curriculum in Britain in the 1960s but the focus of family life/parenthood education has appeared more recently. We suggest that this change of emphasis results from a growing interest and concern for the family which has developed in Britain since the mid-1970s and which has resulted in organizations and institutions, other than the formal education system, recognizing the need for education for family life. Clearly, the rationale for family life/ parenthood education will vary with the ideology of the family held by individuals and organizations. Our discussion later in the chapter of the aims of family life education in schools highlights the varying viewpoints of teachers and gives some indication of the views within society as a whole.

Two documents issued by the Department of Health and Social Security in 1974 mark the beginning of the parenthood education movement.[2] Smith, in an interesting paper on preparation for parenthood policy, highlights the opposing views expressed in these two papers, views which continue to be represented in recent debate on the subject. She sees the first paper as supporting Sir Keith Joseph's 'cycle of deprivation' theory, a 'personal pathology' explanation for family difficulties and 'bad' parenting, whilst the second paper challenged this theory and pointed to 'the structure of the social system as responsible for any cycle of deprivation that might exist.'[3]

The debate grew in momentum with a joint initiative by the DHSS and DES who set up a seminar in 1979 to discuss preparation for parenthood. This culminated in the National Children's Bureau project to establish a national clearing house for the dissemination and interchange of ideas and information on schemes and services in the field of preparation for parenthood and support for parents with young children.

At about the same time the National Children's Bureau was setting up its project, a number of other organizations with concern for the family were developing initiatives in parenthood education and support for parents. For example, the National Marriage Guidance Council appointed an Education Projects Officer in 1978 to coordinate and develop its marriage and family life education programmes; the Study Commission on the Family published its first research papers on various aspects of the family in 1980; the National Children's Home started its Family Network service in 1979; and Family Forum, an umbrella organization for organizations concerned with the family, was set up in 1980. Later other organizations developed 'family education' initiatives such as the Family Education Unit of the Community Education Development Centre which was set up in Coventry in 1983.

One of the things that this concerted focus on 'the family' has done is to expose the institution (and the society of which it is part) to a scrutiny which has emphasized change and vulnerability rather than stability and strength as its major features. This contrasts sharply with the sociological studies of the 1960s which on the whole assured society that, in spite of changes, the family was alive and well and living in Bethnal Green with 'hot-lines' to the more affluent suburbs!

Clearly, major changes in society over the last twenty or so years have affected the family in Britain. These changes include:

1 *Sexual changes:* advances in birth control techniques; population explosion issues; availability of abortion: expectations of sexual fulfilment, particularly in women.
2 *Technological changes:* increased use of technical aids in the home; technological changes in industry which are eliminating traditional male skills; coming into being of the 'compu-

ter age' which has further shifted the control of knowledge from the old to the young.

3   *Economic changes*

   (a)   *up to late 1970s* — social mobility weakening extended family ties; increasing demands for emotional satisfaction within nuclear family.

   (b)   *late 1970s and early 1980s* — widespread unemployment affecting traditional male role as bread-winner, forcing young people back into dependency on the family; and reducing opportunities for women in employment, putting strains on family relationships.

4   *Changes in position of women:* more highly educated; more likely to work outside the home (which also means increase in number and variety of men-women contacts); increased variety of career opportunities which may be alternatives to marriage; development of women's movement challenging traditional sex roles and dependency on men, and seeking equal pay and job opportunities.

5   *Moral and religious changes:* reduction of influence of church due to secularization of society; decrease in respect for 'authority' figures in society, police, teachers, doctors, parents; breakdown in community life (and therefore community influences) due to social and geographical mobility and increased urbanization in 1960s and 1970s, and linked with unemployment in 1980s.

6   *General changes:* increase in living standards and prosperity for many, giving more freedom of choice and wider range of choices; widening of gap, mainly because of unemployment, between 'haves' and 'have nots'; increase in media influence.

Facts on the Family in Britain

The facts and figures on the family indisputably indicate changes in the institution resulting from societal changes. Lesley Rimmer of the Study Commission on the Family in the booklet *Families in Focus* (1981), presents and analyzes the statistics. She comments: 'Increasing divorce and remarriage, the rising number of one parent families, more dual-worker families, and the different patterns among ethnic minority groups are changing the meaning of "family" for a substantial minority of parents and children'.[4] The following is a summary of the relevant statistics as updated in the 1984 Social Trends.[5]

Dorit Braun and Kate Torkington

Divorce

There was almost double the number of divorces in 1982 compared to 1971 and this increase has included a growing proportion of second and subsequent marriages ending in divorce. Eighteen per cent of all divorces in 1982 involved at least one partner who had been divorced before compared with 9 per cent in 1971. Age at marriage is strongly associated with divorce: 'If 1980–1981 divorce rates were to persist unchanged, it is estimated that almost three in five teenage bachelor grooms and one in two teenage spinster brides would eventually divorce.' One hundred and sixty nine thousand children under 16 had parents who divorced in 1981, two-thirds of this number were below the age of 11.

Remarriage and Reconstituted Families

Remarriage increased substantially for both men and women between 1961 and 1981, with the remarriage rate being between three and four times higher for men than for women. Divorce and remarriage means a rapidly increasing number of reconstituted families so that more and more children will have more than two parent figures and many step-siblings.

Single Parent Families

Rimmer notes that there were 570,000 one-parent families in 1971. The Family Policy Studies Centre estimated that in 1982 there were one million one-parent families in Great Britain with one-and-a-half-million children under the age of 16. Approximately 13 per cent of all families with children are one-parent families. This does not, of course, take into account the large number of children who at some time during their lives will be part of a one-parent family. West Indian families are slightly more likely to be headed by one parent, Asian families slightly less.

Working Mothers

Unemployment has clearly affected the number of mothers in employment particularly in full-time employment, nevertheless 'the pattern of women's employment is likely to be full-time work with a short break for child rearing'.[6] Working mothers mainly seek part-time work, in 1980 one in six of the working population was a woman engaged in part-time work. The Study Commission on the Family has frequently claimed that without women's wages three or four times as many families would be in poverty.

What is a Family?

The outline of changes in society indicates that controversy and change rather than certainty is likely to be a feature of family life and personal relationships education and nowhere is that more evident than in discussions about what is a family. Clearly, the stereotype of family life that has been with us for so long, now requires some adjustment.

As Segal put it: 'that image of husband out at work and the wife at home with her young baby embodies the idea of family life — like an eternal freeze frame from the video of life'.[7] In fact, from the evidence discussed in the publications of the Study Commission on the Family it emerges that only one in five of all households at any one time includes a working father, with a non-working mother, married to each other and with two dependent children of that marriage.

So if the 'ideal family is no longer typical' and 'functions only as a myth'[8] what other groupings can be called families?

Joan Cooper, Director of the DHSS Social Work Service, at a seminar in Oxford in 1973 offered the following as part of her definition of the family.

A family:
— offers the experience of warm, loving, intimate and con-sistently dependable relationships.
— secures the physical and material provision and care, health, and security of its members either through its own resources or through the competent use of specialized help and services.
— acknowledges its task of socializing children, encouraging their personal development and abilities, guiding their behaviour interests and informing their attitudes and values.
— cooperates with schools and the wider community in

providing educational and learning experiences.
— offers support to the children as they are achieving independence and during the establishment of their own married and family life.[9]

There are several points to make about this definition. First we
need to remind ourselves that this once more presents the 'ideal' of
family life. Many teachers will know from the experience of some of
their pupils and, maybe from their own experience, that family life
provides for them few or none of the satisfactions outlined in the
definition. Second, it implies that families always include or will
have included at some time, two generations. Many writers on the
family concur with this notion, Lynne Segal, for example, defending
a variety of family forms, from a feminist-socialist perspective,
nevertheless talks of families in terms of two generations. Writing
from a Christian perspective, Gladwin in a thoughtful and sensitive
booklet, *Happy Families*,[10] also presents a 'more than one generation' definition of family life: 'The parent-child relationship is very
much at the heart of the family life .... There is something unique
in the relationship of parents and children which gives the family its
place in God's creation as a basic provision for our human development.'

Both these writers, however, refer to the difficulties of describing family in terms of its constituent members, for Gladwin says:
'we may well exclude many households who, without doubt, fulfil
all the central purposes of family life. That is why it is dangerous to
define family in terms of the traditional nuclear family of father,
mother and two or three of their own children. Other types of
families may be doing a marvellous work in providing love and
stability for its members.'[11]

Segal puts it more strongly: 'There are certain types of "families" which certainly do need defending — single parents and their
children, gay couples and lesbian mothers — but they are under
attack because they do not conform to the family ideal.'[12]

If teaching in the area of family life education is to take into
account the social changes outlined and the controversy that sur-
rounds the issue of 'family', then it inevitably will be aimed at
enabling young people to make choices and decisions about their
future lifestyles.[13] The following section considers the aims of family life education.

Aims and Purposes

Courses on family life education generally define their aims within one or more of the following ideological goals:

(i)   breaking the cycle of deprivation and preventing bad parenting;

(ii) raising the level of knowledge about child development;

(iii) improving the quality of individual and family life through health education;

(iv) educating for personal and social development.[14]

Family life education is thus often seen as very much broader than simply the introduction of a course on child care, and teachers need to be encouraged to think through their own aims, and to consider whether or not they are actually achieveable.

The first aim has a strong ideological base which we would question; the cycle of deprivation is a simplistic and judgmental concept[15] and the aim is in any case distant from young people's immediate lives and concerns. The second aim is usually seen by teachers as related to the first. We would question whether or not knowledge about child development does anything to prepare young people for parenthood. However, as an option, the subject itself may be of interest, and the opportunity to study it in such a way as to challenge notions of 'right' behaviour and to critically examine advice offered by child care experts will encourage the notion of choice. A fascinating amount of historical changes in child care advice which could form a basis for such critical examination can be found in the work of Hardyment.[16] The third aim is frequently linked with a view of individuals which regards them as deficient — lacking knowledge and skills required for healthy living. Again, we would question this assumption — the evidence suggests that social and economic factors determine an individual's health, rather than ignorance, for example, see Graham, 1984.[17] In contrast, the fourth aim assumes that people are capable and knowledgeable, and seeks to build on this to increase tolerance, understanding and perceptions of present and future possibilities. In this article we demonstrate our commitment to this last aim.

It is vital that courses should be based on the concerns of young people. The Open University Family Lifestyles and Childhood packs provide practical examples of ways of negotiating the curriculum of family life education with young people. A number of studies have shown that young people would like to spend more time in school discussing relationships and family problems.[18] It is often assumed that youngsters have hazy and unrealistic perceptions of parenthood, but recent research of how girls see future motherhood suggests that their knowledge directly contradicts this stereotype.[19] Current research by the same authors has investigated the relationship between teaching styles and knowledge gained in parenthood classes.[20] The researchers argue that structured group-work approaches, if carefully utilized by teachers, are likely to make more productive use of pupils' existing knowledge than more traditional didactic teaching.[21]

Therefore those who enter the educative process in relation to family life are not empty vessels to be filled with prescriptive information on the subject but are bringing with them a wealth of experience and understanding to share with others. This is true of adults and young people. Ideally, in family life education, they will be: sharing with others their personal experience of family life; having this supplemented by knowledge and information about 'the family' in our own and other societies; discussing openly and in an 'accepting' environment the issues of family life and relationships; and being given opportunities to practise and develop their skills in relationships. All this is aimed at helping them develop confidence and a level of personal autonomy that will enable them to make choices and decisions about their own lives in the present and the future.

However, although the idea of encouraging young people to make choices and decisions about their own lives and relationships is accepted in principle by many professionals involved in family life education, in practice there is little evidence of any major challenge to or even examination of some of the basic assumptions about family life in our society. For example, even if recognition is paid to the many different family forms and structures which had developed in recent years, there is still an assumption that the traditional nuclear family is the ideal family form. The point being made here is not whether or not the traditional nuclear family *is* the ideal but rather that there is little attempt to examine in some depth, the reasons why a particular form should be seen to be better than another. In parallel with assumptions about the family are assumptions about marriage and having children. Since traditional marriage is assumed to be the only form of marriage which secures the continuation of and provides the best support for the family, little attempt is made to address with young people the question of whether to marry at all. The question of whether to have children seems to be similarly avoided. There has been increased acceptance of the idea that the harsh realities as well as the satisfaction of having children should be conveyed to young people. However, this tends to be connected with the prevention of 'bad' parenting in the future rather than with making a careful examination of the pros and cons of having children, in order to help young people to see the need to make conscious choices about whether to have children or not.[22]

To make valid choices and decisions in relation to family life, young people need to have access to information of a factual kind and a balanced presentation of differing views on marriage and family life which will in some cases reinforce and in others conflict with their own experiences of family life. These personal experiences are the most valuable component of family life education work and can be drawn out and utilized sensitively and skilfully by the caring teacher.

Each individual's knowledge about the family is highly subjective and value-laden. However, where attitudes and experiences are shared in the classroom, not only can knowledge about families be increased; tolerance and understanding are also enhanced. This is particularly important in view of the multicultural nature of British society. It is vital that pupils in all schools in Britain be given the opportunity to consider the various cultural expectations of family life, marriage and children. It is also vital that this should be done in such a way as to acknowledge all perceptions as valid — the pupils should be free to make up their own minds on their own values once they have reviewed the possibilities. In this way the goals of Family Life Education are identical to those of multicultural education. Both are concerned with raising awareness of attitudes and stereotypes, with acknowledging choices and decisions, and thereby enhancing self-esteem.

Where is Family Life Education Taught?

A number of reviews of family life education have been completed recently. A major research project funded by the DES and based at the University of Aston looked at preparation for parenthood. The researchers looked at LEA provision, and conducted in-depth case-studies of five schools in five authorities[23]. In addition the National Children's Bureau conducted a questionnaire jointly with Aston and sent it to all Directors of Education. The findings of both these studies are reported in detail in chapter 3 of Pugh and De'Ath.[24]

The Aston project found that there was virtually no part of the secondary school curriculum where parenthood education was not taught. Some subjects have parent or family life education as their main aim — courses in child care, child development, parentcraft education, preparation for family life, child and family studies. But many more have a broader aim of which family life education is a part — courses in health education, personal and social education, education for personal relationships, moral education, religious education, biology, English, group and tutorial work and so on.

Child Care and Development Courses

Traditionally the majority of family life education takes place in child care and development courses. Courses in parentcraft were pioneered by the National Association for Maternal and Child Welfare fifty years ago, but it was not until the 1960s that interest increased and today more than 10,000 pupils a year are taking their examinations. The syllabus for these courses has just been revised and 'Family Concern', a course in Human Development and Family Life, is available at basic and general levels.

The first CSE examination in child care was introduced in 1971, and since then the subject has grown rapidly with 34,000 students entering in 1982. In 1980 the first 'O' level in child development was introduced, and 1983 saw an 'O/A' level in psychology: child development.[25]

These courses provide for many girls a motivation, interest and self-confidence which other subjects often fail to do. They also offer young adolescents practical experience with young children and perhaps their first opportunities for taking on adult responsibilities, in their placements in playgroups, nurseries and with childminders.

Some courses are also attracting boys. A survey by the British Federation of University Women of the extent of preparation for parenthood available in secondary schools, found that 68 per cent of the 151 schools in their sample offered courses and that these were taken by 39 per cent of all girls and 9.6 per cent of all boys. Just under half of these pupils were not examined.[26] The involvement of boys in child-development courses seems more likely when the subject is offered as a non-examinable part of the core curriculum rather than as an option, and when male teachers, as well as female, teach it.

However, all too often even these courses address issues primarily of concern to women, and neglect a male perspective on for example birth, or fatherhood.[27]

The vast majority of pupils taking child care and development courses are girls. Such courses are often seen as vocational, for less able girls, who may want to look after children, and who may well be mothers in the fairly near future. In many schools the way in which options are presented to the pupils ensures that few boys are encouraged to take the course; this can confirm the traditional view of women within the family, as housewives and mothers, with prime responsibility for childrearing.[28]

The content of some courses can also be criticized; many have now moved away from bathing babies and making layettes and fluffy animals, towards a fuller consideration of emotional and psychological needs of young children, but there is some evidence from young parents that the courses they did in school were largely irrelevant to their needs as parents. A study of the content of CSE child-care syllabi, and a comparison of these syllabi with the anxieties and needs of 150 parents showed that attitudes and feelings caused far more problems than did bottles and nappies.[29]

Examination-based courses may help to achieve status as an academic discipline for the relatively new subject of child development. However they also tend to limit the syllabus, resulting in an emphasis on teaching topics which are examinable. Unfortunately the most valuable aspects of family life education are inherently unexaminable: developing self confidence, awareness of choices, awareness of one's own and others' attitudes .... Teachers frequently blame the examination syllabi for restricting their teaching style, and for reinforcing traditional attitudes to child care. Few syllabi encourage young people to critically examine child care advice.

Personal, Social and Moral Education

There has been an increasing emphasis on encouraging schools to develop their own policy of personal, social and moral education in a number of LEAs — for example Devon, Nottingham and Birmingham. PSME is seen as embracing not just subject areas such as English, religious education, careers, health education and home economics but also as concerned with the ethos of the whole school — its' system of pastoral care and of discipline, its' use of tutorial time, its' relationship with the local communities ...

Personal and social education includes the teaching and informal activities which are planned to enhance the development of knowledge, understanding, attitudes and behaviour
concerned with oneself and others; social institutions, structures and organizations; and social and moral issues.[30]

The emphasis in personal, social and moral education is on
enabling pupils to acknowledge and fully understand their own
value position in relation to the values of society, and of other
pupils' in the class. This is central to the aims of family life education as we have identified them. Family life education is not a
primary aim of PSME, but a secondary one. This in itself increases
the likelihood that the family will be studied in its' social context.

Subject Areas

The NCB study[31] found that: 'in twenty-five authorities *home
economics* was an important site for family-life education'. On the
whole subjects were fairly practical and included such topics as
catering, food and nutrition, home safety, homecraft, money, management and child care. Subjects were again mostly optional and
taken almost exclusively by girls.

In twenty authorities *social studies* had relevance to parent
education, including community studies, social and political awareness, citizenship and the City and Guilds Community Care course.

Eleven authorities mentioned *religious education*, which incorporated personal development and relationships, social and political awareness, moral education and sex education.

Biology was noted by ten authorities.

The Aston study also showed an 'unexpected amount of
parenthood-focussed teaching appeared to be in progress' in *English*, where in one school it was described as 'permeating the
syllabus'.[32] Most teachers found parenthood, family life and personal relationships a rich source of material. Drama sessions and the use
of role-play can also make a useful contribution to the development
of decision making and problem-solving skills.

This short review of the vast range of possibilities for teaching
family life education reveals some of the major difficulties to its
successful implementation:

(i) Family life education occurs across the curriculum. There
     is, therefore, a need for coordination and cooperation

across departments in a school. Not infrequently young people face overkill on some topics and total neglect of others.[33]

(ii)   Family life education, when implemented in the way we suggest, involves discussion of attitudes and values which may conflict with those of the pupils' parents. Teachers need to find ways of involving parents in negotiating the content of family life education, and indeed of PSME.

(iii) Similarly, family life education is likely to involve young people in considering the attitudes, needs and demands of their local community, and in making use of the resources of that community — in placements in under 5 settings, inviting guest speakers from local organizations. At the same time a variety of professionals in any one locality are working in family life education outside the school — health visitors, social workers, youth workers, nursery nurse trainers, marriage guidance counsellors. Coordination of efforts, as well as negotiation of who should do what, when, would do much to make best use of local community services.

(iv)   The interest, concerns and experiences of the pupils themselves can often be overlooked by teachers in their efforts to construct courses which incorporate the demands of their subject, the examination syllabus (if there is one), and the needs of the team of staff involved in the personal, social and moral education of the school.

It is not surprising that teachers of family life education can feel overwhelmed by the contradictory demands made of them. The way out of the muddle is negotiation — with colleagues, parents, members of the community and pupils. In addition, many teachers require training and support to complement the programme which makes use of their skills as facilitator and negotiator, rather than, as is traditionally the case, purveyor of knowledge. These aspects are considered in the remainder of this chapter.

Negotiation

It is important that the coordination of family life education should be part of the school's policy for PSME otherwise the danger is that there will be duplication, confusion and even contradictions. The experience of many LEAs and schools is that successful coordination of PSME (often defined as health education) requires the involvement and status of senior members of staff.[34] Their influence on curriculum decisions and on timetabling is likely to be crucial. Staff also need to discuss and negotiate the range of knowledge, attitudes and skills relevant to family life education, and to discover the extent to which these are currently provided for across the syllabus. They then need to identify gaps in provision, and identify opportunities to fill those gaps. The Open University *Lifestyles* pack (1985) contains several activities which can be used by staff in a school for these tasks. Similarly the Schools Council Health Education Project 13–18 Coordinators Guide (1983) contains a variety of ideas to coordinate the broader area of health education. Ideally, the negotiations of aims, and of needs will be done collaboratively with pupils and their parents. It is possible to run courses jointly with and for teachers, pupils and parents. This was done with support from marriage guidance in Dudley and Luton,[35] and with support from the Health Education Inspectorate in the ILEA.[36] The experience of such collaboration leads us to suggest that teachers are often unnecessarily fearful of parental involvement. Finding ways to involve all parents of teenagers, rather than the few keen PTA members, can be an enriching and rewarding experience for all concerned. Parental values may be in conflict with those of the school over some issues, but given the opportunity to explore each others values and perspectives, there is room for learning and compromise. It is said that teachers often assume that they are in conflict with parents when the reality is more likely to be that parents are their strongest allies in the education of teenagers. Later in the article we outline experiential learning methods which can be used in working collaboratively with parents as well as with other members of the community.

Schools already involve a range of organizations in the family life education work. Health authorities are perhaps the most obvious source — health education officers often provide support in planning and resourcing work in schools; health visitors and school nurses frequently give talks on aspects of their work to pupils. Schools place pupils in playgroups and nurseries, and may develop links with organizations such as the Pre-School Playgroup Association and the National Childbirth Trust. A whole host of other agencies may be invited into schools to give talks for family life education programmes — NSPCC, Spastics Society, Royal Society for the Prevention of Accidents .... In addition these agencies and others — including community workers, youth workers, social workers — are involved in family life education in the community, and have views and skills which can contribute to a school's programme. All too often schools invite an outside agency to send a speaker for a 'one-off' visit, and pay little attention either to preparing the pupils for the visit, or following it up. Nor does the speaker discover how their talk fits in with the school's programme, and its aims. One solution is to invite such agency representatives as 'visitors' to a course, using the active tutorial work 'Receiving a Visitor' technique. The technique is included in their teacher's books and in the Open University Family *Lifestyles* pack (1985). This at least enables the visitor to respond to the interests of the pupils. However, it does not give them scope to use their particular skills and expertise to influence the design of the whole family life education programme and their place in it. To ensure this level of cooperation it is necessary to involve members of community agencies in working with teachers, parents and pupils to negotiate aims for a school's family life education programme.

It is perhaps important to note that negotiation with all those in a locality involved in family life education will require boundaries. Some of these boundaries will be set by the use of a clear title, such as 'family life education' for your meetings. Boundaries can also be set by structuring the meetings. A tight structure does not mean that discussions will not be open-ended. On the contrary, a structure which enables each person present to contribute to the discussions at some level will mean that all views are heard and discussed. Thus we do not suggest calling a meeting for all those involved in an area and asking 'what should we be doing?'. Nor do we recommend calling a meeting and telling them all what you have already planned to do. Instead we recommend a highly structured meeting using groupwork techniques to facilitate a debate of what can and should be done. Various activities are possible, but we would strongly recommend a ranking exercise — see, for example, *Family Lifestyles* (1985), *Childhood* (1985), *Debate and Decision* (1979) and *Priorities for Development* (1980) for a detailed description of the activity and a variety of issues to debate. A description of the use of this activity to negotiate priorities can be found in Braun and Eisenstadt (1984).[37] Essentially a ranking exercise asks people to prioritize a range of nine prepared views on a theme, such as aims for family education: these may be written statements, photographs, press cuttings, quotations. The participants have to do this in pairs first, then in fours and then compare results in the whole group. The list of items placed highest represent the whole group's priorities. Another activity usefully follows this, and serves to clarify individual perceptions of the agreed priorities, as well as to ensure a chance to include views not yet discussed; this is the Aims Card Game. This game is included in the *Family Lifestyles* pack (1985) and *Debate and Decision* (1979). The activity asks individuals to write five statements about their priorities in relation to a theme such as 'what is a Family?', on individual cards. These are dealt out in the group, and the game played so that every individual ends up with three statements with which (s)/he agrees but did not write. The chosen statements represent the group's collective priorities, and can form the basis of the course content.

It is, therefore, possible to work with teachers, parents, pupils and members of the community to negotiate aims and purposes for family life education in a way that acknowledges the validity and makes constructive use of all their points of view. This is a sound beginning, but not an end and if it is to truly offer pupils an opportunity to recognize choices and learn decision-making skills, the participatory and negotiated approach needs to be maintained throughout any course. The appropriate vehicle for such approaches is structured groupwork.

The Active Learning, Through Structured Groupwork, Method

Structured groupwork is appropriate for learning about the family and childhood because it places the participants' existing knowledge and experience as central to the learning process. In addition:

(i) It provides a structure for sharing. The activities offer a framework that generates common ground for group discussion.

(ii) It breaks down traditional barriers between learner and teacher. Knowledge is contributed from both and equally valued.

(iii) It enables participants to control their level of personal involvement. Each activity allows the individual to decide how much to share, and encourages an accepting attitude to those who would rather share less.

(iv) Groupwork is appropriate for various ability groups and all ages. Different groups will respond to materials according to their own abilities and needs.

When using structured groupwork the variety of a group's experience becomes a positive advantage to the learning of all the group. This is particularly relevant given our multicultural context. The multicultural classroom can become a forum for exchanging views, values and experiences. In classrooms which do not include pupils of different races, there is every chance that they will never-theless include pupils from a range of cultures — class, religion, region.

Various materials now exist to provide groupwork exercises which can be adapted by teachers for work in family life education. It should be pointed out that many teachers feel they lack skills and confidence to adopt groupwork techniques if they have not them-selves experienced these techniques as participants.[35] The need for. training is vital, and will be discussed further below. It is important that in using the materials on groupwork teachers adapt and select in order that the techniques can be used to fit in with the negotiated course content. Once teachers become skilled in the use of group-work activities they should find it easier to create activities to suit their particular purposes.

Perhaps the best known materials supporting active learning are the active tutorial work books.[39] The methods included in the books have a much wider potential than mere tutorial time use, and a national dissemination/training programme encourages teachers to adapt the techniques for use in their subject teaching. A danger of the active tutorial work approach is slavish adherence to the books, which rules out negotiated learning, and should be avoided. Teachers will need to spend time planning and negotiating what they intend to teach and then select from the book those activities which can help achieve their aims.

A similar approach to the ATW materials is found in the lifeskills teaching guides produced by the Counselling and Careers Development Unit as Leeds University. Lifeskills is based on the belief that teachers can help the personal development of their students by teaching specific personal and interpersonal skills which will promote self-management and individual competence, and equip students to cope with their life roles and tasks.[40] Included in their courses are such skills as communicating effectively; making, maintaining and ending relationships; coping with stress; and being positive about oneself. Programmes for use in health education and in youth services are being developed. This project is also providing in-service courses for teachers working with groups in the class-room.

One danger of the lifeskills approach is that too much responsibility can be placed on the need for individuals to develop skills, and too little on considering the social and economic factors which shape life chances. Teachers using this sometimes have a 'deficiency model' of their pupils — arguing that if only they can be taught certain skills this will improve their success in life. The use of such a model makes it difficult to build on existing strengths of pupils, and denies social factors like unemployment, of which the pupils are often acutely aware.

Active tutorial work and lifeskills have evolved from the structured and developmental models of groupwork with adolescents developed by Button at the University of Swansea for social workers, youth workers and teachers. The main strategy has been to help local education authorities create their own training teams and to support this work Button has published a programme for form-tutors to use in pastoral time with groups where 'young people can learn how to help one another in their personal development and in their ability to cope with present day society'.[41]

A similar approach can be found in the work of Donna Brandes, particularly in the *Gamesters' Handbooks*.[43] These two books contain a range of exercises which develop interpersonal and communication skills. Another resource, especially useful for training others to use groupwork techniques, has been produced by TACADE (1983). Many of their health education packs similarly contain structured groupwork activities and resources.

All the approaches outlined about make particular use of the experience of individuals within groups, in order to develop the knowledge of the whole group. The knowledge developed is especially concerned with personal relationships, and the development of self-esteem. These aspects are an important part of family life education but do not in themselves constitute a whole programme of family life education.

Four recent publications are specifically designed to match the content of family life education to groupwork methods. The Open University *Family Lifestyles* and *Childhood* packs, and the Development Education Centre's *Values, Cultures and Kids*, and *What is a Family?* Photoset, offer practical ways of using pupils' existing knowledge and experience as the central resource in learning about the family and child development.

Values, Cultures and Kids (DEC, 1982) was produced together with a group of Birmingham teachers. It explores methods and resources for teaching about the multicultural dimension of the family and child development. It was originally designed to fit in with Birmingham's Mode III CSE Child Development, but clearly has wider potential. The book illustrates that an examination syllabus is not necessarily a constraint to active learning. It is based on the view that multicultural education is relevant to all schools, in all areas of Britain, and that the presence of a diverse range of ethnic and cultural groups is a positive attribute for a community.

The *What is a Family?* Photoset (DEC, 1984), shares the same premise. It is also included with the Open University *Family Lifestyles* pack. The pack contains teachers notes and twenty-two black and white photographs depicting a wide range of families in Britain. It can be used to open up the debate about family structures outlined already in this chapter. The teachers notes contain practical suggestions for using the photographs with adults and pupils.

The two Open University packs were produced by the Education for Family Life project, which like many other projects in this field, is funded by the Health Education Council. The *Family Lifestyles* pack (Open University, 1985) was produced for teachers, social workers, youth leaders and other professionals to examine their own values and feelings about family life, in order that they may then explore these issues with young people. The pack contains groupwork techniques and a variety of resource materials — advertisements, press cuttings, photographs — and can be used as the basis of in-service work — as well as directly with young people. The pack's materials develop three themes; What is a Family?; Social Roles; and Family Relationships.

The *Childhood* pack (Open University, 1985) has the same target audience, and contains materials on a further three themes: Identity; Practical Experience with Young Children; and The Child, the School and the Community.

Both these packs are presented in ring binders, to encourage users both to be selective in use, and to add other relevant ideas and resources. As with other groupwork materials the packs require users to plan courses and then to select. However, these packs also offer a framework for planning courses and practical techniques for negotiating course content. The framework for planning is based on work originating in another sphere — world studies and development education (see, for example, *Birmingham and the Wider World*).[43] Essentially the framework recognizes distinct, though overlapping, stages of a course:

(i) *Getting Started and Setting the Scene* — establishing the climate for the course; getting to know one another, beginning to work together as a group, negotiating the aims for the course.

(ii) *Enquiry* — exploring a theme of study: developing understanding, empathy, knowledge.

(iii) *Evaluation/Ways Forward* — what was learnt, how was it learnt, and what are the implications for the future work of participants.

Those planning courses for adults and young people can use this framework to plan the basic structure of the whole course, as well as to plan each session of the course. Both the *Family Lifestyles* and *Childhood* packs contain content checklists to help users decide which activities suit their needs at particular stages of a course. *Values Cultures and Kids* (DEC 1982) pages 28–30 reviews the range of materials now available to schools involved in family life education. In addition to text books, the range of voluntary agencies involved in the field produce leaflets and booklets, the Health Education Council produce a wide range of these, and the new *Pregnancy* booklet (1984) is well written and beautifully presented. The Open University Community Education section has also produced a range of packs on family and child health. Teachers can often find relevant material using press cuttings, advertisements and the popular press — teenage magazines for example. However, it is vital that materials should reflect and acknowledge our multicultural society. Many do not.

To help teachers select materials relevant to our multicultural society, a working group of Birmingham teachers produced the following checklist:

(i) Look for obvious racism — if you can't avoid using the materials then make sure you open the discussion on racism.

(ii) Look for stereotyping — for example are all blacks portrayed as good at sport, all Chinese working in 'take-aways'?

(iii) Watch for English only names: where possible substitute with some Asian or other non-English names.

(iv) Be aware of language — watch for racist terms: notice that the word 'black' is nearly always used as a derogatory term, notice if 'immigrant' is used to describe black people: look for 'loaded' words like savage, primitive, superstitious — always show your pupils *your aware-ness.*

(v) Look at the lifestyles portrayed. Are minorities de-picted:

(a) to contrast unfavourably with whites;

(b) only in ghettoes;

(c) only in native dress.

(vi) Look at relationships — for example are black people always in subservient roles?

(vii) Consider the pupils' self-image; is there someone with whom they can possibly identify?

(viii) Check the illustrations. Look for tokenism — do the black people look just like tinted white people? Are the black people described as genuine individuals?

NOTE You may find it difficult to discard your unsuitable mate-rials: if this is the case then you can show your awareness by encouraging discussion as to why the resources are racist or unrepresentative of our muticultural society.

It is clear that a variety of materials exist to support teachers in developing a family life education programme which involves active participatory learning.

However, family life education as we have presented it requires teachers to assume skills and techniques of groupwork and to work with a team of colleagues from very different backgrounds. It will involve a need to rethink the nature of authority within a school; will require negotiation with and involvement of parents, and a fundamental change in relationships between staff and pupils. Clear-ly teachers require training and support.

Training and Support for Teachers

In view of the points made above it is sad to note the dearth of opportunities for training in family life education. Some of the projects described earlier run training programmes, but these are not aimed specifically at family life education, and do not deal with the particular issues of parental involvement or sensitive subject matter. In addition to training provided by ATW, Lifeskills and TACADE, the Family Planning Association is now increasing its courses on personal relationships and sexuality. Many LEAs include family life education as part of a wider subject specialist course — this is especially true, of course, for home economists. The Open University Education for Family Life project's training will only run for two years, and is staffed for two workers, so will be limited in its scope. At the present time, the National Community Education Development Centre in Coventry offers training courses to local authorities for teachers in home/school relationships and in family life education. It is hoped that the Family Education Unit of CEDC, which was set up in 1983, will be expanding further into the field of training in family education for teachers and other professionals. What can be offered at the present time to local authorities by CEDC are short training courses and a consultancy service which will help LEAs, particularly LEA advisers, to run their own training and set up support groups of teachers. Introduction to the use of materials such as the Open University *Family Lifestyles/Childhood* packs would be an integral part of such training and consultancy services. The priorities for all training for teachers in family life education are:

(i) to provide teachers with opportunities to experience for themselves a variety of groupwork techniques;

(ii) to provide teachers with opportunities to try out such techniques with their pupils, discuss with each other any problems they may have had and support each other in finding solutions to the problems;

(iii) to raise teachers' awareness of the controversial nature of family life education; to enable teachers both to recognize their own value positions and to see that these may not be shared with others in the community;

(iv) to develop teachers' abilities to negotiate the content of family life education courses with their pupils, with other members of staff, with parents, and other members of the community.

Notes

1 PUGH, G. (1985) 'Family life education in secondary schools: A national overview', *Family Lifestyles* (PE. 630), Milton Keynes, Open University; and PUGH, G. and DE'ATH, E. (1984) *The Needs of Parents-Practice and Policy in Parent Education*, Macmillan.

2 DHSS (1974) *The Family and Society: Preparation for Parenthood*, London, HMSO; and DHSS (1974) *The Family and Society: Dimen-*

sions of Parenthood, London, HMSO.

3 SMITH, L. (1984) 'Some Philosophical Notions in Preparation for Parenthood Policy' unpublished paper prepared for HEC National Conference, Southampton.

4 RIMMER, L. (1981) *Families in Focus*, Study Commission on the Family.

5 HMSO (1984) *Social Trends*, London, HMSO.

6 Happy Families (1980) Study Commission on the Family.

7 SEGAL, L. (1983) *What is to be done about the Family?*, Penguin.

8 *Ibid.*

9 COOPER, J. (1981) Quoted in GLADWIN, J. *Happy Families*, see below.

10 GLADWIN, J. (1981) *Happy Families*, Grove Books.

11 *Ibid.*

12 SEGAL, L. (1983) *op cit.*

13 TORKINGTON, K. (1985) 'Conscious Choices The Goal of Family Life Education', *Family Lifestyles*, (PE. 630) Open University.

14 PUGH, G. and DE'ATH, E. (1984) *op cit.*

15 RUTTER, M. (1972) *Maternal Deprivation Reassessed*, Penguin.

16 HARDYMENT, C. (1983) *Dream Babies: Child Care from Locke to Spock*, Jonathan Cape, London.

17 GRAHAM, H. (1984) *Women, Health and the Family*, Wheatsheaf Books.

18 BALDING, I. (1981) 'Health Topics Research', *Education for Family Life* (1981) Open University.
CLARK, M. (1981) 'Child Care and Development Courses for Secondary Pupils', University of Nottingham, M.Phil. Thesis.
DOCHERTY, S. (1978) 'Do pupils Want Health and Social Education? A Reanalysis', Scottish Health Education Unit.
BRAUN, D. and EISENSTADT, N. (1984) 'Family Life Education: Whose Aims?', National Conference Health Education and Youth, Southampton University.

19 PRENDERGAST, S. and PROUT, A. (1980) 'What Will I Do? Teenage Sins and the Construction of Motherhood', *Sociological Review*, 28.3.

20 PROUT, A. and PRENDERGAST, S. (1984) 'Parenthood: What Pupils Know and What They Learn', *Education and Health* 2.3.

21 PROUT, A. and PRENDERGAST, S. (1985) 'Some Reflections on Pupils Knowledge', *Childhood*, Open University.

22 TORKINGTON, K. (1985) *op cit.*

23 GRAFTON, T. *et al* (1982) 'Getting Personal: The Teacher's Dilemma', *International Journal of Sociology and Social Policy*, 2.3.
GRAFTON, T. *et al* (1983a) 'Gender and Curriculum Choice in Relation to Education for Parenthood', in HAMMERSLY, M., HARGREAVES, A. (Eds) *Curriculum Practice: Sociological Courses Studies*, Falmer Press.
GRAFTON, T. *et al* (1983b) 'Preparation for Parenthood in the

Secondary School Curriculum', University of Aston, Department of Educational Inquiry.

24 PUGH, G. and DE'ATH, E. (1984) *op cit.*

25 *Ibid.*

26 RUBINSTEIN, V. (1979) 'Results of Questionnaire on Education for Parenthood', British Foundation for University Women.

27 PROUT, A. and PRENDERGAST, S. (1984) *op cit.*

28 GRAFTON, T. (1983a) *op cit.*

29 DOCHERTY, S. (1978) *op cit.*

30 DAVID, K. (1982) *Personal and Social Education in Secondary Schools*, Longman.

31 PUGH, G. and DE'ATH, E. (1984) *op cit.*

32 GRAFTON, T. *et al* (1983b) *op cit.*

33 *Ibid.*

34 McCAFFERTY, I. (1982) 'Coordinating Secondary School Health Education', Nottinghamshire Health Education Unit.

35 PROCTOR, M. (1982) 'The Dudley Family Life Education Project', Unpublished National Marriage Guidance Council Report, NMGC.

36 ILEA (1985) 'Working with Parents — A Pilot Study 1984–1985'.

37 BRAUN, D. and EISENSTADT, N. (1984) *op cit.*

38 McCAFFERTY, I. (1982) *op cit.*

39 Lancashire County Council (1979–) *Active Tutorial Work*, Years 1–5, Basil Blackwell.

40 HOPSON, B., SCALLY, M. (1980, 1981, 1982, 1984) *Lifeskills Teaching*, McGraw Hill. 'Lifeskills Teaching Programmes 1, 2 and 3' Lifeskills Associates.

41 BUTTON, L. (1981 and 1982) *Group Tutoring for the Form Teacher*, Hodder and Stoughton.

42 BRANDES, D. (1979) *Gamesters Handbook*, Hutchinson and Co.
   BRANDES, D. (1984) *Gamesters Handbook Two*, Hutchinson and Co.

43 Development Education Centre (1980) 'Birmingham and the Wider World — A Report', Development Education Centre.

Resources for Family Education

1 *Community Education Development Centre*
   Briton Road
   Stoke
   COVENTRY
   CV2 4LF

   (a) *Coping With Kids* — a collection of materials for use with
                            individuals in group discussions.

   (b) *Working Together* — a set of ten leaflets on early childhood

(discipline, temper tantrums etc)

(c)   *What Would You Do?* — situational flip charts for early childhood education.

(d)   *Early Years* — a pack of child development materials for use in groups, giving information about stages of development and suggestions for how adults might stimulate children.

2   *Development Education Centre*
Gillett Centre
Selly Oak Colleges
Bristol Road
BIRMINGHAM
B29 6LE

(a)   *Birmingham and the Wider World — A Report* (1980)
(b)   *Priorities for Development — A Teachers Handbook for Development Education* (1980)
(c)   *Values, Cultures and Kids — Approaches and Resources for Teaching Child Development About the Family* (1982)
(d)   *What is a Family? — Photographs and Activities About Families in Britain* (1984)

3   *Open University — Community Education Packs*
Learning Materials Service
The Open University
PO Box 188
Milton Keynes
MK7 6DH

The First Years of Life (P911)
The Pre-School Child (P912)
Childhood 5–10 (P913)
Parents and Teenagers (P914)
Pregnancy and Birth (P960)
Getting Ready for Pregnancy (P901)
Understanding Pregnancy and Birth (P902)
Women and Young Children — Learning Through Experience (P593)
Parents Talking — The Developing Child (P590)
Parents Talking — Family Relationships (P597)

4   *Open University, Centre for Continuing Education/Health*

Education Council
Learning Materials Service
The Open University
PO Box 188
Milton Keynes
MK7 6DH

Family Lifestyles (PE630) (1985)
Childhood (PE631) (1985)

5   *TACADE*
2 Mount Street
Manchester
M2 5NG

Satow, A. and Evans, M. (1983) *Working with Groups* — A handbook for those wishing to run courses on group work; provides useful suggestions and a variety of discussion sheets on aspects of group functioning and dynamics.

6   *Health Education Council*
78 New Oxford Street
London
WC1A 1AH

Many leaflets, booklets and posters available.
Free publications catalogues available on request.

Pre-Vocational Education

Roger Fielding, Ross Maden and
Catherine Village

Introduction

Attempts to show the relationship between social education and
pre-vocational education would be very much easier if the target
of pre-voc could remain the same while we fired our shots.
Unfortunately the scene is rather like a football match in which the
goal posts are moved every time a shot is taken. It is also like a
football match in the sense that there is a different referee for each
game and the referee's decisions are always greeted with derision by
the crowd. Another hallmark of pre-vocational education is that it
must have a set of initials, for example, CPVE, TVEI, C and G 365,
RSA, Voc Prep, YTS, BTEC. The effect of this is to create insecur-
ity amongst teachers and lecturers who do not know what the latest
set of initials stand for and conversely to create a feeling of superior-
ity amongst those who do.

Pre-vocational education was given a great stimulus with the
surprise announcement in November 1982 of the Government's
Technical and Vocational Education Initiative (TVEI). In January
1983 LEAs were invited to submit proposals for the new funds that
had been made available, via the Manpower Services Commission
(MSC), to finance TVEI schemes. By March 1983 sixty-six proposals had been received. Fourteen were accepted and these first projects began in September 1983 with £46 million promised for five
years covering 13,830 students and 144 schools and colleges. In
September 1984 a further forty-five LEAs began MSC-funded projects and in September 1985 the remaining LEAs introduced TVEI
programmes.

TVEI is by no means the only expression of vocational education. The Government's White Paper *17+ : A New Qualification*,

published by HMSO in May 1982, recognized that existing provisions for post-16 study did not adequately cater for students 'with modest examination achievements at 16+ who have set their sights on employment rather than higher education, but have not yet formed a clear idea of the kind of job they might tackle successfully'.

The Joint Board for Pre-Vocational Education was established by the Business and Technician Education Council (BTEC) and the City and Guilds of London Institute (CGLI) at the request of the Secretary of State for Education and Science to develop and administer a new, national qualification to be called the Certificate of Pre-Vocational Education (CPVE). It was hoped that by replacing all the various and different qualifications offered by all the various and different examining bodies with one single, recognized, national qualification that one, more widely credible and less confusing certificate would emerge.

This new CPVE first became available, by dual certification, for the academic year 1983–84 for students over 16 successfully completing the following courses with full-time study — CGLI Foundation Courses, CGLI Vocational Preparation (General) (CGLI 365); BTEC general awards in Business Studies and Royal Society of Arts (RSA) Vocational Preparation (Clerical) and (Distribution) courses and RSA Basic Clerical Procedures. Forty thousand young people were enrolled on this basis during 1983–84. The new award was available in its own right for the first time as from September 1985 and over 600 submissions for approval of CPVE schemes were received by the Joint Board.

Pre-Vocational Education and Social Education

Pre-vocational education aims to provide young people with opportunities:

  (i)   to assist their transition from school to adulthood by equipping them with basic skills, experience, attitudes, knowledge and personal and social competencies required for adult life;

  (ii) for a personally relevant educational experience which encourages learning and achievement;

  (iii) for acquiring a qualification embodying national standards which will give recognition for their attainments;

(iv)   for an accepted basis for progression to continued education, training and/or work.

The specific objectives which would be needed to fulfil these aims would include

(i)   the ability to communicate effectively in a variety of ways including reading, writing, talking and listening, using signs and diagrams;
(ii)   development of practical numeracy;
(iii)   an awareness of the implications and uses of modern technology and its application in everyday life;
(iv)   development of manipulative and physical skills;
(v)   the development of social skills by creating opportunities to work in groups;
(vi)   growth of self-confidence and adaptability;
(vii)   a capacity to tackle problems through experiencing a variety of situations in which strategies can be developed towards satisfactory conclusions;
(viii)   a knowledge of the world of work and the roles of young people in it;
(ix)   an appreciation of the economic, political and environmental factors which influence everyday life;
(x)   a readiness to seek employment or further education and training through an understanding of pathways available.

These objectives are not specifically related to subject areas and should not be seen as discrete core elements.

This list of objectives is not just about pre-vocational education but is equally applicable to social education. The objectives cover a range of educational experiences which are relevant whatever a young person seeks to do in the future.

The rapidly changing nature of our society allied to the inability of government or industry to predict with any degree of accuracy future manpower needs make it imperative that schools and colleges do not go down the road of narrow job-specific training, which may or may not exist when young people leave full-time education. This is an important principle that needs to be made explicit especially to young people, parents and employers whose expectations of the educational service are often quite different from teachers and lecturers.

Finally, pre-vocational education can be seen as a response to those who see the educational world as a highly elitist system based on academic failure. For example, if you do not fail at CSE, you can go on to fail at 'O' levels; if you do not fail at 'O' levels you can go on to fail at 'A' levels. By comparison other educational systems in the western world have a system geared to success. For example, 90 per cent of those students who stay on in full-time education in the USA to the age of 18 successfully graduate. Pre-vocational education will enable many youngsters to gain success and self-confidence that would not be available to them by traditional academic provisions.

Perhaps the most important aspects of PVE are the changes in methodology and classroom practice which it stands for. These are summed up in such terms as 'experiential learning', 'student-centred learning' and 'negotiated curriculum'. Pre-vocational education marks the end of the authoritarian teacher and the appearance of the tutor as a facilitator of and partner in learning. Only time will tell whether these fine phrases are hollow rhetoric or authentic practice. The change of role from 'expert' to 'facilitator' is demonstrated by the initiatives being developed under the name of 'enterprise'.

Enterprise and Pre-Vocational Education

There is undoubtedly a move within education to introduce 'enterprise' into the curriculum. This can take many forms but has found primary expression in the practice of operating school businesses. School businesses may be operated successfully in a number of contexts involving students of all ages and abilities. While school businesses can be successfully integrated into primary education (Jamieson, 1985a)[1] in what follows the focus is on secondary schooling.

The Context of the School Business

There are a number of contexts in which a school business could successfully operate:

    (i)   in a student's free time after school, during the evening or at the week-end;

    (ii) during the general studies periods of sixth-form students;

    (iii) during the core curricular time of fourth and fifth year students (within 'life skills' or similar courses);

(iv) during option subject time for fourth and fifth year students (as part of a business studies or commerce course for example);

(v) during appropriate lesson time for students in years 1 to 3;

(vi) during one complete week for all students with normal schooling suspended;

(vii) within vocational education schemes for students of all ages following TVEI schemes, 14–16 schemes such as the City and Guilds Vocational Preparation (General) scheme (CGLI 365), students taking the Certificate of Pre-Vocational Education (CPVE), and other schemes, in the sixth-form.

Why Run a School Business?

Specifically within the area of vocational education there are a number of good reasons for setting up a school business:

(i) A school business may demand contributions from a number of areas of the school curriculum — business studies, craft, communication skills, numeracy. Their involvement in the school business can help these areas of the curriculum to achieve greater industrial and vocational relevance, at the same time as illustrating their occupational applications and enhancing the students' real understanding of commerce and industry.

(ii) Running a school business requires a skills-based student-centred approach with negotiation and decision-making having central importance in the process. Running a school business then, can also be a vehicle for staff development and the introduction of new pedagogical approaches within the classroom.

(iii) Running a school business is also a very effective way of integrating the various modules and components of a vocational education programme or TVEI Scheme.

(iv) Running a school business also provides a common focus for staff, leading to improved cooperation and team-teaching, as well as developing a genuine interdependence amongst members of the course team.

(v)   A school business can provide simulated work experience at a time when real placements may be hard to guarantee.

(vi)   A school business illustrates in a practical and experiential way many of the central features of business studies modules as well as requiring the acquisition and application of basic skills.

(vii)   A school business can also act as a highly effective motivational device giving new purpose to students in subjects they may otherwise have found difficult, irrelevant or 'boring'.

Setting up a School Business

In what follows two main approaches to the setting up and operation of school businesses are reviewed — the national and formally-organized Young Enterprise Scheme and school-based 'mini-company' projects.

Young Enterprise

The growth of vocational education has been accompanied by a growth in the resources available for introducing enterprise into the curriculum by way of setting up and operating school businesses. However, one of the most widely known schemes — Young Enterprise — has been providing practical business experience to young people since 1963. During the academic year 1984–85 17,000 young people were running more than 700 in schools and colleges as part of the Young Enterprise Scheme (*Times Educational Supplement*, 2 August 1985) and the National Council of Young Enterprise hopes to increase this to 30,000 by 1988 (Jackson, 1985).[2]

Young Enterprise is based on a similar scheme — Junior Achievement — run in the USA. This was first established in 1941 and still operates successfully — in excess of 600,000 young people took part in 1983–84 (Young Enterprise 1985a).[3]

Young Enterprise Ltd. is a registered charity supported by industrial and commercial sponsorship and subscription fees. Each of four regions in the United Kingdom is managed by a full-time Director, although smaller voluntary area boards, made up of industrialists, educationalists and others, maintain and foster specific activities within their areas.

An important feature of Young Enterprise is the emphasis

placed on the voluntary commitment of students outside normal schooling. Young Enterprise, in fact, has in the past seen their scheme as being entirely voluntary and quite distinct and apart from school work or vocational training (Young Enterprise, 1982; Jamieson, 1985b).[4] More recently, however, they have recognized the contribution their scheme could make to TVEI, CPVE, YTS, and BTEC course (Young Enterprise, 1985b).[5]

It is usual for Young Enterprise companies to meet with their advisers — volunteers from industry and commerce — for around two hours, one evening a week, between September and June. The role of the advisers is to guide and advise without imposing their views or taking too leading a role. The students will form a company and register this with Young Enterprise, appoint staff to the Board of Directors, sell shares, produce, market and sell goods. After a life of around eight months the company will go into voluntary liquidation and repay all shareholders with an appropriate dividend. There is a national competition for the 'best' company and a written examination based on the practical learning experiences of the students. Students are awarded a Young Enterprise Certificate on successful completion of this examination.

Young Enterprise aims to give young people experience in order to help them:

(i)   develop initiative and self-confidence;
(ii)   widen knowledge of team-work;
(iii) improve powers of leadership;
(iv)   form positive relationships with adults;
(v)   give and receive advice and criticism;
(vi)   gain awareness of previously unrecognised skills;
(vii) choose future career paths and further education;
(viii) appreciate the values of an enterprise economy;
(ix)   understand the way in which business works.[6]

Mini-Companies

School businesses can, and do, operate outside of the formal Young Enterprise Scheme, of course. There is an increasing amount of resource material available for teachers who might wish to run school businesses in their own way with schemes they can tailor to the specific requirements of their own situation. These alternatives can be broadly labelled as 'mini-companies', and their history can be traced back to the EEC Transition from School to Working Life

Project (Jamieson, 1985b; Bray, 1983).[7] One of the aims of the mini-company experiments within the EEC project was to include less able fourth and fifth year students and to integrate the work into the school curriculum (Jamieson, 1985b). One of the first of the resources available to teachers to run their own mini-company was a complete kit (Bray, 1984)[8] including guidance and much of the documentation necessary. Such mini-companies have the advantage of flexibility to lend themselves, appropriately adapted, to the needs of any specific vocational education scheme.

Having decided a mini-company has a constructive role to play in curriculum development the key questions which must follow are organizational and practical. Some of these questions are listed below:

— Shall we form a 'real' company that trades with the world outside school or is it to be a simulated exercise?
— What shall we produce or what service shall we provide? Who will take this decision?
— Which pupils should be involved and for what length of time?
— Does the enterprise require any money? If so, how should it be raised? Should workers be remunerated? If the enterprise makes a profit, what should be done with it?
— How should the organization be structured? Should it reflect the structure of a small business, or large company? A partnership, a limited company, or a co-operative? Should there be a separate managerial tier?
— What is to be the role of the teachers in the mini-company?
— If the mini-company is to operate in the 'real world' how are the legal obligations to be discharged, for example, product liability, health and safety questions?[9]

The first questions relate to the kinds of goods and services which may best be offered, the methods of raising finance and the procedures needed to get the business going and to keep it going.

The goods and services offered will best be determined by the interests, abilities and aptitudes of the students themselves and the nature and needs of the local community. Throughout the early planning of a school business it is vital that the students play a leading role. Unless the students have a definite feeling that it is their business venture, and their responsibility, the exercise will not achieve all it could.

A school business may be set up in a number of different forms from sole trader, partnership, cooperative or private limited company. In some circumstances it may well be practical to set up several school businesses each operating independently of the others. Individual students may operate as sole traders, small groups of students may set up as partnerships or cooperatives, while a larger group may decide to operate as a private limited company.

The issue of finance, and the means by which the initial capital is raised, is closely linked to questions about the form of business organization adopted. In the case of sole traders, partnerships and cooperatives funds may be raised through bank loans, borrowing from family, friends, the Parents Association or School Fund, or even through fund-raising events. In the case of a private limited company, funds would be raised through the sale of shares to other students, staff, family and friends.

The way in which funds are raised will partially determine what must happen to the profits when the business is liquidated at the end of the exercise. Profits will be distributed to the shareholders, in accordance with the number of shares purchased, in the case of a private limited company. Sole traders, partnerships and cooperatives must repay all loans with appropriate agreed interest first and any remaining profits might be retained by the students themselves, donated to School Fund, passed on to the next year's school business or donated to a favourite charity.

In practice the level of profits is largely an artificial figure determined by the costs imposed by the organizing school. Even trading with money in the 'real world' involves a degree of simulation and a school business may or may not be charged nominal rentals for premises and workshops, rates, electricity bills and wages.

While the students — and any shareholders — will be keen to make a profit it is important to remember that the aims of the exercise are educational and even making a loss may be a lesson well learnt.

While each method of operation has its own peculiar characteristics, selling shares and operating a private limited company seems to offer distinct advantages.

Some Advantages of Running a Private Limited Company

(a) The selling of shares provides a reasonably straightforward source of capital. Shares may be sold for any amount and in any multiples to raise starting capital.

(b)   The sale of shares encourages wider interest in the school business than would otherwise be the case. The issuing of a prospectus informs other students, teachers and parents about the school business and the purchase of shares gives others an interest in the success of the business.

(c)   Having friends, other students, teachers and parents as shareholders gives the students running the business a real responsibility for other people's money. It takes the school business a stage further into the 'real world'.

(d)   The fact of having shareholders leads to the need to hold at least one shareholders' meeting — perhaps at the end of the course when the company is liquidated. Again this can be an excellent vehicle for the acquisition and application of important skills.

(e)   Setting up a private limited company gives increased relevance and importance to understanding the legal procedures involved in the 'real world' when setting up a private limited company. Students may compile Articles of Association and Memorandum of Association for their own company even though the company will not need in any way to be formally and legally incorporated.

The running of a school business, then, in one form or another, can be a most effective way of introducing enterprise into the curriculum. In addition, it can make a tremendous contribution towards meeting the many demands of vocational education. The process of running a school business demands a skills-based approach to teaching and learning; of necessity negotiation with students and student decision-making becomes central; course team cooperation and team teaching become almost inevitable; integration of the students' curriculum is achieved and opportunities for the acquisition, application and demonstration of core and basic skills are provided.

Work Experience

Work experience programmes are now widespread in one form or another and not only do they pre-date the formulation of this pre-vocational education concept but they are not often integrated into social education programmes. Usually work experience is organized by the careers teacher and isolated from other learning experiences. Yet when one analyzes the objectives of work experience they are of direct relevance to social education. The following have been identified as some of the learning objectives of work experience:

Personal Development of Pupils

  (i)   Work experience should enable all pupils to experience the success and frustrations of seeing a project through to its completion.
 (ii)   Pupils will adopt a new role, i.e. that of a worker as opposed to pupil, and respond to different routines.
(iii)   It will increase their awareness of their responsibilities for their own actions and how their actions affect others, and enable them to practise their decision-making skills.
 (iv)   They will experience the inter-dependence of peoples jobs and the variety of jobs within a workplace, and help to ease entry problems into new surroundings after school.
  (v)   Their experience will have significant influences on their attitudes towards schooling, education and training.
 (vi)   They will develop aspects of communication skills, especially oral skills and develop job hunting techniques through interviews and practice self-presentation.

Dealing with Other People

  (i)   Pupils will be able to experience working as part of a group and learning to work with new people in a work situation, and it offers the opportunity to work *with* adults, often for the first time in a different way.
 (ii)   They have access to the experience of adults and see how adults react in different situations. Also they are able to observe the different styles of authority and how to respond to them.

Knowledge

  (i)   Pupils will be expected to gain an understanding of the importance of wealth creation, and the work of trade unions at the workplace level.

Table 1

TASK: TALKING ABOUT MY JOB	CLASSROOM PREPARATION/FOLLOW UP
1 Write a **job specification** (i.e. a list of **all** the things you need to do in your job). Write a **person specification** for your job, i.e. what skills/knowledge/attitudes do you need to do the job well.	1 The class could be divided into groups to work on job and person specifications, those that exist in the school, for example, teacher, caretaker. Invite along a personnel or work study specialist from a local firm to explain how they do job evaluation.
2 Write to a new work experience student taking over your job and give advice about what to do on the first day. How should they behave with fellow workers, and with the supervisor/boss?	2 What are the formal and informal rules of the school? How do pupils learn the informal? How are the rules maintained?
3 Who tells you what to do at work? How do they tell you? Who tells them what to do? What would happen if nobody told you what to do?	3 Draw a model of the school authority structure. Examine school notices/instructions and compare them with notices/instructions in a workplace. Divide the class into groups with the same task but with different authority structures (authoritarian, democratic, laissez-faire) — what happens?
4 Explain what would happen if you were late to work (once, twice, frequently). What would happen if you made a bad mistake at work? (What would be a bad mistake?)	4 Compare the school rules for lateness with those of a couple of employers. Do the same with other discipline offences. Invite in a trade union official and a manager to talk about how they deal with discipline. Work through a discipline case study from industry.
5 Explain to a new work experience student what to do if they need to complain about something at work. Who would they go to? What would they say? Any advice on how to say it? Would the advice depend on what it was?	5 Examine the school complaints procedure. What would you do if you were being bullied? What would you do if you couldn't get on with a particular teacher?
6 What parts of your job do you like doing best? What parts of your jobs do you like least? What other jobs in the organisation would you like to do? — why is that?	6 Ask an adult to come into the class and talk about the features he/she likes about the job, and the things they dislike.
7 Draw a plan/take a photo (ask permission) of your work area. Show the layout of everything.	7 Draw a plan of the classroom, design and technology rooms, or science laboratories. Why are they designed like that? Invite a work study engineer or architect to talk about the design of the working environment.
8 Label the main pieces of machinery in use. Were they there five years ago? Ten? Twenty? How long will the present machinery last? When might it be replaced? What would they replace it with?	8 What is the technology involved in school? Ask the same sort of questions that you would of the workplace.

214

9 What areas are dangerous in your work area? Why are they dangerous? How do you know they are dangerous?

10 Describe in detail how two pieces of machinery work or write some operating instructions for a new work experience student.

11 What jobs could be done by either sex? How are jobs divided up by sex at your workplace?

12 How could your job be done more effectively? Why don't they do it like that?

---

9 Analyze the school for dangerous areas. What signs would you design to warn people of danger?

Invite a health and safety officer or a trade union official with health and safety responsibilities to discuss these issues with the class.

There are a number of health and safety case studies that can be used.

10 Describe in detail how a piece of school machinery works or write some operating instructions for a VCR or OHP.

Examine some industrial operating instructions. Write a booklet for the local junior school on an industrial process.

11 Invite an equal opportunities employer to the school to discuss what they needed to do to promote equal opportunities.

12 Examine certain tasks at home or school from the point of view of efficiency — make recommendations.

Set up a school production line (making something with Lego bricks or paper) and let groups do an efficiency exercise on it — experiment with various methods of organization. Use a work study engineer as a consultant.

Table 2

TASK: TALKING TO PEOPLE AT WORK	CLASSROOM PREPARATION/FOLLOW UP
1 What jobs do they do? What is their job title?	1 Play a production line game to show the division of labour. Make a flow chart.
2 What do they like about their job? What do they dislike about their job? Are there any other jobs in the organization they would like? Why?	2 Get students to rank a dozen or so occupations in order of desirability — examine the reasons for the ranking. Invite different adults other than teachers into school to talk about their jobs and satisfactions/dissatisfactions.
3 Who is their immediate boss? Who are **they** in charge of?	3 Draw a diagram of who is in charge of whom at the workplace.
4 What training and/or qualifications did they need for the job? Are they the same now or have they changed?	4 Compare the methods of training for their jobs with those at school. How might school have equipped you better for the job?
5 Has the job changed much in the 5/10/15 years? Any retraining required?	5 Invite in some long serving employees and trade unionists to talk of past times and the changes.
6 How much would somebody like them earn? Are there any fringe benefits? What would a new employee starting at the bottom earn? How would they go about getting more money?	6 Estimate average earnings of a group of well known occupations and check against the data. Cost common fringe benefits. Run a wage bargaining simulation with a local trade unionist and manager acting as consultants.
7 What would they do if they wanted to complain about something? (a) workplace too hot/cold/smelly? (b) the way they were being treated by a supervisor?	7 Simulate some justified complaints about school, how would they go about it? Simulate an industrial complaint and use industrialists and trade unionists as consultants.
8 What would happen if the organization closed down? (a) what would they personally do? (b) what would happen to the customers/clients/patients, etc.? (c) what sorts of reasons would cause a closure?	8 Find out about redundancy rights, unemployment claims, etc. Invite in a personnel officer and a trade unionist to discuss the problems.
9 Who did you meet at lunchtime/breaktime? Compare with worktime. How are the informal lunchtime groups made up?	9 How do you choose who to have lunch with? And at breaktime? After school? Would you like lunch with a teacher?
10 What did you talk about during lunchtime/breaktime?	10 Invite some adult workers into school and discuss their work/leisure interests.
11 What did they wear?	11 Discussion of school uniform questions. What jobs in society have clear cut uniforms and why? Examine photos of work people and try and deduce their jobs. Examine the reasons behind the judgments.
12 How far have they travelled to work? What means of transport have they used?	12 Do a journey to work exercise for pupils/teachers in the school. Contact the local planning department for maps, journey to work analysis. Contact the local bus company about bus scheduling.

(ii) They will experience new and different types of equipment, see the effects of new technology at the workplace, and gain knowledge of the realities of health and safety issues.

(iii) Pupils will learn about a different disciplined environment and organization structure from that of school and be made aware of the disciplines of work.

(iv) They will face prejudice in the workplace, whether it be the young v the old; black v white; or men v women.

(v) In addition the overall experience will enable pupils to gain an alternative perspective on society, and enable parents to reflect on the transition of their children to young adults.

We are beginning to see now an attempt to tackle the wider curricular implications of work experience. Many teachers find a striking fear on the part of pupils in dealing with adults outside school and some pupils experience extreme discomfort in even making a simple telephone call. Much work is now being carried out in the area of self-presentation, confidence boosting and learning from fellow students. This is a small beginning from which other ideas and spin-offs are coming. Pupils inviting their work experience employers into school for a social gathering organized by themselves or a business venture group has been one response; more regular contact with employers for use of facilities in school time has been another; teachers spending some time in industry yet another.

However the objectives of work experience cannot be fully realized unless there is time given to classroom preparation and follow up. Examples of what can be attempted here are taken from Holmes, Jamieson and Perry (1983).

The Future for Pre-Vocational Education

There are massive implications in developing skills associated with the various PVE initiatives with young people. It requires quite fundamental changes, not in what we teach, but how young people learn. There needs to be a change in methodology which puts the emphasis on how young people learn as opposed to how we teach. It was summed-up by the teacher who asked an offending pupil 'Jones, are you learning anything?'. The reply went straight to the heart of the problem 'No, sir, I am listening to you'. The traditional emphasis on acquiring knowledge by didactic teaching methods needs to be realigned to an emphasis on how young people can use knowledge. Moreover, there is no justification for confining pre-vocational education only to 'non-academic' pupils. The need for 'social and life-skills' is as important for graduates entering employment as it is for 16 year olds. Some indications exist that pre-vocational education will be seen as an alternative to academic education though there is some hope that when CPVE becomes available as a part-time route that it may take the place of general studies in the sixth-form and become acceptable for those taking three 'A' levels as well as those looking for a one-year full-time course. In time it is likely that all youngsters between the ages of 16 and 18 will be treated with financial parity thus allowing them to choose the most appropriate course provisions for their needs, instead of the present system where many young people decide on the basis of financial rather than educational benefits.

Pre-16, the advances of pre-vocational education will continue and there will need to be close monitoring to ensure that provisions post-16 genuinely build upon the knowledge, skills and experiences that have already been gained by that age. We should welcome the spread of pre-vocational education into the general curriculum provisions for all young people providing it allows more of them to gain self-confidence and experience success than is the case with the present system. Many young people leave the education system at the earliest opportunity feeling failures. Their self-esteem is fragile, their confidence is low and they regard themselves as failures, mainly because of the widespread pre-occupation with achieving the magic 'five 'O' levels'. Any innovation which attempts to change the balance of our educational system from one of failure to one of success should be welcomed.

Notes

1 JAMIESON, I., (1985a) 'Industry and Primary Schools' *in* Jamieson, I (Ed) *Industry in Education; Developments and Case Studies*, London, England.

2 JACKSON, D., (1985), 'What is Young Enterprise' in Young Enterprise (1985a) *Young Enterprise: Learning Through Doing*, London, Young Enterprise Ltd., information brochure.

3 YOUNG ENTERPRISE (1985a), *op cit.*

4 Young Enterprise (1982), *Young Enterprise: The Scheme*, London, Young Enterprise Ltd., information brochure.
5 Young Enterprise (1985b), *Learning by Doing* reprinted from *Works Management*, London, Young Enterprise Ltd., information brochure.
6 Young Enterprise (1985a) *op cit.*
7 Jamieson, I. (1985b) (Ed) *Industry in Education: Developments and Case Studies*, London, Longman; Bray, E., (1983) 'Mini-co's in schools' in Watts, A.G. (Ed) *Work Experience and Schools*, London, Heinemann
8 Bray, E., (1984) *The mini-co kit*, York, Longman Resources Unit.
9 Jamieson, I. (1985b) *op cit.*

Resources

Colin Barnett, Ruby Chambers and Ken Longman *Learning from experience — A Training Manual in Personal Effectiveness*, Macmillan.

Elizabeth Bray, *Directors' Handbook 1: Setting Up Your Mini Company*, Longman.

Elizabeth Bray, *Directors' Handbook 2: Running your Mini Company*, Longman.

Elizabeth Bray, *Mini Co. Forms*, Longman.

Sue Carroll and Patricia McQuade, *The Voc Prep Manual*, Framework Press.

CSV, *No Bed No Job — Homelessness Amongst Young People*, CSV.

CSV, *Joe & Jackie — The Great Job Hunt*, CSV.

CSV, *The Survival Game — Working it Out*, CSV.

CSV and National Westminster Bank, *Life Skills Training Manual*

FEU, *Tutoring Profiles*, Longmans for the FEU.

FEU, *How Do I Learn?*, Staff Development Publication.

Terry Parker, *A Simulation from CSV*.

Urban Studies and Community Education

Anne Armstrong

> This is better than school, Miss, why can't we do this all the time?

This is a comment that I have often heard from children working in urban studies centres. It reflects an enthusiasm for learning which can be transmitted to the school classroom through urban studies practice. It comes out of the immediacy and relevance of what the children are asked to do. Sometimes my best returns from teaching have come watching the smile of understanding that crosses the pupil's face when he or she makes sense of a complex sociological or political concept from the basis of the pupils' own local research. It is, of course, always pleasant for teachers to work with students who do not want to go or want to come back tomorrow.

Urban studies is one of the ways of making this magic and it has an important contribution to make to social education. Although it grew out of environmental education, it has taken on board a concern for sociological, political and economic issues. Urban studies is a separate but closely-related movement to community education. The two are dealt with together in this chapter in terms of their contribution to social education, because of shared philosophies and because both offer a special approach to dealing with political education. The chapter is divided into five sections:

(i) The history of urban studies and its links with community education.
(ii) Urban and local studies in the classroom.
(iii) Some examples of projects.
(iv) Setting up a resource base and where to go for help.
(v) Getting over the problems.

The History of Urban Studies and Its Links with Community Education

The historical development of both urban studies and community education have made them what they are today because they have evolved and are continuing to do so. Keith Wheeler sees the dawn of urban studies in man's alienation from nature during the Industrial Revolution (Martin and Wheeler, 1975). Patrick Geddes could have been said to have invented urban studies when he started to link environmental improvement with education, but the movement did not really take concrete form until the 1960s. At the time of the post-war building boom there was a growth of public interest in an education which would help people to understand the built environment and facilitate participation in decision-making. Out of the enthusiasm for participation of the sixties came urban studies and somehow, despite the failure of any real development in the participation movement, it has survived and grown.

In the late sixties various organizations began to invest time and energy in urban education. Some were created for this purpose such as the Civic Trust's Architectural Heritage Group and others like the Council for Environmental Education shifted their emphasis to embrace the urban world. But the most important development was the creation of the Education Unit of the TCPA (the Town and County Planning Association) who started to publish BEE, the *Bulletin of Environmental Education*. It is significant that it was an environmental, rather than an educational, pressure group that took the step, thus ensuring that the urban studies movement was firmly linked to concepts of urban and social improvement. The unfortunate consequence of these origins is that some educationalists were, and continue to be, suspicious of what they saw as planners daring to suggest something new to them and it has been particularly difficult to get sociology teachers to see the value of urban studies. (Perhaps the geographers find it easier to make the link through the environment).

Teachers concerned with social education should be particularly interested in the link with the concept of participation. It was soon realized by those who wanted to produce active adults able to participate in decision-making that they had to find methods of teaching which were different from the traditional methods which sadly seem to produce a passive result. For you cannot hope to create active adults if you spoonfeed them and ask them to be totally passive in the classroom. In fact some urban studies enthusiasts felt that it was impossible to teach urban studies in school and devoted themselves to setting up urban studies centres, separate places where both students and adults could study the urban environment and tackle local issues.

Urban studies centres are closely linked to many of the institutions that have grown up out of the community education movement because they offer their resources to the whole community not just those in the school system. The forty-two existing centres are promoted by CUSC, the Council for Urban Studies Centres which was also set up by the TCPA's Education Unit. Examples of the work-based centre will be given later in the chapter.

However, the educational practices developed in both community education centres and urban studies centres can, to some extent, be adapted to the classroom. The starting point is the local issue and there is nothing to stop schools building up their own resources on local issues and trying to adopt a new approach to learning about them. The hardest thing for a school to achieve is the symbiotic interaction between different groups of learners, which can happen in an urban studies centre when for example the representatives of a tenants' group arrive to type and print some minutes and can talk to the school group which is studying housing in the area. Perhaps community schools find it easier to facilitate such relationships because they have the push and the enthusiasm for building up local contacts and try to find many different ways to bring people into the school.

The Community Education Movement grew out of Herbert Morrison's work in Cambridgeshire in the 1920s. He started from the notion that the village primary school could have a much wider social role than simply educating 5–11 year olds. Out of this has come a wide-reaching campaign which includes the deinstitutionalization of education, making more efficient use of plant and offering education as a life-long possibility. Like urban studies, the community education movement contains a wide variety of opinion. At one end of the spectrum there is the dual use of educational plant providing educational activities for every age. At the other end there are people striving for real community control of education resources and the curriculum. Thus some education authorities have put their efforts into developing community schools and colleges whilst other authorities and independent groups have concentrated their efforts on setting up alternative centres and bases which could in some way be said to mirror urban studies centres.

It is impossible in this short chapter to discuss adequately all the complex issues which affect the community education movement. As Colin Fletcher (1980) says, at present community education takes a bewildering variety of forms. It is only possible to see how both it and urban studies have already affected and could improve social education in schools. The two movements meet in their basic philosophy. For example, they both believe that the student's active contribution to the learning process is essential and that he or she should be relating directly to real life and they are both suspicious of imposed and academic knowledge. Emphasis is thus placed on developing learning skills rather than acquiring facts. The teacher's role changes to be a facilitator and a catalyst and the end product is a change in understanding and ability. It is thus very hard to assess.

A first reaction to such a brief description is always, 'well, that is what we are doing anyhow'. Certainly many of the ideas are old ones but in my experience they are rarely put into practice in the school, especially the secondary school, where the pressures of the timetable, the examination system and the organization of the institution discourage this radical approach. I would, however, suggest that if it is not adopted, not only will large and important elements of social education fail, but we may also be facing educational failure on the whole front. As Chris Webb, Director of the Notting Dale Urban Studies Centre says,

> It is no longer any use to bring out the old recipes, usually aspic based, to attempt to cope with these issues [of urban crisis]. There is no proven link between the experience of learning or being taught a subject in school and becoming a caring, struggling adult! Yet much of the curriculum industry prefaces its self-descriptions with these inherently overblown and fanciful assumptions. (BEE 117 January 1981)

Urban and Local Studies in the Classroom

Urban studies has derived its own methodology of bits and pieces borrowed and adapted from elsewhere, as an intrinsic part of what it is. It is the way in which urban studies is done that makes it different from most other forms of environmental education and in fact from most educational practice.

The content of urban studies is special too for the content of urban or local (it can be adapted to the rural situation) studies is a local issue. The word issue sometimes puts teachers off because of its political and thus dangerous connotation. However, it is possible for even the faint hearted to adopt an issue-based approach because it need not necessarily culminate in protest marches or rebukes from the school governors. An issue can be relatively safe such as a heavily-trafficked street with no pedestrian crossing, thus an issue is not a hypothesis testing which the geographers seem to be doing at the moment. The setting of a hypothesis puts too much stress on collecting objective data and discourages the pupil from evaluating personal subjective opinion including his or her own. Ideally the issue should give the teacher or students the opportunity to study a problem first-hand and relate it to the wider context. The process of issue selection should be done with the pupils but teachers must decide beforehand whether they can cope with the most sensitive and difficult issues which may be chosen by the pupils such as racism and class. Both the urban studies and community education proponents would say that these are issues which should be tackled and the best way to tackle them so that they do not seem apart and abstract is in a local issue. It is useful to recall the chapter on the curriculum and the community in David Hargreaves' book *The Challenge for the Comprehensive School*. This discusses in more detail the problems and potential of building an issues-based curriculum which is more relevant to the majority of school children.

Before giving some real examples of urban studies projects some of the methodology will be explained through an abstract example. However it must be remembered that there is no prescribed way of doing urban studies as the reader will soon discover through pursuing the recommended reading at the end of the chapter.

Nine Basic Steps

1   The students are introduced to the idea of the urban studies project.
2   The students visit the buildings, streets, institutions or whatever is to be studied. They should be near the school or urban studies centre and certainly in first instances areas should be already known by the students so that they can contribute directly to the project. Through something like a town trail the students are introduced to a variety of issues related to the history, geography, sociology, economics,

ecology and aesthetics of the place. Most urban studies teachers prefer taking an integrated approach because it is so difficult to compartmentalize the environment into artificially defined subject areas. However, we are often forced, when working with secondary groups, to make the project fit the demand of a particular subject syllabus. Fortunately it is possible to fit urban studies into all curriculum areas.

3   On the trail the students will be asked to observe, discuss and make first judgments about what they see. Tony Fyson (1973) describes the aims of this process thus:

> ... to make the student visually inquisitive about the town scene and lead him to form discerning judgments, not as a passive recipient of other men's ideas but as an informed critic who demands the best of his urban environment.

They are then able when back in the classroom or at the urban studies centre, to select the issue they would like to study. They would be encouraged to work in groups because of the value of cooperative learning, and to find an issue which is related to their own experiences and interests. In fact the concepts of urban studies fit well into those developed by the collaborative learning enthusiasts and have the advantage of being real. This stage is always an interesting process of negotiation and compromise both for the groups of students and for the teacher. A class can arrive at the decision to study five different issues or just one from five different points of view.

4   Once the issue is chosen the students work cooperatively to plan their own research, decide what data needs to be collected and from where, what they can observe for themselves and who else needs to talk to them. They may well end up by redefining the study several times over as it goes on but this adds to the educative process. Groups who have never planned their own work before are often lost when asked to do this. The teacher must be careful to guide gently and resist the temptation to step in and do it for them. Feeding students pre-digested work sheets and projects is no way to stimulate the mind or encourage active learning.

5   The next stage is to complete the research although this may be linked with the following stage, that of analysis. It is hard to give more than a flavour of what might happen

because it is important to allow flexibility and respond to events as they occur. Most urban studies projects will include direct observations, using the opinions of others, using written and graphic evidence and using available statistics and reports. At this point another warning needs to be given to teachers we feel that students need to have data processed before they can be used. An important part of urban studies is to allow people to handle materials in their raw forms so that the students will build up confidence and skills and be able to use such things when there is no teacher around. Every student can do this with the right help and motivation. Talking to other people and finding out that people have differing ideas is another important part of the project. Some people will also include the use of photography, video tape recorders and so on to develop skills in using such equipment, and communication and as a motivating tool.

6 Stage six is analysis but this of course cannot in reality be separated from stage five because it should be going on throughout. Role-play and simulations are often used to reinforce the analysis and students may well be helped at this stage to link their study to wider issues. They may in fact do this for themselves by asking questions. I have seen 9-year-olds at Notting Dale Urban Studies Centre who have been studying local housing start to question national policies of housing allocation!

7 Students can then be asked if it is appropriate to suggest solutions. When looking at a physical problem they might be asked to come up with a design solution and test their ideas on an expert. When studying a social issue they might want to suggest policy changes. Whatever the case they should be asked to back up their solutions with the information they gathered along the way. Being asked to produce a solution to a problem lifts the approach neatly away from the impersonal hypothesis-testing and ensures that the student develops his or her own thing.

8 The next stage can be a presentation of these ideas back to the whole class and other interested visitors such as adults who have been involved in the study. This technique is borrowed directly from design education 'crits' and provides a good focus for the study provided students do not think of the presentation as being all-important. It need not be formal but it should encourage all the class and visitors

to comment, challenge and compliment. It demands the development of useful communication skills which seem usually under-developed in schools where too much emphasis is placed on the written and private end product.

9   The final stage is the one which is most difficult to achieve. It is that of ensuring that the projects lead into action and it is especially difficult to achieve when the issue chosen is wide and sensitive. Students could for example present solutions to local racist behaviour but they might not be able to do anything about it. Some teachers get around this by guiding students towards issues that they can influence such as internal school design or organization. Others accept that action must sometimes be low key and be as simple as writing to local councillors in the planning office. I was once involved with a primary school group who noticed that the nearby post box had lost its sign saying when the post was collected. They wrote to the post office about it and a few weeks later the sign was replaced. It was a very small achievement but they felt very proud.

Some Project Examples

Below are eight brief descriptions of urban studies projects, most of which I have been involved with, that begin to demonstrate how urban studies can be made available to all ages and can be taught as an integrated study or fit in one subject area. Longer descriptions of these and other projects can be found in back copies of BEE.

1   *A primary group looks at pedestrianization*
    This project was done by a mixed third and fourth year class from a junior school. Most of the research work was done at our Urban Studies Centre but the follow-up work was done in the classroom. The group decided to look at the question of whether or not the local shopping street should be pedestrianized. They first divided into groups to study various aspects of the problem from the point of view of shoppers, shopkeepers, vehicle drivers, officials and others. They soon discovered that there was a conflict of view between the local council and the GLC (Greater London Council) and thus had to investigate this relative power. Each group made direct observations such as a traffic count

or a shop use survey and they all talked to the public and officials.

After several weeks of research we used a role playing game to focus their ideas to which end we asked them to play the parts of the various factions. Before playing the game students were asked to say whether or not they thought the street should be pedestrianized. The majority said 'no'. Then they played the game which includes a planning evaluation designed to give insight into the ways in which planners make decisions. After playing the game which highlighted sometimes painfully the relative powerlessness of some groups and individuals, we asked them again whether they still thought the street should have traffic in it. This time they said they thought it should be pedestrianized. In a way it is not important what conclusion they came to but it is important that they saw the process of changing their minds.

2 *A secondary group looks at the same issue*
As part of a CSE social studies course a fourth year group looked at another aspect of the pedestrianization issue. They chose to look at the road that would need to be widened to accommodate the traffic from the closed street. The study was meant to teach them about local government but through a local studies approach rather than didactically. They used techniques of photography and local interviews and we were also careful to ensure that they talked to different officers and politicians with a variety of opinion.

However we had to allow the study to change half way through as you often have to do in urban studies projects because they had a particularly interesting and not altogether comfortable experience when talking to a GLC councillor. This led them into all sorts of questions about the role of the politician and into the whole issue of the closure of the GLC.

3 *An integrated study for first years in a secondary school*
Employment is an important issue to tackle in social education and provides a good focus for an integrated study. The whole information technology centre network grew out of a study by FE students on local employment possibilities based at Notting Dale Urban Studies Centre. One local secondary school decided to take an integrated approach to teaching humanities in the first two years and used the

summer term of the first year to focus on employment. The project was school-based but involved drafting in several additional adults/teachers including the Divisional Industry-School Coordinator who initiated and steered the work. The whole first year, working in classes, followed trails in local employment areas, visited firms and tried to come to grips with issues in the local economy.

The culmination of the project was a focus on the old White City Stadium site which had recently been cleared but whose future had not been decided. The study told them much about the mismatch between employment opportunities and the local adult communities' needs. When the children played a simulation game about replanning the site they were concerned to provide something that would offer work to local people.

4 *A critical look at MSC training*
In an area where there is a high incidence of unemployment amongst school leavers it is important to open students' minds to training possibilities but it is also important to teach them to be critical. With a social studies teacher we organized a project with another fourth year group of secondary pupils where in school they learnt something about employment and training and were then sent to visit local MSC training projects. We found that they were already aware of issues of payment on some schemes but we helped them ask pertinent questions of tutors and trainers about what the training involved and job opportunities afterwards.

5 *A special day on women's issues*
In urban studies we usually encourage teachers to give a good chunk of time to a project because it can take a while for students to come to grips with an issue and to learn the skills necessary to pursue the project. However practical limitations can mean that it has to be a one-off exercise. These can be valuable especially if the students can spend at least a whole day following one issue. It is also possible to organize a day event where students from different schools and different ages can meet and work together.

One such day was organized to celebrate International Women's Day in 1985. We invited adults and women and female students to meet at the Urban Studies Centre. They were given a variety of issues to look at including design in the shopping centre and mother and toddlers provision in the park. Two of the most successful projects are worth mentioning because they could be adapted to a school base. One group looked at women and safety. They walked around the area identifying problems and talking to other local women. They then tackled the officials about what action should be taken. Another group looked at what it was like to work as a woman. They looked at council employees and came up with some interesting conflicts which it would have been hard to raise in an abstract situation in the classroom.

6   *New technology and urban studies*

It is important to teach children applications for information technology and to get away from academic computer studies. This can be done through an urban studies project and in the case described below can also lead to that highly desired 'action' which is often mentioned.

A junior school teacher asked for information about trees in the area around his school and was told that the council did not have this sort of information but that they could do with it. He then set about collecting information on local street trees with his class. The project included survey work, talks with an arboriculturalist and with planners, and making a tape slide show telling other schools how to do a tree survey. The children collected the data on their school computer and eventually handed a print-out to the Town Hall containing all the information that they had asked for in the first place.

7   *A motivator in communication studies*

Another interesting project was undertaken by a local English teacher with a group of 12-year-olds. She designed an agreed programme of work with a teacher in a Swedish school. The programme in itself was nothing extraordinary. It included half term blocks of work on the individual pupils, their homes, the school, and the local area. The classes used the written word, photography, drawing and videos. What made it special was the link with the Swedish children who were of course doing their part in their English lessons. It was what we sometimes call an environmental exchange and parcels of work crossed the North Sea six times a year. Both teachers said that the project had a great motivational force and included a great deal of social education, especially in terms of explaining the multicultural background of the British group, as well as communication skills.

Urban and local studies do not need to be parochial. Looking at self or a local issue can lead to much higher things. There is the famous case of the closure of the sugar refinery in Hammersmith which could lead to a look at local job losses and what should be rebuilt on the site but might also include a look at EEC sugar policy and its effect on sugar cane growing on the West Indies.

8   *Local studies in the community school*
I mentioned earlier that it was often easier to do school-based urban studies in a community school. This is demonstrated by a City and Guilds Project currently running in my school which will evolve into part of our CPVE course. The group is doing a year's worth of work on local recreation picking up on the life skills elements of the City and Guilds syllabus. It includes a look at local recreational opportunity, the role of the Council, the effect of public transport, sports hall management, publicizing recreational programmes and planning events. Because we are a community school I am able to weave all sorts of real elements into the Project. The students can survey the recreational, educational and sports provision in the school, buy and test equipment for us, help publicize our facilities and plan some of our programmes. Also because we are a community school and have a close relationship with all sorts of individuals and organizations around us it is easy to bring them into such projects.

Working With Adults and End Products

All the projects so far described have included adults but it is of course possible to work in exactly the same way with an adult group. Sometimes something very exciting can come out of it in terms of an end product. However the best end product from urban studies that I know of did not grow out of any formal adult education class. A group of council tenants were able to design, oversee the building of and then run their own community centre on an estate in North Hammersmith. They did this with the help of the Notting Dale Urban Studies Centre, using the Centre's re-

sources to make them aware of local needs. Incidentally the awareness in part came from local school children's research.

Another good example of an exciting end product involving
children comes from much further north, in Glasgow. There the
Glasgow Eastern Area Renewal Group (GEAR) ran a competition
for children to redesign areas of open land that they were about to
improve. They committed themselves to implement the prizewin-
ning plans. The group that won, a junior school class, then had to
face the local residents, amend their plans and work alongside a
landscale architect but they eventually saw their proposal built.

Getting Over the Problems

Urban studies is not easy to do especially if you work in a situation
where community education has not been widely developed. It is
time consuming. It demands a change in teaching style. There are no
text books to do the work for the teacher. Sometimes it leads into
political difficulties and sometimes it is hard to make colleagues see
that it is worthwhile and that it fits into their educational aims.
There are however ways round most problems.

The first and perhaps the most difficult problem to overcome is
to achieve the change in teaching style. A teacher who is used to
being the fount of all knowledge and to imparting carefully prepared
lessons to the class perhaps using a well-tried and trusted textbook
will be at a loss. The need to change classroom practice has been
recognized by many including those who set up the College of St.
Mark and St. John Training Project in the East end of London. As
John Rayner (1981) says,

> The teachers in schools, so often contemptuous of what they
> saw going on in colleges of education, continued neverthe-
> less to endorse the programme followed by their apprentices
> even after the system showed signs of breaking down. The
> system was certainly showing signs of breaking down in
> inner-city areas: pupils were refusing to accept their role as
> pupils and their teachers in consequence were unable to
> sustain theirs.

There are many deep fears about letting go, some of which
relate to the fear that the class will be undisciplined and control will
be gone. However, the educational rewards of doing so are great.
One way round the problem is to introduce more adults into the

classroom. Working with small groups makes the move easier. In these difficult economic times it is hard to find more teachers but team teaching is one solution. Alternative non-teachers such as local experts, students or parents can come in to help in the urban studies project. Good urban studies needs a high teacher/pupil ratio.

The next problem to overcome, especially in the secondary school, is the tyranny of the timetable and later the exam syllabus. It is hard if not impossible to do a good project in one double lesson a week. There is hardly time to go out which will be necessary at some point and there is no time for follow-up. The way round this is to persuade colleagues to cooperate. An integrated approach to areas of learning is probably best but if this is not achievable it may be possible to plan projects with teachers from different subject areas either to bargain for time or to agree to teach about the same issue from different viewpoints. The exam syllabi will cause problems in the later years but it is possible to bend many exams round to include some element of local studies. In CSE courses there are no problems and 'O' and 'A' level geography, sociology and history field work can be made to fit in. Preoccupational courses like CPVE and TVEI also contain possibilities. Many schools have personal or social development lessons which are not exam orientated and local studies can be made to fit into English and Art where there is a will. Some schools also choose to abandon their timetable and run an activities week. Here is a perfect opportunity to have the whole school involved in a variety of local studies, such as the one organized by Forest Gate School, Newham in 1984 (see BEE 166).

Another pedagogical difficulty is the thorny question of assessment. There is no doubt that it is difficult to assess one's success in urban studies if one's goal is to produce an adult capable of participating in local and national affairs. One can easily assess whether the pupil has acquired the necessary skills to observe, record, analyze and communicate and it may be that we have to accept that this is what any formal assessment will be about.

The political nature of urban studies raises further problems. First, teachers have to accept that they are dealing with a form of political education. They then have to decide where they stand on the issue of teacher neutrality and perhaps put their own stand in the context of the school. Although there have been recent government rumblings about the danger of some political education, the present government gives full support to the learning of political literacy. We thus have to show that taking an issue-based approach in urban studies is one of the best ways of acquiring those skills. To a worried headteacher or governor it is important to point out that urban studies is not trying to pass over one particular set of values or ideas. It is also important to point out that we always try to get students to see each side of any argument and to be thoughtful before making up their own minds. Some teachers try to steer away from over-sensitive issues and in the end it is their choice, but it is a pity because it is certainly important to face difficult urban issues with the children who have to live with them. It can also be argued that everyone should be encouraged to deal with them.

The last problem that needs to be pointed out is the difficulty that the individual teacher has in making time to prepare for an urban or community studies project. It is very time-consuming making contacts, collecting resources and making appointments. This is why it is so important that teachers are not left in isolation trying to develop this area of a curriculum. A school should have a policy which commits it to a community studies approach so that teachers can share resources and contacts and so that examinable activities, non-examinable activities and extra-curricular activities can all feed off each other. It is so exciting when the person you invited to talk at assembly on handicap can suggest contacts for the social service club and help prepare a module for the fourth year's personal development studies. This is when the time spent in making the contact in the first place is repaid as a good investment.

Conclusion

I want to end by underlining some of the ideas presented in this chapter on community education through urban studies. It is essential that the approach is issue-based and that it deals with issues that are relevant to the student's life. It is also essential that the teacher's role as an information giver is reduced to a minimum. Often the teacher knows as little about the issue or the area as the students but he or she does have skills to share and knows how to find things out. Teachers thus become facilitators and catalysts.

In community education through urban studies it is important to allow the students to define their own research and to give them access to the raw data that they might have to face in later investigations. Students should be encouraged to base their analysis and problem-solving on that research, which includes their own views and the views of others. They must always be made to present their ideas back so that they have a focus for the project and so that they develop their ability to communicate. Finally we should try to find ways of ensuring that urban studies leads whenever possible into action, however small, so that the students see that there is a purpose to the project and so that they will know how to take creative action later.

Things will move slowly. As David Hargreaves (1982) says:

> Community schools and community education are in their infancy; courses in community studies are still few and somewhat experimental. There is an emerging literature on community education which is rich in ideas, cautious in its pretensions and critical of the achievements so far; and that literature treats in depth many of the issues and arguments that have to be neglected here. Changes in curriculum and pedagogy are substantially slower than changes in structure and organization, as we learned in the case of comprehensive reorganization. Change in the content and method of teaching has to be grafted on to existing practice. Or, to put the matter another way, existing practice can show a remarkable resistance to apparent change. Teachers, like everybody else, do not much care for having their deep assumptions questioned and changed. The culture of individualism is as deeply ingrained into the fabric of schools as the cognitive-intellectual tradition and can easily survive what appear to be radical changes.

All I can add is that whilst I understand why things move slowly, they had better start moving soon. Otherwise we will be failing the individuals we educate and the society of which they are part.

References

FLETCHER, C. and THOMPSON, N. (Eds) (1980) *Issues in Community Education*, Lewes, Falmer Press.

HARGREAVES, D.H. (1982) *The Challenge for the Comprehensive School*, London, Routledge and Kegan Paul.

MARTIN, G.C. and WHEELER, K. (Eds) (1975) *Insights in Environmental Education*, Edinburgh, Oliver and Boyd.

Ann Armstrong

RAYNER, J. (1981) *Teachers for the Inner City: The Work of the Urban Studies Centre*, report of the College of St. Mark and St. John Training Project, Calouste Gulbenkian Foundation.

WARD, C. and FYSON, A. (1973) *Streetwork*, London, Routledge and Kegan Paul.

Further Reading

BEE (Bulletin of Environmental Education).
A magazine promoting the development of urban studies. Eleven issues a year, £10 back copies available through Streetwork, 189 Freston Road, London W10 6TH.

Council for Urban Studies Centres (CUSC) Reports:
CUSC Information Pack (Urban Studies Centres in Great Britain), £2.50.
Urban Studies in the 80s, £1.50.
CUSC State of the Art Report, £1.95.
All available from Streetwork, 189 Freston Road, London W10 6TH.

Department of the Environment (1979) *Environmental Education in Urban Areas*, London, HMSO.

MATRIX, *Making Space: Women and Man-made Environment*, Photo Press, available from MATRIX, 8 Bradbury Street, London E8.

Ward, C (1979) *A Child in the City*, Harmondsworth, Penguin Books.

Sources of Help

Streetwork Urban and Local Studies Unit/CUSC
Able to supply lists of urban studies centres, information on curriculum development, BEE and some individual help on getting started, 189 Freston Road, London, W10 6TH, tel 01 968 5440.

Community Education Development Council
Able to provide general information on community education and lists of local centres. Also able to give contacts for local CEA groups. Briton Road, Coventry, tel 0203 440814.

Appendix

A Brief Bibliography for Social Educators

General

ASSESSMENT OF PERFORMANCE UNIT (1982) *Personal and Social Education*, London, Department of Education and Science.
The report which argues that social education cannot be assessed.

BALL, C. and M. (1979) *Fit For Work?*, London, Writers and Readers Publishing Cooperative.
An early examination of schooling in the light of youth unemployment.

BATES, I. *et al* (1984) *Schooling For The Dole?*, London, Macmillan.
A classic neo-Marxist critique of the new vocationalism in schools. Should not be ignored by social educators. Includes an analysis of social education at Eltham Green, Peter Dawson's former school, by a teacher in the department.

DAVID, K. (1982) *Personal and Social Education in Secondary Schools*, York, Longman.
The Schools Council's survey of social education.

DAVIES, B. (1979) *In Whose Interests? From Social Education to Social and Life Skills*, Leicester, National Youth Bureau.
Argues that an instrumental definition of SLS has replaced the more liberal social education but the arguments also apply to much social education.

DAVIES, B. and GIBSON, A. (1967) *The Social Education of the Adolescent*, London, University of London Press.
An authoritative account of social education in youth work.

DEFORGE, Y. (1981) *Living Tomorrow: An Inquiry Into the Preparation of Young People For Working Life in Europe*, Strasbourg, Council for Cultural Cooperation of the Council of Europe.
An early survey of Project No. 1 of the Council for Cultural Co-operation. Free from Strasbourg.

EDUCATION FOR THE INDUSTRIAL SOCIETY PROJECT (1983) *An Education For Life and Work*, Edinburgh, Consultative Committee on the Curriculum. A Scottish perspective on the task facing secondary schools.

ELLIOTT, J. and PRING, R. (1975) *Social Education and Social Understanding*, London, University of London Press.
A rather esoteric collection of papers from well known 'applied' philosophers of education.

ENTWISTLE, H. (1970) *Education, Work and Leisure*, London, Routledge and Kegan Paul.
A prescient discussion of schooling and work written when 'leisure' had not yet become a problematic concept.

FREIRE, P. (1972) *Pedagogy of the Oppressed*, Harmondsworth, Penguin.
Difficult but still a most penetrating analysis of education.

FURTHER EDUCATION UNIT (1980) *Developing Social and Life Skills*, London, FEU.
A fascinating study of assumptions underlying the motives of SLS tutors. Where do *you* stand?

Gow, L. and McPherson, A. (Eds) (1980) *Tell Them From Me*, Aberdeen, Aberdeen University Press.
Another powerful collection of the views of school leavers on school life.

HARGREAVES, D. (1982) *The Challenge for the Comprehensive School*, London, Routledge and Kegan Paul.
Radical proposals for reform of secondary education by the Chief Inspector for ILEA.

HEMMING, J. (1980) *The Betrayal of Youth*, London, Marion Boyars Pubs. Ltd.
A passionate, but coherent, argument for changing the structures and the ethos of secondary schools.

LEE, R. (1980) *Beyond Coping*, London FEU.
A comprehensive exploration of social education in a variety of contexts.

McPHAIL, P. (1982) *Social and Moral Education*, Oxford, Blackwell.
Although the emphasis is strongly on moral education, some fundamental issues are discussed.

RENNIE, J. *et al* (1974) *Social Education: An Experiment in Four Secondary Schools*, Schools Council Working Paper 51, London, Evans/Methuen.
Detailed account of a failed attempt to adopt a 'community campaigning' approach to social education.

ROGERS, C. (1983) *Freedom To Learn For the 80's*, Columbus, Chas. E. Merrill Pub. Co.
A classic discussion of formal education from a humanistic perspective.

SCOTTISH SOCIAL EDUCATION PROJECT, *Social Education: The Scottish Approach; Social Education: Notes Towards A Definition; Social Education: A West German View; Social Education: The Conference Approach; Social Education: A Resource Guide; Social Education*

Through Curriculum Subjects; Social Education Through the Informal Curriculum; Social Education: Using Media.

WAKEMAN, B. (1984) *Personal, Social and Moral Education: A Source Book*, Tring, Lion Publishing.

An excellent handbook for the classroom teacher.

WATTS, A.G. (1983) *Education, Unemployment and the Future of Work*, Milton Keynes, Open University Press.

An up-to-date and thoroughly informed discussion of the predicament in which secondary schooling finds itself in the face of youth unemployment.

WILLIAMSON, H. (1984) *Boys for the Jobs* (reprint with new Preface), Cardiff, Sociological Research Unit, University College.

A critique of social and life skills courses.

WHITE, R. and BROCKINGTON, D. (1978) *In and Out of School: the ROSLA Community Education Project*, London, Routledge and Kegan Paul.

A blueprint for a system of 'living, experiential' teaching and learning.

WHITE, R. (with D. BROCKINGTON) (1983) *Tales Out of School*, London, Routledge and Kegan Paul.

Students' views of school with commentaries by assorted professionals.

Curriculum

COMMITTEE ON THE CURRICULUM AND ORGANIZATION OF ILEA SECONDARY SCHOOLS (1984) *Improving Secondary Schools (The Hargreaves Report)*, London, ILEA.

A radical review of secondary schooling with a strong 'social education' perspective.

CRAFT, A. and BARDELL, G. (Eds) (1984) *Curriculum Opportunities in a Multicultural Society*, London, Harper and Row.

A comprehensive application of multicultural education principles to secondary school subjects.

DUFOUR, B. (Ed) (1982) *New Movements in the Social Sciences and Humanities*, London, Maurice Temple Smith Ltd.

Contains many chapters relevant to the social education curriculum.

GLEESON, D. and WHITTY G. (1976) *Developments in Social Studies Teaching*, London, Open Books.

Still a relevant and helpful analysis for social educators.

HARBER, C. and BROWN, C. (1983) 'Social education and the social sciences', *Curriculum*, 4, 1.

Argues that social education is often too loose and sloppy about social phenomena.

A Brief Bibliography for Social Educators

IFAPLAN (1984) *Education for Transition: The Curriculum Challenge*, Brussels, IFAPLAN.
A useful (and free) discussion document based on the EEC 'Transition' project.

McGUIRE, J. and PRIESTLEY, P. (1981) *Life After School: A Social Skills Curriculum*, Oxford, Pergamon.
Disappointingly pedestrian.

PRING, R. (1984) *Personal and Social Education in the Curriculum*, London, Hodder and Stoughton.
A recent philosophical discussion which included practical suggestions.

SCRIMSHAW, P. (1981) *Community Service, Social Education and the Curriculum*, London, Hodder and Stoughton.
A useful research study.

VARLAAM, C. (Ed) (1984) *Rethinking Transition: Educational Innovation and the Transition to Adult Life*, Lewes, Falmer Press.
A collection of research papers on social education from the EEC 'Transition' project.

WHYLD, J. (Ed) (1983) *Sexism in the Secondary Curriculum*, London, Harper and Row.
A very useful commentary and handbook organized by subjects.

WILCOX, B. *et al* (1984) *The Preparation for Life Curriculum*, Beckenham, Croom Helm Ltd.
A detailed report on the Sheffield EEC Project.

Methods

BARNETT, C. *et al* (1985) *Learning Through Experience*, London, Macmillan.

BELBIN, E. *et al* (1981) *How Do I Learn?*, London, Further Education Unit.
A useful perspective which may be new to many teachers.

BOUD, D. *et al* (Eds) (1985) *Reflection? Turning Experience into Learning*, London, Kogan Page.

BRANDES, D. and GINNIS, R. (1986) *Student-Centred Learning*, Oxford, Blackwell.

BRANDES, D. and PHILLIPS, H. (1979 and 1984) *The Gamesters' Handbook No. 1*, London, Hutchinson; *The Gamesters' Handbook No. 2*.
Hundreds of games for teachers and group leaders.

BUTTON, L. (1971) *Discovery and Experience*, London, Oxford University Press.
This is the original theory behind active tutorial work.

BYV SOCIAL EDUCATION PROJECT (n.d.) *Social Education as a Teaching*

Method, Birmingham, BYV Social Education Project.

A short paper describing and evaluating a course in an inner-city comprehensive school.

CLAXTON, G. (1984) *Live and Learn: An Introduction to the Pyschology of Growth and Change in Everday Life*, London, Harper and Row.

A readable and eclectic theory of experiential learning.

COLANGELO, N. *et al*, *The Human Relations Experience: Exercises in Multicultural Nonsexist Education*, Monterey, CA, Brooks/Cole Pub. Co. A wealth of useful exercises particularly for staff development.

DEARLING, A. and ARMSTRONG, H. (1983) *The Youth Games Book*, 2nd edn, I.T. Resource Centre.

More games and group exercises for a teenage clientele.

HAMBLIN, D. (1981) *Teaching Study Skills*, Oxford, Blackwell.

HOPSON, B. and SCALLY, M. (1981) *Lifeskills Teaching*, London, McGraw Hill.

Probably the best account of social education methods available.

IRVING, A. (Ed) (1983) *Starting to Teach Study Skills*, London, Edward Arnold.

Sensible discussion and practical case studies across the curriculum.

JAQUES, D. (1984) *Learning in Groups*, London, Croom Helm.

PIKE, G. and SELBY, D. (1985) 'The global classroom' *Social Science Teacher*, 14, 3.

Fifteen exercises to encourage participatory learning.

PRIESTLEY, P. *et al* (1978) *Social Skills and Personal Problem Solving*, London, Tavistock Pubs.

Written for all the helping professions but a source of much wisdom and clear strategies for social education.

PRIESTLEY, P. and McGUIRE, J. (1983) *Learning to Help*, London, Tavistock Pubs.

Excellent source book for advice on values, interviewing, counselling and group work.

RICHARDSON, R. (1979) *Learning for Change in World Society*, London, World Studies Project.

An excellent compendium of teaching ideas.

RICHARDSON, R. *et al* (1979) *Debate and Decision: Schools in a World of Change*, London, One World Trust.

A very useful guide to staff development in experiential learning.

SCOTTISH COMMUNITY EDUCATION CENTRE (1982) *Social Education: Methods and Resources*, Edinburgh, SCEC.

A useful companion for teachers.

SMITH, M. (1981) *Creators not Consumers* (2nd edn), Leicester, National Association of Youth Clubs.

An invaluable discussion of social education in youth work. Teachers should not ignore it.

TABBERER, R. and ALLMAN, J. (1983) *Introducing Study Skills: An Apprai-*

sal of Issues at 16+, Windsor, NFER-Nelson.

An important research report containing many practical observations.

WOLSK, D. (1975) *An Experience-Centred Curriculum: Exercises in Perception, Communication and Action*, Paris, UNESCO.

A thoughtful discussion of experience-based learning with exercises.

World Studies Journal, 5, 2, The Learning Process.

Thorough review of all the new learning styles. Available from World Studies Teacher Training Centre University of York.

Index

achievement
  and social education, 57–8
active tutorial work, 60, 95, 96, 97,
  193, 194, 197
AFFOR (All Faiths for One Race),
  65
alcohol, 146
  see also health
Alcohol Syllabus, 11–19, 153
Alvarado, M., 133
Anatomy of a Gang, 96
Asian Resource Centre, 65
assessment, 21–41
  definition of, 22–3
  ethics of, 33–4
  formative, 23
  and social education, 32–40
  and student profiles, 35, 36–40
  summative, 23
  techniques of, 35–40
  uses of, 34
Association for the Teaching of
  Social Sciences, 98
Aston, University of, 185–6
Atlantic College, 91
audience research, 127–8,
  129–31
audiences
  and genre, 130
  as 'makers' of meaning, 129–31
  and mode of address, 130

and positioning, 130
research on, 127–8, 129–31

Balding, J., 144, 146
Birmingham
  case study of social work project
  in, 62–9
Birmingham Young Volunteers
  Social Education Project, 59–70
  achievements of, 68–9
  aims of, 62
  case study of school in, 62–9
  and crime, 67
  history of, 59–61
  and race, 64–7, 68
Blackfyne Comprehensive School
  (Durham), 94
Brandes, D., 194
Brandt, W., 74
British Federation of University
  Women, 186
Brockington, 61
Bruner, J., 56
*Bulletin of Environmental
  Education,* 221
Business and Technical Education
  Council (BTEC), 204, 209
  Joint Board for Pre-Vocational
  Education of, 204
Button, L., 194
BYV